BLUE GUIDE

THE VENETO

ALTA MACADAM
WITH ANNABEL BARBER

SOMERSET • LONDON

BLUE GUIDE THE VENETO
2nd edition

Published by Blue Guides Limited, a Somerset Books Company
Unit 2, Old Brewery Road, Wiveliscombe, Somerset TA4 2PW
blueguides.com
'Blue Guide' is a registered trademark.

© Blue Guides 2026
Maps and plans © Blue Guides
Front cover: *Madonna* (detail) by Francesco Bonsignori,
Museo del Castelvecchio, Verona © Blue Guides
Back cover: Punta di San Vigilio, Lake Garda © Blue Guides
Interior photos © Blue Guides except pp. 20 and 133, Wikimedia Commons
and p. 14 © Kate O'Sullivan.

Typesetting and pre-press by Anikó Kuzmich.

All rights reserved. No part of this publication may be reproduced or used in any
form or by any means—photographic, electronic or mechanical—without the
permission of the publisher.

The publishers have made reasonable efforts to ensure
the accuracy of all the information in this book; however, they can accept
no responsibility for any loss, injury or inconvenience sustained by any
traveller as a result of information or advice contained in it.

Every effort has been made to contact the copyright owners of material reproduced
in this guide. We would be pleased to hear from any copyright owners we have
been unable to reach.

Statement of editorial independence: Blue Guides, their authors and editors,
are prohibited from accepting payment from any restaurant, hotel, gallery
or other establishment for its inclusion in this guide or on www.blueguides.com,
or for a more favourable mention than would otherwise have been made.

blueguides.com
'Blue Guide' is a registered trademark.
We welcome reader comments, questions and feedback:
editorial@blueguides.com

ISBN 978-1-916568-09-9

CONTENTS

THE VENETO REGION 5

THE VENETIAN LAGOON
The northern Lagoon 10
Chioggia 11

PADUA 15
The Scrovegni Chapel 17
Musei Civici Eremitani 21
Caffè Pedrocchi 23
The University 23
Palazzo della Ragione
  and the market places 24
The Duomo, Baptistery and
  Museo Diocesano 26
Il Santo (Basilica of St Anthony) 27
Prato della Valle, Santa Giustina
  and the Orto Botanico 33
Other things to see in Padua 34
Practical tips 37

THE BRENTA RIVIERA 39

THE EUGANEAN HILLS
The spa towns 43
Villas and gardens 44
Arquà Petrarca 45
Monselice 46
Este 48
Montagnana 50
Practical tips 51

ROVIGO AND THE PO DELTA
Rovigo 53
The Polesine 54
Practical tips 57

VICENZA
Along Corso Palladio 59

Teatro Olimpico 62
Museo Civico 64
Piazza dei Signori and the Basilica 65
The Duomo and Museo Diocesano 67
Santa Corona 68
North of Corso Palladio 70
In the bend of the Retrone river 72
Outside Porta Castello 73
Sanctaury-Basilica of Monte Berico 74
Villas on the outskirts 75
Practical tips 76

THE VENETO VILLAS 77

BASSANO DEL GRAPPA AND MAROSTICA
Bassano del Grappa 83
Marostica 87
Practical tips 89

VERONA 90
Piazza Brà and the Arena 91
Piazza delle Erbe and
  Piazza dei Signori 95
Sant'Anastasia 98
The Cathedral complex (Duomo) 101
On the left bank of the Adige 103
Museo di Castelvecchio 108
San Zeno 109
San Fermo 111
Other sights in Verona 112
Practical tips 115

SOAVE, THE MONTI LESSINI AND VALPOLICELLA
Soave 117
The Monti Lessini 118
The Valpolicella region 119
Practical tips 120

TREVISO AND CASTELFRANCO VENETO

Treviso	121
Castelfranco Veneto	132
Cittadella	135
Practical tips	136

ASOLO, CONEGLIANO AND VITTORIO VENETO

Asolo	138
Valdobbiadene and Prosecco	145
Conegliano and Vittorio Veneto	146
Practical tips	148

FELTRE, BELLUNO AND THE DOLOMITES

Feltre	150
Belluno	153
The Dolomites	155
Practical tips	157

LAKE GARDA

The Lombard side of the lake	159
The north end of the lake	169
The eastern shore of Lake Garda	169
Practical tips	172

PRACTICAL INFORMATION

Getting around	175
General tips	176
Accommodation	178
Eating in the Veneto	178

GLOSSARY OF TERMS 181

INDEX 184

MAPS

Veneto north	192
Veneto east	193
Veneto west	194
Veneto overview	195

TOWN PLANS

Padua	
Town centre	16
Scrovegni Chapel	19
Basilica of St Anthony (Il Santo)	29
Treviso	
Town centre	123
Verona	
Town centre	92–3
Sant'Anastasia	99
San Fermo	111
San Zeno	110
Vicenza	
Town centre	61
Santa Corona	69

THE VENETO REGION

The Veneto stretches from the delta of the Po in the south to the alpine border with Austria in the north and from the Adriatic in the east to Lake Garda in the west. It is inextricably linked to the great maritime city of Venice, to whom much of its territory once belonged and to whom many of its cities historically owed allegiance. However, Venice was settled from the Veneto, and not vice versa, and it is on the mainland that the story begins. Venice itself is a separate subject and is covered in its own Blue Guide. This volume is the story of the *terraferma*.

A SHORT HISTORY OF THE VENETO

Celts and Romans

The early history of Italy is being continually rewritten as new sites emerge and interpretations develop. If one starts, however, with the Bronze Age (2200–1000 BC), its culture seems to have been remarkably homogenous—but there is a break about 900 BC (with the coming of the Iron Age) when the indigenous peoples of northern Italy develop distinct cultures. A determined migration of Celts, probably impelled by population increase and the breakdown of societies to the north, took place in the late 5th century. It was not peaceful. By the early 4th century, Celtic warbands were raiding further south, reaching Rome in 390 BC.

Roman retaliation was inevitable, and the ill-disciplined Celtic warriors were no match for a Roman legion. After Celtic tribes helped the Carthaginian Hannibal in his invasion of Italy in 218, total subjection of northern Italy followed. Roman citizens were settled on the land in what were called *coloniae*, in sites originally chosen for strategic reasons. In contrast to the *coloniae* were the *municipia*, earlier urban settlements which were Romanised. Padua and Verona are examples of these, Romanised settlements which appear to have been originally founded by the Celtic Veneti. Many *municipia* flourished as a result of their position on roads or rivers. And with the Roman peace, the region prospered. Land was drained and vast quantities of grain were produced. The foothills provided excellent grazing for sheep. The elite enjoyed a comfortable lifestyle, as the remains of villas around Lake Garda bear witness.

From the Fall of Rome to the Holy Roman Empire

The collapse of Roman civilisation was gradual. 476 traditionally marks the end of the Western Empire, but there was no abrupt transition. Many of the 'barbarians' had by now become Romanised, and in any case they were a small minority in a Roman population. When the Ostrogoth Theodoric became ruler of much of Italy in 493, it is estimated that his followers numbered 100,000 in a native population of four million. He ruled through Roman bureaucrats and was sympathetic enough to Roman culture to restore buildings in Rome.

The first abrupt break with the Roman past came with the invasion of northern Italy by the Lombards in 568. The Lombards were a mix of peoples from northern Europe, forged by their king Alboin into a military force who would cooperate when attacked by the Byzantine troops from the south or the Franks from the north. One reason for the Lombards' continuing success was a succession of charismatic kings who kept the allegiance of these dukes and through them sustained what remained of urban life. By the 8th century most Lombards had become Catholics, using Roman law alongside their own.

The Lombards met their match in 753 or 754, when Pepin the Short, King of the Franks, came over the Alps. Their kingdom collapsed and in 773, Pepin's successor, Charlemagne, received the iron crown of Lombardy in the old capital, Pavia. In 800 Charlemagne was crowned 'Roman Emperor' by Pope Leo III in Rome. The Holy Roman Empire, which passed from the Franks to German kings in the 10th century, was to survive until dissolved by Napoleon in 1806.

The rise of the city states

The problem for northern Italy was that the relative roles of pope and emperor were never clearly defined. The Church remained strong on the ground; the emperors claimed overall responsibility as successors of the Lombards. This, however, was also northern Italy's opportunity. Many cities, though greatly diminished from the days of the Roman Empire, had remained relatively intact, while in a sheltered lagoon in the northern Adriatic tenacious settlements of refugees from the Lombard invasions were being forged into a trading community. These refugees, the Venetians, were nominally part of the Byzantine Empire (their first patron saint, Theodore, was a soldier martyr from Asia Minor), but they were determined to achieve independent control of their destiny. Contemporary documents from the 8th century show trading links between Venice and Constantinople, Sicily, the whole of north Africa, Syria and France. Trading prosperity on the mainland was supplemented by the rise of a landowning class (made up, it appears, of both Frankish and Lombard aristocrats) on the plains. The rivers opened again to trade, and it was only now that cities such as Ferrara, well placed on the Po, became important.

Politically the most remarkable development was the rise of communal government. In the 11th century the weakening of imperial rule led to revolts by many northern cities, a sign of a strong local identity. There was also increasing irritation with the power of the Church, and bishops were expelled from a number of cities. Communal government can be seen as the political structure which filled a vacuum, with different social groups all interested in a share of power: local landowners anxious for a foothold in the local city, a rising merchant class, administrators whose knowledge of Roman law was instrumental in defining the checks and balances of communal government.

The most common form of communal government consisted of 'consuls' (an echo of Roman times), who took responsibility for internal order and foreign relations with an assembly of 'the people' who could check the misuse of power. The assemblies ratified major decisions such as the making of peace and war, the approval of alliances and the acceptance of new laws. It was the ability to create and sustain a legal structure of government which was especially important and which provided the impetus for cities to set up their own institutions for the study of the arts and law (notably Roman law). So were born the first universities, among them that of Padua, founded in 1222. They were organised on communal lines as if the teachers were the consuls and the students the citizens. Communal activities also spread to trade, and fraternities of citizens were formed for charitable purposes. In 1300 there were an estimated 48 guilds or trade associations in Verona and 38 in Padua.

The wealth of these cities was boosted by trade. The Italians were pioneers in every aspect of commerce from banking to the design of ships. They dominated the Mediterranean trade routes, their tentacles penetrating deep into the Islamic world. Venice competed with its rival Genoa for trading concessions from the Byzantine emperors. In Padua, the vast Palazzo della Ragione, built first in the early 1200s and then rebuilt a hundred years later, acted as law court and assembly hall, with shops for merchants on the ground floor. Its size was also a symbol of the city's wealth and status. The ambiguous attitude to wealth creation in a Christian society is beautifully illustrated in Padua. Giotto's frescoes in the Scrovegni Chapel were commissioned by a wealthy merchant who sought, by his piety, to distance himself from the usury of his father, who had been named by Dante amongst the denizens of Hell.

From *comune* to Seigniory

Despite its successes, northern Italy always remained vulnerable to invasion from its nominal overlord, the Holy Roman Emperor. Frederick Barbarossa, elected in 1152, waged five campaigns over 30 years, although at last he was forced to accept the independence of the *comuni*. Barbarossa's grandson Frederick II launched further campaigns between 1225 and 1250, but again was unsuccessful. The invasions placed immense burdens on the *comuni*, with factions in the cities supporting either the emperors (the Ghibellines) or the papacy (the Guelphs). These factions were often a mask for local ambitions and the combination of marauding imperial armies and social tensions was devastating. 'O servile Italy, breeding ground of misery, ship without a pilot in a mighty tempest' wrote Dante, himself a Guelph. After his exile from Florence in 1302, Dante's wanderings around the courts and universities of northern Italy—he sheltered in Verona and taught at Padua—are symbolic of a troubled age. He yearned for the return of a strong emperor who would rule under the auspices of the papacy.

The *comuni* were idealised by later generations but, as Dante's experience suggests, their history was also filled with factional in-fighting and popular unrest. One pragmatic response was to elect, often from outside the city, a *podestà*, an official given wide powers for a fixed period of time. This proved the forerunner of the next development in northern Italy: the emergence of the seigniories, governments based on one man, with power then being passed on to the next generation of his family. As with communal government it is difficult to generalise: sometimes the lord enjoyed popular support, in other cases he emerged from aristocratic in-fighting, and the path to power was invariably tortuous. The Della Scala of Verona are an example of such a family. The Visconti of Milan are another, whose dominance over Lombardy was extended to Bologna (1350), Genoa (1353), and ultimately into the Veneto.

The stories of individual seigniorial families are too varied to be followed here, but while many cities of the Veneto were dominated by Venice, which maintained its republicanism, many others have monuments to the rule of a single family. The lives of the *signori* were often precarious, with the result that their residences were as much fortresses as palaces. A good example is the Castelvecchio of the Della Scala in Verona (1350s), still with its tall battlements.

In their time, the *signori* attracted both praise and blame. For those who retained the ideal of *libertas*, the ancient rallying cry of republican Rome, revived by the *comuni*, they were tyrants, 'a breed of cruel destruction', as one opponent of the lords of Milan put it. Others stressed that strong rule brought an end to factional squabbles and that the *signori* were often effective patrons.

The rise of France and Spain

A new period of vulnerability for northern Italy began in 1494, with a sequence of invasions from French, Spanish and imperial troops. The cities were no match for these well organised states, although they tried to play one off against another. It was Venice who encouraged the French to attack Milan, their main rival on the mainland, in 1499. The French in their turn were defeated in 1525 by the new Holy Roman Emperor Charles V. Charles, whose territories already extended across Europe from Spain to Austria, now stamped his rule on northern Italy. Venice was allowed to survive as a republic (and she regained much of her mainland territory) but Milan became a capital of a province of the Holy Roman Empire.

The 16th century saw another challenge with the opening up of trade routes round the Cape to the Far East and across the Atlantic. Mediterranean trade fell into decline and wealth creation shifted to the more lively and untrammelled (by guilds) economies of England and Holland. The prosperous merchant families began to transform themselves into an aristocracy living on the land, and villas and palaces replaced the warehouses of earlier centuries. The cultural interests of these patricians were broad, as can be seen from their patronage of Palladio in Vicenza. The Palladian villa was designed to exploit the aesthetic appeal of the landscape without losing touch with the labour on the land, which was required to sustain the ideal.

The universities of northern Italy had long had an international clientèle. (Teaching was, of course, in Latin, still the universal language of scholarship.) The Palazzo del Bo, the 16th-century core of the university of Padua, is filled with the insignia of students from all over Europe. The area was now also attractive to collectors, prominent among them Thomas Howard, 2nd Earl of Arundel, who in a seminal trip to Italy in 1613 was enthused by Italian art and architecture. His purchase of several chests full of Palladio's drawings proved the catalyst by which Britain became the first country outside Italy to adopt Palladianism. Italy was being redrawn as a place to go for cultural improvement, the Grand Tour providing the 'gap year' experience for the European aristocracy.

The 18th century and Napoleon

The outbreak of the French Revolution in 1789 was greeted in Italy with a mixture of fear and enthusiasm. The momentous significance of the event hit Italy when one of the revolution's generals, Napoleon Bonaparte, arrived over the Alps and bullied the Venetian Republic into an ignominious dissolution in 1797: defaced Lions of St Mark (for example in Verona) bear witness to this. Having conquered the Veneto, Napoleon then transferred control of the region to Austria. The rest of northern Italy was incorporated into the Kingdom of Italy, with Napoleon as its monarch. Napoleonic rule broke down the intricate network of legal and administrative boundaries and replaced them with a centralised state. Some Italians responded to the siren song of reform and of new opportunities in government, but primarily the kingdom, like all Napoleon's fiefdoms, existed to be milked for taxes and men. By 1812 Italians were fighting Napoleon's battles all over Europe, and suffering heavy casualties. Few regretted the collapse of his empire in 1814.

Unification: the Kingdom of Italy

In the settlement which followed at the Congress of Vienna (1814–15), Austria retained control of the Veneto. The Austrians were not particularly brutal rulers, but the Italians had a growing sense of national consciousness, partly a reaction to Napoleonic rule, but also given inspiration through the impassioned writings of Giuseppe Mazzini (1805–72), the founder of the revolutionary movement 'Young Italy'. This was the period known as the Risorgimento, literally the 'resurgence', denoting an awakening of nationalist feeling. The sophistication of Italian intellectuals can be seen from the meeting rooms of the Caffè Pedrocchi in Padua (opened in 1831), which were dedicated to the great civilisations of the past. Such people needed to be treated sensitively but the inept response of Metternich's Austria ensured that Italy was at the forefront of the revolutions of 1848. The mountain kingdom of Piedmont became the focus of nationalist hopes. A constitutional monarchy, it also had, in Camillo Cavour (1810–61), an able and pragmatic statesman. In 1859 Cavour engineered the support of Napoleon III in a war against Austria which led to the absorption of Lombardy and later central Italy into a new Kingdom of Italy under the Piedmontese monarch Vittorio Emanuele II. After the killing fields of Magenta and Solferino, Napoleon III began to question the wisdom of what he had set in motion. Bismarck had no such qualms. His Prussian armies conclusively defeated Austria in 1866, after which Venice itself was joined to the new Kingdom of Italy.

This historical introduction has covered the background to the major historical monuments a visitor is likely to encounter. Themes of invasion (the appalling fighting in the Veneto of the First World War), centralised rule (the Fascist era), desires for independence (the Northern League of the 1980s and 1990s), and a growing underlying prosperity persisted through the 20th century. The twenty-first century brings its challenges. The north has, like the rest of Italy, deep-rooted social and political problems which the visitor often passes by. However, the cities of the region are alive and immensely proud of their heritage. Restoration work is effective and expert. There are happy signs of a post-industrial society which will sustain ancient traditions. The 'Slow Food' movement in a region where good food and wine has always been linked to courteous hospitality offers much to be thankful for.

by Charles Freeman

THE VENETIAN LAGOON

The Venetian lagoon stretches in a broad arc from Jesolo in the north to Chioggia in the south, with the great city of Venice in the centre. It is protected from the open sea by a long series of low-lying sandbars and islands: the Lido di Jesolo, Lido di Venezia, Pellestrina. Immediately to the east lies Istria, now part of Croatia. Many of the settlements in the lagoon are ancient; in fact, Venice itself was colonised from here.

THE NORTHERN LAGOON

QUARTO D'ALTINO
On the mainland north of Venice is Quarto d'Altino (*map Veneto East C1–2*). Situated at the point where the Dese, Sile and Piave rivers enter the lagoon, it was already settled by the 7th century BC and later became the Roman *Altinum*, at the junction of several Roman roads. It is difficult to imagine it today, because Quarto d'Altino is a tiny place, just a couple of scattered buildings on either side of a narrow road amidst flat farmland, but this was once a thriving town and the beauty of its country villas was admired by the Latin poet Martial. Today, part of the Roman city has been excavated and what has been revealed can be seen in the **Parco Archeologico di Altino**, right beside the road (*open April–Oct, all day on Tues–Sat and on Sun afternoons*), which contains the finds, including mosaic pavements, stelae, Roman portrait busts (1st–2nd centuries AD), glass, amphorae and architectural fragments. A Roman road, thought to be part of the Via Claudia, has been exposed. The town was still densely populated in the 4th century AD, but after its destruction by Attila the Hun in the mid-5th century, and subsequently by the Lombards, and after floods and malaria had taken their toll, it was finally abandoned in the mid-7th century. The people took refuge on the island of Torcello and are thus directly involved with the early history of Venice. It is from Torcello that Venice was founded and many Roman stones from Altino were reused in the buildings of Venice, Torcello and Murano.

NB: A short way further along the road, on the opposite side, is the Trattoria Antica Altino (closed Mon).

JESOLO AND ERACLEA
Protected within a deeply indented bay, along the banks of the Sile, **Jesolo** (*map Veneto North C4*) gives its name to a long tongue of land, the Lido di Jesolo, a popular seaside resort with numerous hotels and campsites. The old town of Jesolo preserves a handful of handsome old buildings and a fine church, dating from 1927 but on

ancient foundations and in a historicist style. In ancient times, Jesolo was known as *Equilium*, since horses were bred on the marshes here. There was a Roman *mansio*, or stopping place for travellers here, whose remains were excavated in 2013–16; and traces of the old town walls (Antiche Mura) can be seen on the town's northern outskirts. For control of the affairs of the lagoon, Equilium was the rival of Heraclea, immediately to its north. Modern **Eraclea** (*map Veneto North C4*), on east bank of the Piave, preserves the old name of what was (in the 7th–8th centuries) the episcopal and administrative centre of the Venetian lagoon, named after Emperor Heraclius. The site of the ancient city was near Cittànova and has been identified by aerial photography. It was formerly surrounded by a lagoon, and it recalls Venice in plan, with a central canal and many smaller canals. From 750 onwards the inhabitants migrated to the safer islands of Malamocco and Rialto, and a leader from Heraclea is thought to have become the first Doge of Venice. Heraclea then rapidly declined as its lagoon silted up and Venice grew in importance.

CAORLE

Founded by refugees from Concordia (*see Blue Guide Friuli-Venezia Giulia*), Caorle (*map Veneto North C4*) is an ancient fishing village and now a popular seaside resort near the mouth of the Livenza. It preserves a very picturesque old centre of cobbled streets and low-rise houses, near the waterfront, dominated by the venerable **cathedral** of 1038. Caorle was a bishop's see for twelve centuries (until suppression under Napoleon). In the cathedral apse, behind the high altar, is a magnificent Pala d'Oro, consisting of six panels of gilded silver, excellent examples of medieval metalwork. The two endmost panels depict the *Archangel Gabriel* and the *Virgin Orans*. Scholars dispute the identifications of the others. According to tradition, the Pala d'Oro was the gift to Caorle of Caterina Cornaro, Queen of Cyprus (*see p. 141*). The find and distinctive cylindrical campanile was built in the 11th century. It can be climbed and on weekend nights in July an atmospheric light show re-enacts a 'Burning of the Bell-tower' (*Incendio del campanile*). To the north is a beautiful lagoon with fishing huts and interesting wildlife

CHIOGGIA

Chioggia (*map Veneto East C3*), one of the main fishing ports of the Adriatic, lies at the southern extremity of the Venetian lagoon, connected to the mainland by a bridge. It is not part of Venice but it can be reached by bus and ferry from the Venice Lido and the island of Pellestrina. Its unusual urban structure—dating from the late 14th century—survives, with numerous narrow straight streets (known as *calli*) packed very close together on either side of the main Corso and a network of canals. The Bocca di Chioggia is one of the three entrances to the lagoon from the open sea.

Chioggia's history has been interwoven with that of Venice since it was first settled by inhabitants of Este, Monselice and Padua in the 5th–7th centuries. Always loyal to Venice, Chioggia was destroyed by the Genoese in 1380; but the Venetians

View of Chioggia.

succeeded in shutting the Genoese fleet in the harbour immediately afterwards. Genoa's subsequent surrender marked the end of the struggle between the two rival maritime powers. The Chioggia saltworks, first developed in the 12th century, were the most important in the lagoon and survived up until the 20th century. Today it is the most important town in the lagoon after Venice and though much of its life is devoted to tourism, it is still a working fishing port and is a pleasant and interesting place to visit.

EXPLORING CHIOGGIA

The **Corso del Popolo** is Chioggia's wide main street, crowded for the *passeggiata* in the early evening. At its northern end is a column surmounted by a Lion of St Mark. Heading east from here, over a bridge across a canal, and then across another canal used by the fishing fleet, you come to the church of **San Domenico**. Inside on the right is a painting of *St Paul*, the last known work by the great Venetian painter Vittore Carpaccio (signed and dated 1520). On the right and left of the choir arch are a *Deposition and Saints* by Leandro Bassano and *Christ Crucified and Saints*, attributed to Tintoretto.

Corso del Popolo itself leads south through the heart of Chioggia. Next to a sturdy brick campanile, which functions as the city's clock tower, is the church of **Sant'Andrea**, which has, in the apse, a small oval painting of *St Andrew* by the local painter Antonio Marinetti (1719–90), known as 'Il Chioggiotto'. Further on, past the long, white, arcaded Town Hall, is the church of **San Giacomo**, with a ceiling fresco of St James, with remarkable perspective, also by Il Chioggiotto. Further on again, opposite where Calle Muneghette opens off to the right, is **Palazzo Poli**, once home to the great playwright Carlo Goldoni and to the portrait artist Rosalba Carriera (plaque). At the far end of the Corso is the large, brick **Duomo**, its interior reconstructed by Longhena in 1624. The chapel to the left of the sanctuary contains a number of fine paintings, including one by Tiepolo (*Torture of Two Martyrs*). Behind the Duomo is a canal, a short way along which you will find the entrance to the **Museo Diocesano**, arranged around a modern cloister. Among the highlights are a polyptych of the *Madonna with Four Saints* by Paolo Veneziano; a *Madonna and Child* by Cima da Conegliano; and a *St Barbara* by Giovanni Bellini (the lower part is not original).

Beyond the squat **Torre di Santa Maria** (or Porta Garibaldi), the old entrance to the town, guarding a bridge, the road widens out into a roundabout, to the left of which is the very plain ex-church of San Francesco, now the **Museo Civico della Laguna Sud** (*museo.chioggia.org*), the museum of the southern lagoon, which documents Chioggia's maritime history.

'And the beast which I saw was like unto a leopard, and his feet were as the feet of a bear, and his mouth as the mouth of a lion...' Giusto de' Menabuoi's 1378 interpretation of St John's vision in Revelation, in the Baptistery of Padua's duomo.

PADUA

Padua, in Italian *Pádova (map Veneto East B2)*, is one of the most ancient cities in Italy with a famous university (the second oldest in the country) and a large student population. It is a busy, lively place, visited for its numerous important works of art (including frescoes by Giotto), for its busy markets, and for its famous shrine of St Anthony. Padua is the place where the saint carried out many miracles and his burial chapel, 'Il Santo', is visited every year by millions of pilgrims. Donatello was just one of the famous Renaissance artists who carried out works of art to embellish the city, which was a leading centre of Humanism in the 15th century. The centre of the old town is characterised by pleasant arcaded streets and narrow cobbled lanes, but other districts had to be rebuilt after damage in WWII. Like all larger towns in the north of Italy, it has less overtly friendly outskirts.

Highlights of Padua, from a visitor's point of view, are the Scrovegni Chapel, with frescoes by Giotto; the Basilica of the Santo, with the tomb of St Anthony and works by Donatello; the magnificent medieval Palazzo della Ragione and the markets that surround it; and the venerable University, which can be visited on a guided tour. A short distance away is Palladio's magnificent villa La Malconenta.

HISTORY OF PADUA

The Roman historian Livy, born near *Patavium* (Padua) in 59 BC, claimed that the cities of the Po valley were founded by Antenor, Aeneas' fellow refugee from Troy. In reality the site was probably already occupied before the 8th or 7th century BC by palaeo-Venetic tribes. It received full Roman franchise in 89 BC. The town prospered under Byzantine and Lombard rule and declared itself an independent republic as early as 1164. The foundation of the university in 1222 attracted distinguished teachers to Padua, including Dante and Petrarch, as well as numerous students from England, and the city came to be known as *La Dotta* ('The Learned'). In 1237–54 Ezzelino da Romano was tyrant of Padua, then after the suzerainty of the Carraresi (1318–1405) the city was conquered by the Venetians, and remained a faithful ally of Venice until the end of the Venetian Republic. Along with Venice, it was ceded to Austria in 1797 and its celebrated coffee house, Caffè Pedrocchi, was an important meeting-place for patriots during the Risorgimento. It became a command post for troop movements during WWI and the armistice that followed Austria's defeat at the battle of Vittorio Veneto was signed at Villa Giusti on the southeastern outskirts. Today, Padua is a fairly prosperous town with many light industries.

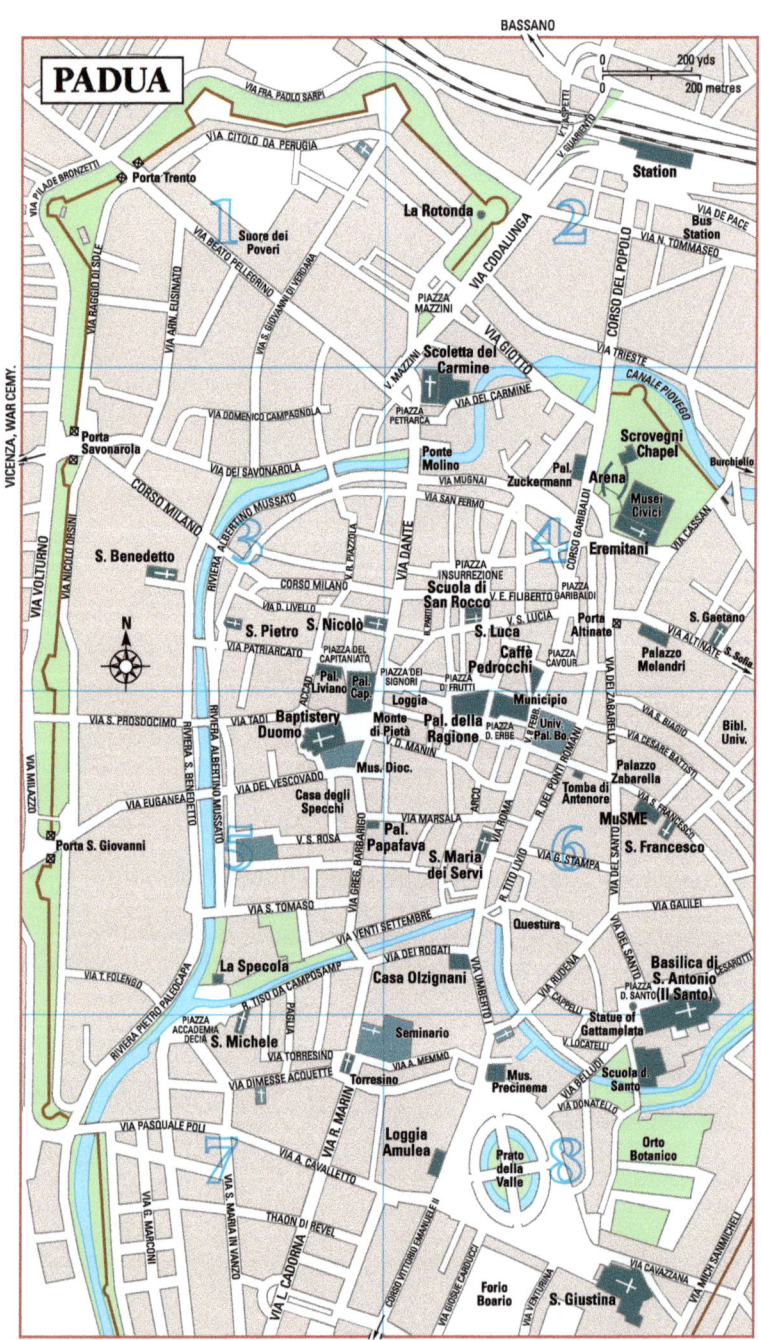

ART IN PADUA

Giotto's frescoes in the Cappella degli Scrovegni gave rise to a flourishing local school of 'Giottesque' painters (including **Guariento** and **Giusto de' Menabuoi**). The Veronese artist **Altichiero** (c. 1330–95), who was active in Padua in the 1380s, was one of the most creative interpreters of Giotto's achievements. Though he lacks the robust individuality of Giotto, and though he is less daring with colour, he is nevertheless the most important northern Italian mural painter of the late 14th century, with a love of pageant and of decorative elements that marks him out as an artist in the Gothic tradition. The Renaissance came to Padua with the arrival of **Donatello** in 1443, to work on his equestrian statue of Gattamelata and the high altar of the Santo. The painter **Mantegna** produced a superb fresco cycle in the church of the Eremitani between 1454 and 1457 (almost totally destroyed in WWII). In the late 15th century **Bartolomeo Bellano** (1434–96) and his pupil Andrea Briosco, the great metalworker known as **Il Riccio** (1470–1532), created some of the finest small bronze sculpture of the Renaissance. Riccio's almost exact contemporary, **Giovanni Maria Falconetto** (1468–1534), was a painter but also an important architect: the two pretty little buildings he designed in Padua (where he died) for the erudite Venetian Alvise Cornaro, as ideal retreats where he could meet the great literary figures of his day, are his masterpiece.

THE SCROVEGNI CHAPEL

Map Padua 4. Book visit in advance; cappelladegliscrovegni.it. There is a cap on the number of visitors allowed in the chapel at one time and a series of automatic doors to preserve the interior microclimate. Visits are timed and last approx 15mins. Combined tickets are available Tues–Sun with Palazzo Zuckermann and the Musei Civici Eremitani.

This simple little barrel-vaulted chapel is the most famous monument in Padua, entirely decorated with frescoes by the greatest early Italian master, Giotto. The chapel was built by Enrico Scrovegni in 1303, next to his palace (now demolished), in expiation for his father's usury. Dante, who may have been in Padua at the time Giotto was at work on these frescoes, singles out Scrovegni's father in his *Inferno* as one of three noblemen famous for their usury (although none of them is named by the poet, they are identifiable by the description of their coats of arms).

Giotto may also have designed the chapel itself when he was commissioned to carry out the frescoes since its scale fits the painted decoration so precisely. The cycle was painted in just two years, when he was at the height of his power. The scenes, whose colour scheme with its strong blues is exceptionally well preserved, depict the history of Christian redemption through the lives of Christ and the Virgin and reflect the painter's deeply religious spirit. Giotto's influence on all subsequent Italian painting can here be understood to the full: his painting has a new monumentality and sense of volume which had never been achieved in medieval art. Here for the first time, Biblical narrative is given an intensely human significance.

The frescoes are arranged in three bands, beginning at the top of the south wall nearest to the sanctuary.

Stories of Joachim, Anne and the Virgin

1. Joachim, father of the Virgin Mary, is expelled from the Temple after his offering is rejected by the priests, since after 20 years of marriage to his wife Anne, God has not blessed them with children;
2. Joachim retires in sorrow to a sheepfold (greeted by a friendly sheepdog), leaving Anne alone not knowing what has become of him;
3. An angel tells Anne that she is to give birth to a daughter, and that she will find her husband at the Golden Gate of Jerusalem (her handmaiden sits spinning in the porch);
4. Joachim makes a sacrifice of a burnt offering;
5. An angel appears to Joachim (still in the sheepfold) in a vision and tells him of the imminent birth of the Virgin;
6. The meeting of Anna and Joachim at the Golden Gate;
7. Birth of the Virgin;
8. *Presentation of the Virgin*;
9. The high-priest Simeon orders all unmarried men of the lineage of David to present their rods at the altar, and declares that the man whose rod comes into bud (through the influence of the Holy Spirit) will marry the Virgin;
10. *The Watching of the Rods*, as all kneel in prayer;
11. Betrothal of the Virgin to Joseph (he is shown holding his rod in bud which also bears the Holy Spirit, while the others break their rods in disappointment);
12. The Virgin returns with her seven companions to her father's house in Galilee, accompanied by joyous musicians;
13. God the Father, surrounded by angels, dispatches the Angel Gabriel;
14. The Angel Gabriel;
15. The Virgin Annunciate;
16. *The Pact of Judas*, with the black devil, is paired with the opposite scene:
17. *The Visitation*, in which Mary embraces her older cousin Elizabeth (mother of John the Baptist).

Stories of Christ, from the Nativity to the Ascension

18. *Nativity*;
19. *Adoration of the Magi*;
20. *Presentation in the Temple*;
21. *Flight into Egypt*;
22. *Massacre of the Innocents*;
23. *Christ Disputing with the Elders*;
24. *Baptism of Christ*;
25. *Marriage at Cana*;
26. *Raising of Lazarus*;
27. *Entry into Jerusalem*;
28. *Clearing of the Temple*;
29. *Last Supper*;
30. *Washing of the Feet*;
31. *The Kiss of Judas*;
32. *Christ before Caiaphas*;
33. *Flagellation* and *Crowning with*

SCROVEGNI CHAPEL

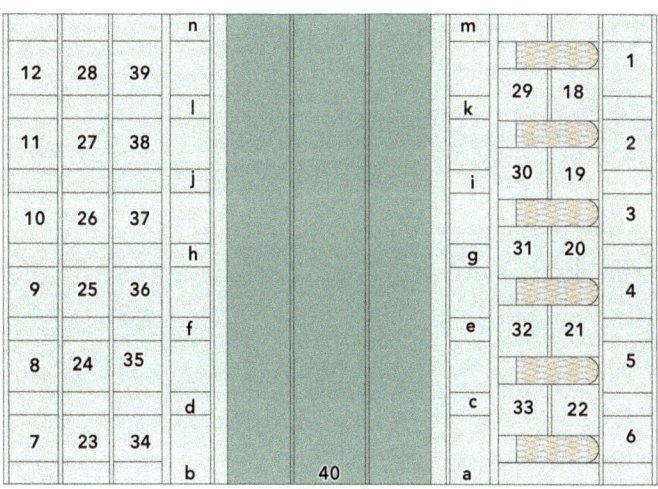

Thorns;
34. *The Way to Calvary*;
35. *Crucifixion*;
36. *Deposition*;
37. *Resurrection*, with the Angels at the empty tomb and the soldiers asleep (and the *Noli me Tangere* on the left);
38. *Ascension*;
39. *Pentecost* and *Descent of the Holy Spirit*;
40. *Last Judgement*. The west wall is entirely occupied by this scene, full of fascinating figure studies, although it is the most damaged part of the cycle since the wall was the most exposed to the elements, after the portico and Scrovegni palace were demolished in the 19th century and the plaster was removed from the chapel façade. Above the door, in front of the Blessed, Scrovegni kneels before the Cross and presents his Chapel to the Virgin; on the right the contorted figures of the Damned in Hell are shown dominated by the huge monstrous Devil.

The Kiss of Judas, one of the famous scenes by Giotto in the Scrovegni Chapel.

Frescoes of the Virtues and Vices

Around the socle on the two long walls are very beautiful monochrome allegorical figures of the Virtues and the Seven Deadly Sins or Vices, among the most original and striking part of the entire cycle. The seven Virtues are all turned towards the fresco of Paradise on the west wall, and the seven Vices on the opposite wall look in the direction of Hell. The panels in between, in imitation of marble, were painted with a technique used by the ancient Romans known as *stucco lustro*, similar to encaustic painting which involved the use of wax.

Nearest to the *Last Judgement* wall, the winged figure of **Hope (a)** is counterbalanced by **Despair (b)**, killing herself with a cord as the tiny Devil drags her towards the abyss on the west wall. **Charity (c)** has a triple flame on her head and holds a vase of flowers, while horned **Envy (d)**, enveloped in flames, is bitten on the forehead by a serpent issuing from her own mouth. The majestic figure of **Faith (e)** is crowned with a diadem and holds a Cross, while **Unbelief (f)** is represented by a helmeted warrior holding an idol. The serene figure of **Justice (g)** holds weighing scales, perfectly balanced, while **Injustice (h)** is shown as a judge armed with a sword and double hook sitting isolated in his fortress protected by trees, painted with extraordinary skill. **Temperance (i)** is a draped figure prevented from using arms, and **Anger (j)** is an ugly woman tearing at her dress. **Fortitude (k)** is also a female figure, fully protected by armour with the head of a lion on her head. **Inconstancy (l)** is represented by a girl vainly trying to balance herself on a wheel as it turns, while her veil flies away. **Prudence (m)** has two heads, one elderly and one youthful holding a mirror, while opposite **Folly (n)** is a pot-bellied grotesque figure wearing a headdress of feathers and defiantly shaking a mace.

On the altar are three very beautiful statues of the Virgin observed by two angels (or deacons) commissioned by Enrico Scrovegni at the same time as the frescoes from the greatest sculptor of the time, Giovanni Pisano. The **tomb of Enrico Scrovegni**, with his effigy, is on the wall behind. The frescoes here are by followers of Giotto.

Outside in the garden are the walls of a **Roman amphitheatre** (1st century AD), an 'arena': the Cappella degli Scrovegni used to be known as the Arena Chapel.

MUSEI CIVICI EREMITANI

Map Padua 4. Paper tickets for the Scrovegni Chapel should be bought or picked up here. Combined tickets are available with Scrovegni Chapel and Palazzo Zuckermann. padovamusei.it.

This huge museum is housed in the former friary to which the church of the Eremitani belonged, consists of the Archaeological Museum and the Medieval and Modern Art Museum, with paintings and sculpture.

Museo Archeologico

Exhibits include pre-Roman and Roman material and an Egyptian collection in honour of the great Egyptologist Giovanni Belzoni (1778–1823), who was born in Padua. The son of a barber, he met his English wife during his time as a strongman with a travelling circus. His discoveries in Egypt made his name. He was the first European to enter the tomb of Ramesses II at Abu Simbel and supplied the British Museum with many of its largest Egyptian statues, including a famous bust of Ramesses. In this collection, the two fine black basalt statues of the ancient Egyptian goddess Sekhmet, were given by him to his native city.

Museo d'Arte

The art collection gives an overview of painting in the region from the 13th–18th centuries. There are works by famous masters such as Giotto (a Cross painted for the Scrovegni Chapel), and also by important local artists such as Guariento and Giusto de' Menabuoi, who, inspired by Giotto, launched a revival of the Padua school in the

14th century. The work of the Venetian artists Michele Giambono can be compared to that of his Paduan contemporary Francesco Squarcione. Here too are works by the Venetian painters Marco Basaiti and Giovanni Bellini. Sixteenth-century Venetian art is well represented, with examples by Giorgione, Veronese, Tintoretto and Titian. Titian was an influence on the early work of the Padua-born painter Il Padovanino. Sculpture includes pieces by Canova and small bronzes by Il Riccio.

The church of the Eremitani
This Augustinian church, built in 1276–1306 with a façade of 1360, was almost completely destroyed by bombing in 1944 but has been extremely well reconstructed.

South (right) side and sanctuary: There are Giottesque fresco fragments on the south wall by Giusto de' Menabuoi and Guariento and in the **sanctuary**, on the left wall, are frescoes by Guariento (1361–5) of scenes from the lives of St Philip and St Augustine, allegories of the planets and the ages of man.

The second chapel to the right of the sanctuary, the **Cappella Ovetari**, contains all that remains of a famous fresco cycle by Mantegna, the destruction of which was the greatest individual disaster to Italian art in WWII. Mantegna began work here in 1454 when he was only 23 and he took three years to complete the frescoes. He was clearly influenced by Donatello, who had begun work on his sculptures for the Santo (*see pp. 29–30*) ten years earlier. The *Martyrdom of St Christopher* on the right wall was detached and removed before the War and so is in a better state than that on the other wall of the *Martyrdom of St James*, which was partially recomposed from shattered fragments. Behind the altar can be seen the wonderful *Assumption*.

North (left) side: In the **Cappella Sanguinacci**, left of the sanctuary, the 14th-century votive frescoes include some by Giusto de' Menabuoi. On the north wall, the large **monument to the law professor Marco Benavides** (1489–1582) is by the Florentine sculptor Bartolomeo Ammannati and shows how greatly he was influenced by Michelangelo.

West end: Near the west door are two 14th-century **hanging funerary monuments**. The one to Jacopo II da Carrara has an epigraph supplied by Petrarch.

Palazzo Zuckermann
Across the road from the Eremitani, Palazzo Zuckermann is a monumental building of 1912/14 by Filippo Arosio. Its spacious Neoclassical interior houses the Museo Bottacin and the Musei Civici's applied arts collection.

Niccolò Bottacin (1805–76) was a wealthy textile merchant and a keen collector of coins and medals. His collection spans the pre-Roman to the modern Venetian era. The paintings and furniture all decorated his residence in Trieste. The applied arts collection offers well-displayed examples of ceramics, majolica, glassware, silver, furniture, textiles and costumes.

CAFFÈ PEDROCCHI

Map Padua 4. caffepedrocchi.it.

In its heyday, this café was one of the most celebrated in Italy. The building, fronted by twin neo-Doric loggias, is named after its founder, Antonio Pedrocchi, and was built on this triangular site in 1831–7 by Giuseppe Jappelli in an eclectic style. It became famous soon after it was opened, as a meeting place for intellectuals, and used to be kept open 24 hours a day. In 1891, Pedrocchi's adopted son left the building to the city of Padua on condition that it would remain a café. It has done so. And though its glory days have passed, the ground-floor rooms are still decorated in white, green and red, the colours of the Italian flag.

The upper floor was added in 1842. A grand staircase, with a stuccoed apse at the top, decorated with the dancing Muses, leads up to a series of salons and meeting rooms, originally used for earnest intellectual discussion and political plotting, and now as a venue for corporate events and weddings. Each room is decorated in a style that evokes a great civilisation of the past. The Egyptian Room was inspired by Jappelli's friend Giovanni Battista Belzoni (*see p. 21*) and is decorated with mock porphyry and painted stucco statues. There are also Etruscan, Greek Room, Roman, Moorish, Gothic and Renaissance rooms, and an elaborate ballroom, the Rossini Room, decorated in Napoleonic, Empire style.

Museo del Risorgimento e dell'Età Contemporanea

This **museum**, on the upper floor of Caffè Pedrocchi, documents the Risorgimento period and also the later history of Italy up to the end of WWII. This is particularly appropriate since it was here that a revolt against the Austrians was planned in 1848. The displays are well done and extremely interesting.

At the back of Caffè Pedrocchi is another neo-Doric loggia and a neo-Venetian wing, a nod to the architect Giuseppe Jappelli's native city. From here you look south, down Via VIII Febbraio. On your right is the Town Hall (*Municipio*) and on your left, the University.

THE UNIVERSITY

Map Padua 6. Open Mon–Sat for guided tours, also in English, of around 30mins. See unipd.it/en/tours-and-tickets.

The University of Padua, founded around 1222, is the second oldest university in Italy (after Bologna). It was nicknamed 'Il Bo' (*bue*, or ox) from the sign of an inn which used to stand on this site. Renowned as a medical school, it flourished in the 15th and 16th centuries, when it was the only university in the Venetian Republic.

Over its entrance is a Venetian Lion and the Latin inscription '*Gymnasium Omnium Disciplinarum*', labelling it at a school of all disciplines, offering a truly 'universal' education.

It was from this university that Elena Cornaro Piscopia (1646–84) received her doctor's degree, in philosophy, the first woman to do so. Other alumni include the surgeon Fabricius, master of William Harvey (who discovered blood circulation), who took his degree here in 1602. Founder of the Royal College of Surgeons Thomas Linacre (1492) and the future physician to Queen Elizabeth I John Caius (1539) also qualified here as doctors, and the anatomist Vesalius (1540) and Fallopius (1561, who lends his name to the fallopian tube) were among the famous medical professors (Fallopius died in 1562 and is buried in the Magnolia Cloister of the Santo).

Tours of the University include this main building, **Palazzo Bo**, and the Modernist Palazzo Liviano. Highlights of Palazzo Bo include the Aula Magna, covered with the coats of arms of rectors and 19th-century frescoes; Galileo's wooden *cattedra*, a teaching desk supposed to have been made as a sign of affection by his pupils so that they could see him better (the great scientist taught physics at the University from 1592–1610, a period he looked back on as the best of his life); and the anatomical theatres, the oldest in Europe (1594). Built by Fabricius, it was in use until 1874.

Palazzo Liviano (*map Padua 3*), built in the 1930s by Giò Ponti, an architect from Milan, is an interesting piece of Rationalist design. It is a *Gesamtkunstwerk*: the furnishings, even down to the coat hooks, are also designed by Ponti, and the frescoes are by artists chosen by him. From here, you can visit the **Hall of the Giants** (Sala dei Giganti), part of the old Palazzo del Capitanio, which became the seat of the Venetian governor of Padua in the mid-16th century. The Hall is decorated with the enormous likenesses of illustrious men of history, role models for their flawless conduct in military, political and administrative affairs. The enfilade begins with Romulus and ends with Charlemagne. Included too are a handful of men of letters, either natives of Padua or whose careers brought them into contact with it.

PALAZZO DELLA RAGIONE & THE MARKET PLACES

The immense Palazzo della Ragione (*map Padua 6*), the former *Palais de Justice*, stands at the commercial and administrative heart of old Padua. Its double porticoes overlook market places, in Piazza delle Erbe (vegetables) and Piazza dei Frutti (fruit). It is one of the most extraordinary buildings in Italy, built by Fra' Giovanni degli Eremitani in 1306–8, although the huge roof had to be reconstructed in 1756 after storm damage. The food shops beneath the vaulted lower arcades are an extension of the busy fruit and vegetable markets held outside on weekday mornings.

Interior of Palazzo della Ragione
Open 9–6 or 7 except Mon. Usual entrance from the outside staircase on Piazza delle Erbe. Wheelchair access from the Municipio courtyard.

Detail of the symbolic and allegorical depictions of the months, on the walls of Palazzo della Ragione.

The interior of the Palazzo della Ragione is extraordinarily impressive: it is certainly one of the largest interior spaces in all Italy, 82m long, nearly 30m wide and 26m high, and it quite takes your breath away. Its splendid proportions can only be fully appreciated when temporary exhibitions are not being held. It contains just three objects: the *Pietra del Vituperio*, a block of stone which once served as a stool of repentance for debtors (a reminder that this hall was built as a hall of Justice), a freely suspended pendulum which reproduces Jean Foucault's experiment in 1851 by which he proved that the earth rotates, and a giant wooden horse, which calls to mind the Trojan Horse but is in fact a copy of Donatello's *Gattamelata* (*see p. 31*), made for a fête in 1466.

In 1313 Giotto and his assistants were called in to decorate the walls. Those frescoes where destroyed in a fire in 1420 and it fell to the far less well-known painters Nicolò Miretto and Stefano da Ferrara to repaint them: it is not known how closely they followed the original scheme. However, they are very well preserved and extremely interesting. The 333 panels of religious and astrological subjects are divided according to the months of the year: each represented by nine scenes in three tiers, with an allegory of the month together with its sign of the Zodiac, planet and constellation, as well as the labours of the month and astrological illustrations. A touch screen, also in English, supplies details of the frescoes.

Under the Palazzo are the excavations of Roman and medieval buildings that once stood on this site. Beneath the arcades is the **Sotto Salone**, a covered parade of shops selling cheese, meat and other produce.

The market places

The two market places, **Piazza dei Frutti** and **Piazza delle Erbe**, both have slightly raised pavements in the centre. In the former is a particularly good view of Palazzo della Ragione and the tall medieval tower known as Torre degli Anziani.

Close by, to the west, is a third picturesque market place, **Piazza dei Signori**, an elongated space also with a raised pavement in the centre and a tall column topped with the Lion of St Mark, a typical feature of cities that came under Venetian control. At one end of it is the little smoked-salmon-coloured church of San Clemente, and opposite it, the **Torre dell'Orologio**, adapted in 1532 by Giovanni Maria Falconetto to accommodate an astronomical clock dating from 1344 (the oldest in Italy). The archway under the clock-tower leads into **Piazza del Capitaniato**, shaded by acacia trees. At the far end of it is a café/bar, where you can sit and have a drink and a snack.

THE DUOMO, BAPTISTERY & MUSEO DIOCESANO

Map Padua 5.

The exterior of the Duomo, the cathedral of Padua, is extremely plain, since it was never given a façade. The interior dates from a reconstruction in 1552, to a design by Michelangelo, though his plans were much altered. The chapels have paintings dating from that time or later. The sanctuary is the result of a redesign of 1997.

Next to the Duomo is the **Baptistery** (*for times and tickets, see battisteropadova. it; online booking recommended*). Built at the end of the 12th century, the interior was entirely covered with wonderful frescoes by Giusto de' Menabuoi (1378). They are his best work and one of the most interesting medieval fresco cycles in Italy. In the dome is *Christ Pantocrator* surrounded by a host of angels and the Blessed; in the drum are scenes from Genesis, and in the pendentives, the Evangelists. On the walls are scenes from the lives of Christ and St John the Baptist. In the apse are illustrations from the Apocalypse, including the very memorable beast, just as described in Revelation 13: 'I saw a beast rise up out of the sea, having seven heads and ten horns, and upon his horns ten crowns, and upon his heads the name of blasphemy. And the beast which I saw was like unto a leopard, and his feet were as the feet of a bear, and his mouth as the mouth of a lion…and I saw one of his heads as it were wounded to death…'. The crowns in Giusto's interpretation are mitres. The polyptych on the altar is also by Giusto.

The **Museo Diocesano** (*combined ticket with the Baptistery available; see battisteropadova.it*) is housed in the spacious Bishop's Palace (Vescovado). Among the collection of manuscripts and incunabula, reliquaries, Church silver and vestments, are some exceptional treasures including two beautiful panel paintings of the Madonna, one by Giusto de' Menabuoi and the other by Paolo Veneziano. On the third floor is the huge Salone dei Vescovi with portraits of one hundred bishops of Padua by Bartolomeo Montagna (early 16th century). later artists with works in the collection include Francesco da Bassano and Giovanni Battista Tiepolo.

IL SANTO (BASILICA OF ST ANTHONY)

Map Padua 6. Generally open all day from 6.15am. santantonio.org.

The most famous church in Padua, and one of the great pilgrim shrines of Italy, this magnificent basilica was begun in 1232 as a temple for the tomb of St Anthony of Padua, who was canonised in the same year, just a year after his death. Born in Lisbon in 1195, he was forced in a storm to land in Italy, while on a missionary journey to Africa in the 1220s, and settled in Padua where he preached with great fervour against heresy (a manuscript of sermons annotated in his own hand is preserved in the monastery library here). He was a close companion of St Francis, and is one of the earliest Franciscan saints (and was made a Doctor of the Church in 1946). In 1257 he was declared a patron saint of Padua after it was believed that through his divine intervention the city had been saved from the tyranny of Ezzelino da Romano. Famous as a miracle-worker, he remains one of the best-loved saints in the country and millions of pilgrims visit his church every year.

From the north side of the piazza, the massive **exterior** of the basilica is a wonderful sight, with its six Byzantinesque domes and towers of different heights. At the east end is the Gothic apse and the separate domed Chapel of the Relics, and the idiosyncratic façade combines several different styles. The exterior flank makes its greatest impact when approached either from Via del Santo or Via Cappelli.

Interior of the Santo

Cappella di Sant'Antonio

In the dark interior, this is the chapel to which all visitors are first drawn. It contains the greatly revered **tomb of St Anthony (A)**. The green marble sarcophagus is touched every day by hundreds of devout worshippers, many of whom leave ex-votos, candles, or messages for the saint. From the 13th century onwards, indulgences were granted by the pope to pilgrims who visited the tomb.

When it was decided to reconstruct the chapel in the late 15th/early 16th century, the classical design is presumed to have been drawn up by Tullio Lombardo. It seems that his pupil Giovanni Minello directed the work, and his son Antonio was also involved. It is one of the most beautiful works of the Italian Renaissance. It has blind arcades on all four sides, delicate carving with busts in roundels and a carved architrave. The monumental entrance screen, supported on four lovely marble pillars and two exquisitely carved pilasters, was added by Giovanni Maria Falconetto in 1532. High up in niches are five statues of the patron saints of Padua, including St Justina on the left by Antonio Minello. Falconetto also supplied the rich stucco vault inspired by the decorations discovered in Nero's Domus Aurea in Rome.

What most claims the attention, however, are the nine large sculptured panels at eye level around the walls. Though probably designed as a set by Tullio Lombardo, they were carved by different hands (and over several decades, from 1500 to 1577). Each panel has life-size figures in both high and low relief, commemorating miracles of St Anthony in front of an architectural perspective in different marble. They are framed by blind arcades. The panels by the Lombardo brothers incorporate wonderful classically inspired figures. The scenes are as follows:

1. *St Anthony Kneeling to Receive the Franciscan Habit* (Antonio Minello, 1517).
2. *The Jealous Husband Prevented from Killing his Beautiful Wife Suspected of Adultery* (Giovanni Rubino, 1524; completed after his death by Silvio Cosini, 1536.
3. *The Young Boy Brought back to Life*, a dramatic scene by Danese Cattaneo and Girolamo Campagna (1571–7). The boy's parents, shown kneeling in the background, had been accused of murdering him because his body had been found in their garden. But the boy is about to reveal the name of his assassin, shown on the extreme right, wringing his hands in despair. In the background is Padua's Palazzo della Ragione.
4. *The Virgin Carilla Brought back to Life*. She is shown coming back to life from drowning while her mother looks on. Signed by Jacopo Sansovino (1540–50), 'Florentine sculptor and architect', it is in a style quite different from the other panels, by sculptors from the Veneto. The Santo basilica is shown in the background.
5. *Parrasio Brought back to Life* (Antonio Minello, 1528; finished by Jacopo Sansovino, 1532). Parrasio was St Anthony's nephew and had been drowned.
6. *The Heart of the Dead Miser Found in his Strong Box instead of in his Body*, a clear message against usury (Tullio Lombardo, 1525).
7. *The Irascible Youth's Severed Leg Restored to Him* (after confessing to the saint, he had amputated it in repentance, and here the saint is shown reattaching), also by Tullio Lombardo.
8. *The Glass Dropped by the Unbeliever Adelardino Remains Unbroken* (begun by Giovanni Maria Mosca, finished after 1529 by Paolo Stella). This was a posthumously performed miracle of St Anthony: but Adelardino (in armour) has just dropped the glass and his companions are crowding round to see if it is still intact.
9. *The Newborn Babe Identifying his True Mother, Accused of Adultery by her Husband* (Antonio Lombardo). This classical relief, the first to be completed, clearly influenced the others.

The altar in front of the saint's tomb has eleven bronze statues by Tiziano Aspetti added at the end of the 16th century. A door leads into a dark chapel off which is the **Cappella del Beato Luca Belludi (B)**, St Anthony's companion, who is buried

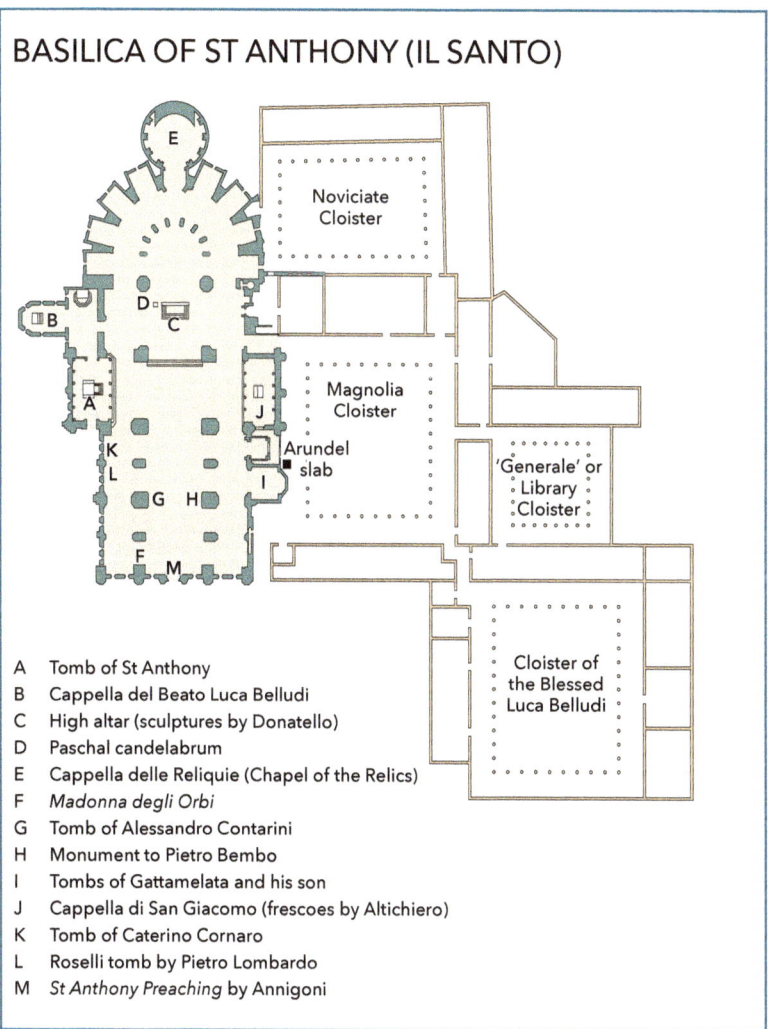

here. It is decorated with early frescoes dating from 1382 by Giusto de' Menabuoi, relating the story of this little-known Franciscan's life. It includes a scene of Padua itself enclosed in its walls.

Sanctuary

Donatello produced the wonderful bronze statues and reliefs for the **high altar (C)** in 1446–9 but it has suffered many vicissitudes and its present reconstruction dates from 1895 (it is not known just how Donatello intended to arrange the sculptures, nor do we know what the original altar looked like). The sanctuary is dark and the works are very difficult to see clearly unless you ask one of the custodians to unlock the gates at a time when Mass is not being held.

Above twelve charming reliefs of angel musicians (only four of which are by Donatello's own hand), on either side of Christ as the Man of Sorrows, are four remarkable gilded bronze reliefs set in to the altar (two on the front and two on the back) which constitute some of Donatello's greatest works. The superb details in low relief are highlighted in gold and silver leaf. They depict four of St Anthony's miracles: three of them later depicted in marble in the Chapel of St Anthony (the *Miser's Heart*, the *Irascible Boy*, and the *New-born Babe*; *see above*), but the fourth, that of the mule which belonged to a non-believer kneeling before the Host, is the only depiction of this particularly charming miracle in the Santo and symbolises Anthony's crusade against heresy.

At the ends are the symbols of the Evangelists. The altar is crowned with seven superb bronze statues: in the centre is the Madonna rising from her throne, a disturbing figure in an unusual pose, holding the Christ Child in front of her; she is flanked by the four patron saints of Padua (Prosdocimus, considered Padua's first bishop; Justina and Daniel, two Paduans who were martyred for their faith; and Anthony), together with St Francis and another great Franciscan, St Louis of Toulouse. It is clear that they were all designed to be seen from below. The bronze Crucifix above, another masterpiece by Donatello, is his first documented work here but was not made for the altar; it was probably intended for a more conspicuous position in the nave. On the back of the altar is a large stone relief of the *Entombment*, perhaps by an assistant of Donatello.

On the left of the altar is another bronze masterpiece: a **paschal candelabrum (D)** on a marble pedestal, the most important work of Il Riccio (1515), who also carried out two of the twelve exquisite small bronze reliefs with Old Testament scenes on the wall of the choir here. The others were made some 20 years earlier by Riccio's master, Bartolomeo Bellano, who may have worked in Donatello's workshop.

At the far east end is the **Cappella delle Reliquie (E)** (Chapel of the Relics), housing the rich treasury with more than a hundred reliquaries. Among the relics are some fragments of St John Paul II and, in a magnificent reliquary of Florentine workmanship, the tongue of St Anthony, which is shown in solemn procession on the 'Festa della Lingua' in mid-Feb.

Nave

The basilica has been used over the centuries as the burial place of Padua's most eminent citizens. On the first north pillar, the greatly revered 15th-century painting of the *Madonna degli Orbi* **(F)**, in gilded robes, faces the tomb of Antonio Trombetta (d. 1518), his erudition indicated by the piles of books on either side of his bronze bust. The tomb is by Il Riccio. Against the second north pillar is the **tomb of Alessandro Contarini (G)**, a Venetian general who died in 1553, by Sanmicheli with a bust by Danese Cattaneo (pupil of Sansovino) and statues by Alessandro Vittoria. The design of the **monument to Cardinal Pietro Bembo (H)**, humanist scholar, secretary to Leo X and friend of Raphael, who died just a few years earlier, is quite different: its simple classical lines have been attributed to Palladio. The bust is by Danese Cattaneo.

Donatello's celebrated equestrian statue of the 15th-century *condottiere* Erasmo da Nardo, known as Gattamelata ('Honey Cat').

In the first south chapel, on the left wall, is the **tomb of Gattamelata (I)** (*see below*), and (right wall) that of his son. They were erected in 1458 by order of Gattamelata's widow.

In the south transept is the wonderful **Cappella di San Giacomo** (or San Felice) **(J)**, designed in 1372–7 and entirely frescoed by Altichiero with stories from the life of St James of Compostela and a huge scene of the *Crucifixion*.

In the north aisle is the Baroque **tomb of General Caterino Cornaro (K)**, by Juste le Court (1674), next to a beautiful **monument by Pietro Lombardo (L)** commemorating Antonio Roselli, who died in 1466.

On the west wall, above the main portal, is *St Anthony Preaching from a Walnut Tree* **(M)**, a fresco by Pietro Annigoni (1985).

The equestrian statue of Gattamelata

Outside the Santo, rising against the sky from an exceptionally high base, is this famous masterpiece by Donatello, made in 1447–53, the first great bronze equestrian monument cast in Italy since the Roman era and the first to be exhibited in a civic piazza. Gattamelata (Erasmo da Nardo) was a Venetian *condottiere* and protector of the Venetian Republic. He died in 1443 and had a state funeral in Venice, but he was buried here in the Santo according to his wishes: it is thought to have been his widow who commissioned this work from the greatest sculptor of the time. The rider dominates the sculpture, sitting squarely astride his charger, a horse clearly influenced by Classical prototypes, including the ancient Horses of St Mark's in Venice and a 4th-century BC bronze horse's head owned by the Medici, which the young Donatello would certainly have seen (it is now in the Museo Archeologico in Florence). The canon ball under the horse's front left hoof cleverly resolved the sculptor's problem of stabilising horse and rider. The monument was instantly acclaimed and Alfonso V of Aragon, King of Naples, decided that he, too, wanted to be immortalised by Donatello, and asked the Florentine merchant Bartolomeo Serragli to try to arrange this. But Donatello only ever carried out the horse's head (now in the Museo Archeologico in Naples).

The stone reliefs on the base are good copies of the damaged originals which the artist sculpted a few years earlier (now in the vestibule of the Biblioteca Antoniana). Unfortunately today the horse and rider are beset with pigeons. While at work on this monument, Donatello lived in the little house opposite the basilica façade (marked by a plaque).

Monastery of the Santo and Museo Antoniano

Adjoining the basilica is the huge Franciscan monastery, with four handsome Gothic cloisters. In the **Magnolia Cloister**, named after its huge magnolia tree, is a modest slab which marks the burial-place of the entrails of Thomas Howard (1586–1646), Earl of Surrey and Arundel, English statesman and connoisseur. Inigo Jones had accompanied the Earl and Countess of Arundel on their Grand Tour in 1612–15, and the Earl is remembered for his interest in Classical sculpture: his collection known as the 'Arundel Marbles' was left by his grandson to the Ashmolean Museum in Oxford.

The **Museo Antoniano** (*well signposted; santantonio.org; closed Mon*) has sculpture, tapestries and inlaid wood panels, as well as works attributed to Tiepolo and Giovanni Battista Piazzetta and a lunette frescoed by Mantegna. The **Biblioteca Antoniana** (*open to scholars*) contains MSS and incunabula.

Scuola del Santo and Oratorio di San Giorgio

In Piazza del Santo outside the basilica are the two almost-matching brick façades of the Scuola del Santo and the Oratorio di San Giorgio. The **Oratorio** (*santantonio.org; closed Mon*), from 1377–84, is entirely frescoed by Altichiero di Zevio. The cycle is now a UNESCO heritage site. The large colourful scenes illustrate the life of Christ (entrance wall), with a *Coronation of the Virgin* above the *Crucifixion* (on the opposite wall). The side walls have scenes from the lives of the saints: St George is shown with the Dragon but also in much less well-known episodes of his life such as when he made a pagan temple collapse, and his death by decapitation. Harrowing scenes of martyrdom follow St Catherine and St Lucy's confessions of their Christian faith.

The **Scuola or Scoletta** (*same website and opening times*) contains paintings of the miracles of St Anthony, carried out in 1511 by Venetian artists: the young Titian painted three of the scenes (the *Jealous Husband*, the *Irascible Youth* and the *Newborn Babe*; *for explanations of the scenes, see p. 28*).

PRATO DELLA VALLE, SANTA GIUSTINA & THE ORTO BOTANICO

Map Padua 8.

Prato della Valle is the largest 'piazza' in Italy, surrounded by a miscellany of arcaded buildings. This huge area was used from Roman times for public spectacles and fairs but by the 18th century it had become an unhealthy marsh and so the land was reclaimed and laid out in 1775, under the inspiration of Andrea Memmo, a distinguished Venetian who took up public office in Padua in the same year. He gave his name to the central island, **Isola Memmia**, which is approached by four bridges decorated with fountains and encircled by a canal bordered by 18th-century statues of famous citizens (including Memmo himself), as well as professors and students of the University. The huge space is still used for a weekday market (fruit and vegetables, in the mornings) and for a larger market on Saturdays.

On the west side of the Prato is the **Loggia Amulea**, built in 1861 in the Venetian style with two Gothic loggias in brick and marble, with statues of Giotto and Dante. On the north side, Palazzo degli Angeli houses the charming **Museo del Precinema** (*minicizotti.it*), which illustrates the history of the magic lantern shows which predated the cinema. It also has a collection of stereographs.

The Basilica of Santa Giustina

This Benedictine church (*abbaziasantagiustina.org*) was designed by Il Riccio in 1502 but modified by its builder Andrea Moroni. It has eight cupolas, four of which are invisible in the interior, and was built to protect the relics of two of Padua's patron saints, St Prosdocimus (the city's first bishop) and St Justina, an early martyr.

The interior is huge. In the south transept is the **Arca di San Mattia**, containing relics of St Matthias, the apostle who was chosen to replace Judas. The relics were purportedly brought to Italy by Helen, mother of Constantine. The tomb chest is supported on stout pillars and has mid-16th-century Greek marble reliefs. Behind it, a door leads into a chapel with a frescoed cupola above a well. Beneath the pavement can be seen a fragment of the original mosaic floor of the Palaeochristian basilica. The altar beyond has a painting showing the finding of the well.

The so-called Corridor of the Martyrs leads down to the **Cappella di San Prosdocimo**, an oratory which retains its domed cruciform architecture dating from as early as 520 but which was decorated in 1565, when the effigy of the saint was carved. The only architectural element which survives from the 6th century is the very rare iconostasis with delicate columns and an inscription. Above the effigy, the roundel with a relief of the saint also dates from this time. The interior used to be covered with very fine mosaics (destroyed in an earthquake of 1117), and a fragment of the pavement can be seen through an adjacent glass door.

In the **north transept** is another marble tomb chest, the **Sarcofago di San Luca**, forming a partner to that of St Matthias in the south transept and said to contain relics of St Luke the Evangelist. It was decorated with alabaster reliefs in 1313.

In the **sanctuary** of the main church (with very fine 16th-century choir stalls), the **high altarpiece of the *Martyrdom of St Justina*** was painted by Veronese in 1575, four years after the Battle of Lepanto, the great Christian naval victory over the Turks, which was fought on St Justina's Day (7th Oct).

Orto Botanico

This is the oldest botanic garden in Europe (*ortobotanicopd.it*), founded in 1545. It is beautifully tended and all the plants are well labelled. It retains its original form and structure with a charming circular walled garden, entered through four symmetrical gates. The geometrical beds are protected by low iron fences, and there are a number of ponds and fountains. The various sections include medicinal and aquatic plants, rare species from northern Italy, and poisonous plants. The oldest plant is a palm tree dating from 1585 and known as 'Goethe's palm' (since he saw it when he visited the garden during his Italian Journey 1786 and it inspired his later 'Essay on the Metamorphosis of Plants'). Now some 11m tall, it survives in a little greenhouse. There are some interesting 19th-century hothouses, where succulents and carnivorous plants are kept, and also a display of the plants first introduced into Italy in this garden, including the lilac, first cultivated in 1565, the sunflower in 1568, and the potato in 1590. There is also a Botanical Museum and a Botanical Theatre, where you can enjoy a film entitled *Goethe: The Life of Leaves*, which imagines the great poet returning to Italy and re-living his Italian Journey.

OTHER THINGS TO SEE IN PADUA

The Reggia Carrarese Chapel

This 14th-century chapel (*Via Accademia; map Padua 3–5; open mornings; closed Mon*), **built by the Carraresi as part of their palace, when they were lords of Padua, preserves frescoes by Guariento of Old Testament scenes, including** *Judith and Holofernes* **and the** *Sacrifice of Isaac*.

The city walls and gates

Porta Altinate (*map Padua 4*) is a gateway that belonged to the 13th-century town wall. The later walls, built by the Venetians in 1513–44, with a circumference of some 11km, survive and the two gates to the west, **Porta Savonarola** (*map 3*) and **Porta San Giovanni** (*map 5*), were built by Giovanni Maria Falconetto, their design derived from ancient Roman architecture.

Commonwealth War Cemetery

West of the centre is a small Commonwealth war cemetery with over 500 graves (*for details, see cwgc.org*). To get there, leave by Porta Savonarola (*map Padua 3*) and continue straight along Via Vicenza and Via Chiesanuova. Turn right up Via della Biscia. (*For more on the First World War in the Veneto, see p. 147*.)

Loggia e Odeo Cornaro

This classical-style **Loggia** (*entrance at Via Cesarotti 37; map Padua 6; visits every half hour; closed Mon; padovamusei.it*) was built in 1524 by Giovanni Maria Falconetto, his first work, for **Alvise Cornaro**, a cultivated Venetian who came to live in Padua and surrounded himself here with artists and intellectuals (Falconetto himself was Cornaro's guest for over 20 years). The Loggia was designed as a stage for theatrical representations (many of them with the participation of Angelo Beolco, known as Ruzante, whose statue stands behind Teatro Verdi; *map 3*) and the vault is decorated with stuccoes and mythological scenes. The delightful little **Odeo**, on the right of the lawn, is a remarkable centrally planned building, built a few years later as the seat of a literary society which Cornaro had founded. Derived from Classical models, it was also designed by Falconetto. Palladio was a frequent guest of Cornaro in 1538–40. The façade, has two stucco reliefs of allegories of Time (Apollo as the Sun and Diana as the Moon, copied from antique Roman reliefs). The tiny entrance admits to a charming central room with an umbrella vault covered with lovely grotesques on a white ground, inspired by similar decorations in the Vatican. The little side rooms have landscapes and stuccoes by Tiziano Minio, including one room entirely decorated with white stuccoes of a triumphal procession. Here Cornaro and his erudite friends would meet to converse and listen to music.

Oratorio di San Michele and La Specola

The **Oratorio di San Michele** (*map Padua 7; open weekend mornings and afternoons*), opening off a little cobbled street beside a canal, is all that remains of the ancient church of San Michele (documented as early as 970). It has detached frescoes by Jacopo da Verona dated 1397 including, above the arch, a charming domestic *Annunciation* consisting of three distinct episodes: on the left is the Angel Gabriel, and in the middle a maid at work in the Virgin's house and orchard (with a chicken pecking at the ground). On the right is the *Virgin Annunciate*, with a dog beside her asleep in his basket on the parquet floor, and a straw-seated chair (reminiscent of those painted by Van Gogh), and linen hanging up to dry, while the dove of the Holy Spirit flies in at the door.

On the other side of the canal rises a very high tower (part of a castle built by Ezzelino da Romano, then modified by the Carraresi) which dominates this part of the city. It was transformed into an observatory in the 18th century and now belongs to the University of Padua's Astronomy faculty. It has a small museum, **Museo La Specola** (*map Padua 5; open only for guided tours; www.beniculturali.inaf.it/musei/padova*), with astronomical instruments made in Padua in the 18th and 19th centuries. The view is remarkable.

Oratorio di San Rocco

Reached from one of the narrow lanes which lead north out of Piazza dei Frutti, this an attractive Renaissance building (*map Padua 4; closed Mon; padovamusei.it*), the chapel belonging to one of Padua's many guilds, was frescoed in 1525 with scenes illustrating the life of St Roch, patron saint of the plague-stricken. The scenes of later episodes in the saint's life, on the left wall, are by Gualtiero, born in Padua, and include a townscape of Padua, and St Roch dying in prison in the company of the dog who befriended him. The last scene, of his funeral, is attributed to Stefano dell'Arzere and is one of the most interesting.

San Francesco and MuSME
The **church of San Francesco** (*map Padua 6*), in a very pretty, narrow arcaded section of Via San Francesco, was begun in 1416 and enlarged in the following century when the second south chapel frescoes by Girolamo dal Santo were painted. Two fine large bronze reliefs from the funerary monument of the natural philosopher Pietro Roccabonella can be seen above the door into the sacristy and above the door in the south transept. They are by Il Riccio. Very close on the same side of the street is **MuSME**, an excellent museum of the history of medicine (*musme.it*).

Santa Maria dei Servi
This church (*map Padua 6*) boasts a Crucifix (in the chapel to the left of the choir), made of wood varnished to resemble bronze. Its attribution to Donatello is now accepted by many experts.

Santa Sofia
Santa Sofia (*beyond map Padua 4*), founded in the 9th century, is the oldest church in Padua. It was rebuilt in the 11th–12th century in a style which recalls earlier churches of the Exarchate of Ravenna. The apse is particularly remarkable.

Scoletta del Carmine
In an unattractive modern area, across the river, is the church of the Carmine (*map Padua 4*), next to which is the Scoletta del Carmine (*only open on Thur; carminepd.it*), chapel of one of the city confraternities. It dates from 1377 but has 16th-century frescoes of the life of the Virgin by Giulio and Domenico Campagnola and Stefano dell'Arzere, notably the *Meeting of St Anne and St Joachim*.

Tomba di Antenore
In a patch of garden beside Via di San Francesco is the so-called **Tomba di Antenore** (*map Padua 6*), the 'Tomb of Antenor', the Trojan prince whom Livy credits with the founding of Padua. When the skeleton of a large man was unearthed in the 13th century, it was supposed to be that of Antenor and so this marble sarcophagus was supplied for it and it was set up on short columns here. Beside it is another sarcophagus dating from 1309.

PADUA PRACTICAL TIPS

VISITOR CARD

The **Urbs Picta Card**, valid for 48hrs or 72hrs, gives free entrance to eight key sights in Padua, plus free travel on public transport. The eight sights are: Scrovegni Chapel, Basilica of Il Santo, Palazzo della Ragione, Church of the Eremitani, Oratorio di San Michele, Oratorio di San Giorgio, Baptistery, Carrarese Chapel.

GETTING AROUND

- **By tram**: The 'Tranvia di Padova' tram service has a useful route (Sir 1) with services every few minutes going north–south through the city centre from the railway station, with convenient stops at Eremitani (for the Scrovegni Chapel), Ponti Romani (for Palazzo della Ragione, market places and Caffè Pedrocchi), Santo (for the Basilica) and Prato della Valle (for Santa Giustina and the Botanical Garden). You can pay on board by contactless.

WHERE TO STAY

€€ **Donatello.** Very well located close to Il Santo, the Basilica of St Anthony. Rooms are furnished in a 'could be anywhere in the world' style but comfortable. *Via del Santo 104, hotel-donatello.net. Map Padua 6.*

€€ **Majestic Toscanelli.** An old-established, boutique-style, family-run hotel near Piazza delle Erbe. Rooms are attractively fitted out. *Via dell'Arco 2, toscanelli.com. Map Padua 6.*

WHERE TO EAT

€€ **Ai Porteghi.** Once a traditional *trattoria*, now revamped but still with a lot of classics on the menu, made with local ingredients. Food is simpler at lunchtime, more elaborate in the evening. Closed Sun and Mon. *Via Cesare Battisti 105, aiporteghibistrot.it. Map Padua 6.*

€€ **Antico Brolo.** Don't be put off by the unprepossessing exterior; this is a long-established, family-run restaurant. Also a pizzeria. Tables in the garden in summer (enclosed in winter). Closed Thur lunchtime. *Corso Milano 22, anticobrolo.it. Map Padua 3.*

€€ **Belle Parti.** A special-occasions place, elegant and refined, with bright white napery. Near Piazza dei Signori. Closed for much of August. *Via Belle Parti 11, ristorantebelleparti.it. Map Padua 4.*

LOCAL SPECIALITIES

Pasticceria Graziati, at Piazza dei Frutti 40 (*map Padua 4*), is famous for its *millefoglie*. The **Lilium** pastry shop at Via del Santo 181 (very close to Piazza del Santo; *map Padua 6*), with its old-fashioned interior, is good for many things, including *panettone* and the *Dolce del Santo*. Made to a secret recipe (of course), this is the signature cake of Padua, originally invented in honour of their patron saint, Anthony. A flaky pastry case encloses many good things. Almonds, raisins and candied orange are always part of the recipe.

MARKETS

Padua retains its atmosphere of a busy market town since it has so many flourishing market places. Stalls selling vegetables, fruit and other produce, meat, cheese, honey, clothing, hardware etc. operate in Piazza delle Erbe (weekday mornings and all-day Sat); Piazza dei Frutti (Mon, Tues, Wed mornings and all day on Thur–Sat); Piazza dei Signori (Tues–Sat mornings) and Prato della Valle (weekday mornings and all-day Sat, with an antiques market on the 3rd Sun of the month. Christmas markets are held from early Dec to Epiphany (6 Jan).

FESTIVALS AND EVENTS

Look out for concerts by I Solisti Veneti, classical music orchestra and organisers of the Veneto Festival. They perform regularly in their home city of Padua, as well as across Italy and internationally (*solistiveneti.it*).

For concerts, theatre and other events in villas around Padua, as well as guided tours, look up Villeggiando (*villeggiando.info*).

On 13 June, Padua celebrates the feast of its patron saint, St Anthony, with processions, pageantry, etc.

University graduation ceremonies take place regularly, when the newly dubbed 'doctor', usually crowned with a wreath of laurels, is fêted in the streets by an army of friends in fancy dress chanting '*Dottore, Dottore....*' and sometimes drenching him or her—and the onlookers—with prosecco, water or worse.

THE BRENTA RIVIERA

The Venetians built the canal known as the Naviglio di Brenta or Brenta Vecchia to facilitate navigation between Venice and Padua, diverting the river itself to the north, to reduce the amount of silt pouring into the lagoon. The magnificent villas for which the area is famous first appeared in the 16th century when, in the face of Turkish expansion in the eastern Mediterranean, Venetian patricians shifted their investments from foreign trade to real estate. Portia's villa of Belmont in Shakespeare's *Merchant of Venice* was just one such. The great farms that grew up here were intended both to generate income and to provide a pleasant escape from the heat and humidity of the lagoon in summer.

The principal façades of the residences faced the water, like the palaces on the Grand Canal—and this was deliberate, because the same festive lifestyle that graced the Venice *palazzi* in winter continued in summer in the villas of the riviera. With the approach of the 18th century, the idyllic pleasures of country life merged with a taste for the exotic, and the architecture of the noble manors became more luxurious and extravagant, with spectacular parks, gardens, aviaries, greenhouses and even private zoos stocked with non-native animals. Meanwhile patricians of limited means (of whom there were quite a few), adventurers (even more) and the *nouveaux riches* rented lodgings in the towns, in order not to miss the great social events of the Venetian summer.

For many, the journey from Venice to the summer villa on the Brenta canal would be undertaken in the family gondola. Others would take the *burchiello*, a large riverboat rowed by crews of oarsmen or pulled by horses—a 'marvellous and comfortable craft', as Goldoni recalls, 'in which one glides along the Brenta sheltered from winter's cold and summer's ardour'. Today, between March and Oct, a motorised *burchiello* lazily winds its way from Venice to Padua or vice versa, for a handsome fee, stopping to visit a couple of the 50-odd extant villas. The trip can also be made by bicycle (there are marked cycling routes) or by bus (*for details, see p. 42*).

Today, many of the villas are still privately owned and some are open to the public (usually between April and Oct). Others, such as Villa Nani Mocenigo between Dolo and Mira and Villa Valmarana between Mira and Oriago, have found a new role as venues for weddings, gala events and conferences.

Villas that are open to visitors, either regularly or by appointment, are described below in the order in which they appear if you depart from Padua.

STRA

The 18th-century **Villa Pisani** at Stra (*map Veneto East B2; villapisani.beniculturali.it*), the largest villa on the Riviera, is named after its original owner, the Venetian doge Alvise Pisani. The interior, with a total of just under 150 rooms, was decorated by

Venetian artists, including Tiepolo, who frescoed the *Triumph of the Pisani Family* on the ceiling of the ballroom (1762). The villa was purchased by Napoleon in 1807 and in 1934 it was the scene of the first meeting between Mussolini and Hitler. In the vast park is a labyrinth, described by Gabriele d'Annunzio in *Fire*. On the opposite bank of the canal rises the long front of the **Villa Lazara Pisani**, 'La Barbariga', with a Baroque central structure and symmetrical 18th-century wings.

DOLO

Dolo (*map Veneto East B2*) was once the principal town of the Brenta Riviera in the 18th century, and still preserves its mill, a *squero* (or boatyard) and one of the old locks. Like most of the places along the Brenta, once individual towns in their own right, is has now succumbed to urban sprawl. To the east of the centre, on Via Brenta Bassa, is the **Villa Ferretti Angeli**, designed in 1596–1608 by Palladio's pupil Vincenzo Scamozzi. Its Ionic pilastered façade is particularly elegant. The park is open to the public. Slightly further east, on the corner of Via Badoera, is the 18th-century **Villa Badoer Fattoretto**, which houses the Museo del Villano, which contains a collection of farm instruments and innumerable curiosities which document farming life near the Brenta.

MIRA

It was at Mira (*map Veneto East B2*) that Lord Byron wrote the fourth canto of *Childe Harold*, while staying at **Villa Foscarini dei Carmini** (on Via Nazionale overlooking the Brenta Canal). On the outskirts to the east are the **Villa Pisani Contarini** (or dei Leoni) on Riviera Trentin (*open for events*) and **Villa Valier**, or 'La Chitarra', on Riviera Matteotti (*open for guided tours by appointment; villavalier.it*). A little further, on Via Nazionale, between Mira and Oriago, is **Villa Widmann-Rezzonico-Foscari** (*to visit, see coopculture.it/en/poi/villa-widmann-rezzonico-foscari*), built in 1719 but remodelled in the French Rococo manner after the middle of the 18th century. The most famous of the villas of Mira, it has a two-storey façade with a curved tympanum, and frescoed rooms.

LA MALCONTENTA

On a bend shaded by willows, on the first stretch of the canal (just before the small town of Oriago), stands the **Villa Foscari**, also known as La Malcontenta (*map Veneto East, C2; still privately owned by the Foscari family; closed in winter; for access and opening times, see lamalcontenta.com*), justly one of the most famous of all the Veneto villas. It was constructed around 1555–60 for the brothers Nicola and Alvise Foscari by Andrea Palladio, and is one of his most successful suburban structures, and the nearest he built to Venice but the only one he sited on the Brenta Canal. It was extremely influential in European country-house architecture. The exterior is very slightly rusticated; the side towards the river is characterised by a noble six-columned Ionic porch, which projects outward and is raised on a tall basement with lateral ramps. It has a thermal window, and four characteristic Venetian chimneys. The interesting interior plan provided for two identical apartments for the brothers on the *piano nobile*, on either side of the central Greek-cross *salone* frescoed by

THE BRENTA RIVIERA

The beautiful Villa Foscari, known as 'La Malcontenta', a supreme example of the architecture of Palladio.

Battista Franco and Giovanni Battista Zelotti. In one of the rooms is the frescoed figure of a woman, whom legend claims to be Elisabetta Foscari (the 'malcontent' of the name), exiled here for betraying her husband.

FUSINA

Fusina (*map Veneto East C2*) is where the Brenta Canal enters the Venetian lagoon: if you are coming down the Brenta from Padua, it is here that you glimpse Venice, just 4km away. This was the place where boats were boarded for Venice, before the railway line was built in the 19th century. The trip took about one and a half hours and provided a splendid approach across the lagoon to the city. It was described by numerous travellers, including Charles Dickens in 1846:

I was awakened after some time (as I thought) by the stopping of the coach. It was now quite night, and we were at the water side. There lay here, a black boat, with a little house or cabin in it of the same mournful colour. When I had taken my seat in this, the boat was paddled, by two men, towards a great light, lying in the distance on the sea...It soon began to burn brighter; and from being one light became a cluster of tapers, twinkling and shining out of the water, as the boat approached towards them by a dreamy kind of track, marked out upon the sea by posts and piles...Before I knew by what, or how, I found that we were gliding up a street—a phantom street; the houses rising on both sides, from the water, and the black boat gliding on beneath their windows. Lights were shining from some of these casements, plumbing the depth of the black stream with their reflected rays; but all was profoundly silent. So we advanced into this ghostly city, continuing to hold our course through narrow streets and lanes, all filled and flowing with water.'

Boats still leave Fusina for Venice; but the journey takes only half as long today as it did in Dickens' time.

BRENTA RIVIERA PRACTICAL TIPS

GETTING AROUND

- **By boat**: The 'Burchiello' service provides regular boats along the Brenta canal between the Portello wharf in Padua (*just beyond map Padua 4*) and Venice (Fusina; *map Veneto East C2*). For the route, timetables and prices, see *ilburchiello.it*. Other operators, offering boat trips that also include visits to one or more of the Palladian villas, are Artemar Tours (*artemartours. it*); Battelli del Brenta (*battellidelbrenta. it*), Delta Tour (*deltatour.it*) and Navigazione Brenta (*navigazione-brenta-laguna.it*).
- **By bus**: ACTV service no. 53E runs between Padua bus station and La Malcontenta. The journey takes approx 1hr and buses leave once an hour. They stop at Stra, Dolo, Mira, Oriago (for La Malcontenta). For timetables, see *actv. it*. Choose the 'Extraurbano' tab and choose the route you want.
- **By bicycle:** For the cycling route along the Brenta canal, see *bicicletta. bonavoglia.eu/itinerari/brenta.html*.

WHERE TO EAT

€€ **Trattoria Nalin.** This restaurant in Mira (*map Veneto East B2*) has been the best-known place to eat on the Brenta Canal for many years. Run by the same family since 1914, it serves excellent fish from Chioggia, simply grilled on an open wood fire. Good selection of wines. Open Wed–Sun. *Via Argine Sinistro Novissimo 29, trattorianalin.it.*
€ **Trattoria alla Vida.** Also in Mira (*map Veneto East B2*). A simple place with a little summer garden. Good fish (and meat too). Closed Mon evening and Sat lunch. *Via Don Giovanni Minzoni 31, trattoriaallavida.it.*

THE EUGANEAN HILLS

The Euganean Hills (Colli Euganei; *map Veneto East A2*), southwest of Padua, are an unexpected sight: a small group of low humps rising abruptly from the plain. Geologically speaking, they are lacoliths, formed when magma forces its way to the surface through a double layer of rock, causing the upper layer to erupt. Covered with chestnut woods, the hills are now protected as a regional park and have pleasant paths for walking. The vineyards produce good wine, both white and red. There are also several spa towns in the area, whose hot thermal springs, rich in minerals, have been well-known since Roman times. Other highlights include a number of fine villas and gardens; and places linked to the area's many literary associations. Petrarch spent the last years of his life, and is buried, in Arquà Petrarca; Byron was an assiduous visitor; and it was at Este that Shelley wrote his 'Lines Written among the Euganean Hills', about the healing power of nature and landscape:

Many a green isle needs must be
In the deep wide sea of Misery,
Or the mariner, worn and wan,
Never thus could voyage on…

In the south part of the Euganean Hills is the charming Arquà Petrarca and, in a landscape bisected by sinuous canals, a chain of historic walled towns: Monselice, Este and Montagnana.

THE SPA TOWNS

Abano Terme is the most famous spa in the Euganean Hills, known for its thermal pools and its curative mud, said to be effective against rheumatism and arthritis. The Grand Hotel Trieste & Victoria was established in 1912 and still retains something of the atmosphere of the golden age of 'taking the cure'. The town has some interesting early 19th-century buildings designed by the Neoclassical architect Giuseppe Jappelli (whose most famous work is the Caffè Pedrocchi in Padua). An example is the colonnaded screen fronting the entrance to the Montirone thermal springs.

Montegrotto Terme has more parks and extensive remains of ancient Roman baths as well as a small Roman theatre. A less grand and rather old-fashioned spa is **Battaglia Terme**, with a park also laid out by Jappelli.

ABBAZIA DI PRAGLIA
Approached by a beautiful, tree-lined driveway, this huge abbey is a Benedictine foundation of 1080, now the largest community of monks in Italy (40 members at

the time of writing). Its members reside either here, or in nearby Teolo or in Venice, or in a their sister foundation in Bangladesh. Today they produce their own range of herbal remedies and teas, natural cosmetics, honey and wine, but are particularly renowned for their skill in restoring books. They also have their own publishing house.

The abbey is open for guided tours (*closed Mon; for times, see praglia.it; free but donation welcomed*). Visitors are shown the cloisters, chapter house, refectory and church. The three peaceful cloisters date from the 15th–16th centuries. The refectory (attributed to Pietro Lombardo, c. 1495) has ceiling paintings by Giovanni Battista Zelotti, 18th-century carved woodwork and, at the back, a frescoed *Crucifixion* by Bartolomeo Montagna (1490–1500), with the Cross shown against a limpid blue sky. The church (Santa Maria Assunta) was built between 1490 and 1548, probably to a design by the great Venetian sculptor and architect Tullio Lombardo (son of Pietro). The vaulted Latin-cross interior has 16th-century Venetian paintings, a 14th-century wooden crucifix over the high altar, and frescoes in the apse by Domenico Campagnola.

There is a shop where you can purchase some of the produce made by the monks.

VILLAS & GARDENS

In a wonderful position in the wooded hills above Luvigliano (*map Veneto East A2*), surrounded by vineyards and fields, is the **Villa dei Vescovi** (*fondoambiente.it/villa-dei-vescovi-eng*). It was built in 1535–42 for the Bishop of Padua, Francesco Pisani, under the direction of Alvise Cornaro by Giovanni Maria Falconetto, and continued by Andrea della Valle in 1567. Both Giulio Romano and Vincenzo Scamozzi were involved in the project. On three sides it has open loggias overlooking the lovely landscape. It contains frescoes by the Netherlandish artist Lambert Sustris (1545), who also worked in Padua. There is a café and a wine bar where you can taste the local wines.

In 1570 Andrea della Valle was also involved in the construction of the **Castello del Catajo** (*castellodelcatajo.it*), just north of Battaglia Terme off Via Maggiore. He built it for Pio Enea degli Obizzi, a captain of the Venetian army, and the contemporary frescoes by Giovanni Battista Zelotti on the first floor depict the exploits of members of the Obizzi family, including one who accompanied Richard I of England on the Crusades, and another who perhaps fought for the English against the Scots at Neville's Cross in 1346. When the building was altered in the 17th century, part of the beautiful garden was created with numerous fountains.

At **Valsanzibio** (*map Veneto East A2*) is the Villa Barbarigo, built in the mid-17th century for the Venetian nobleman Zuane Francesco Barbarigo. Its lovely garden (*valsanzibiogiardino.com*) survives from that time, with numerous pools, fountains and statues, as well as a 400 hundred-year-old boxwood maze.

At **San Pelagio/Due Carrare** (*map Veneto East B2*) the Villa Zaborra (really a castle; it also goes by the name of Castello di San Pelagio) has a **Museum of Flight** (Museo del Volo; *castellosanpelagio.it*) where you can see the rooms occupied in 1917 by the famous eccentric poet and nationalist Gabriele d'Annunzio, who served as a daredevil pilot in the Italian air force and had urged his country to go to war with Austria. It was also from here that he masterminded the dropping of leaflets on Venice, urging her to surrender, and here that he planned his flight to Vienna in 1918. This was followed by the Italian victory over Austria at Vittorio Veneto, and a year later by d'Annunzio's flight to Fiume, which he managed to seize for Italy. The history of these notorious exploits is illustrated, and the museum also provides a broad panorama of air 'transport' from the experiments of Leonardo da Vinci to the era of space travel.

ARQUÀ PETRARCA

This delightful little medieval *borgo* (*map Veneto East A2*), the 'soft quiet hamlet' of Byron's *Childe Harold* (Canto IV), is in a pretty position in the Euganean Hills, where numerous *giuggiole* (jujube) trees grow. This ancient Asian plant, *Ziziphus jujuba*, produces an orange fruit, more or less the size of an olive and rich in Vitamin C, which is harvested in early October (when a festival is held in its honour, the Festa delle Giuggiole). In 1868 the village added the name of the poet Petrarch to its name, since he lived here for the last four years of his life.

PETRARCH

Francesco Petrarca (1304–74) was born in the Tuscan town of Arezzo, the son of a political exile from Florence, a member of the Guelph faction. His family followed the Pope from Rome to Avignon and it was there, in 1327, that Petrarch met 'Laura', the woman for whom his unrequited love was to inspire some of the greatest poetry ever written. He studied at Bologna and was crowned 'Poet Laureate' on the Capitoline Hill in Rome in 1341. Thereafter he taught at the University of Padua, but left the city for Venice in 1362, during a plague outbreak. He came to Arquà in 1370 and died here four years later. Petrarch was a great Humanist and his verse provides a rational and very modern analysis of his sentiments and ideas. His *Canzoniere* is probably the most imitated collection of love lyrics in Western literature and traditionally he was considered the rival only of Dante. He himself considered Dante too 'popular', however, and made mock of the fact that simple artisans knew snatches of his *Divine Comedy* by heart. In his own language, Petrarch aspires to Classical perfection and besides his poetry, he also produced studies of ancient Latin texts, in particular writings by Cicero and Virgil. His influence on the circle of intellectuals who surrounded Lorenzo the Magnificent in 15th-century Florence was profound.

At the top of the village, in Via Valleselle, is the **Casa del Petrarca**, the house Petrarch was given when he was appointed canon of nearby Monselice (*closed Mon; for times, see padovamusei.it/it/biglietti-orari-musei*). Originally restored by Petrarch himself, it was altered in the 16th century, with frescoes painted depicting scenes from Petrarch's most famous works including the *Canzoniere*. Petrarch's stature and influence as a poet has meant that the village has been a site of literary pilgrimage since his death. Byron visited several times between 1817 and 1819, on the last occasion accompanied by his mistress Countess Teresa Guiccioli, a far greater admirer of Petrarch's works than Byron himself. Though disappointed by the condition of the house, at the time in a state of neglect, Byron was sufficiently moved to dedicate numerous stanzas of *Childe Harold* to the village.

In the lower part of the village, above Via Fontana, is the church of **Santa Maria Assunta**, outside which is Petrarch's plain sarcophagus of red Verona marble, supported on four tall plinths in the manner of the tomb of Antenor in Padua (*see p. 36*), and with an epitaph composed by the poet himself: FRIGIDA FRANCISCI LAPIS HIC TEGIT OSSA PETRARCE; SUSCIPE VIRGO PARENS ANIMAM; SATE VIRGINE PARCE. FESSAQ IAM TERRIS CELI REQUIESCAT IN ARCE. ('This stone covers the cold bones of Francesco Petrarca; receive his spirit, O Virgin mother; O thou born of the Virgin, pardon him. Now weary of the earth, may he find repose in the citadel of Heaven.') Inside the church is an altarpiece of the *Annunciation* by Palma Giovane. The **fountain** which gives Via della Fontana its name, beneath a wide stone archway, is of ancient origin. A Latin inscription informs us that a spirit inhabits the water, of which Petrarch once drank.

Traces of prehistoric pile dwellings were found on the shore of the little **Laghetto della Costa**, just over 2km east of the town. The finds from here are in the archaeological museums in Este and Padua.

MONSELICE

Monselice (*map Veneto East A2–A3*), which lies on either side of the Bisatto Canal, was a Roman settlement, a Lombard *gastaldato* in 602, a free commune, a seigniory, and finally a Venetian dominion. The town was particularly valuable strategically for its location on the route from Ferrara to Padua, and for the protection afforded by the sharply rising hill that still dominates the town. Today it is an active industrial and agricultural centre. It takes its name (literally, 'mountain of flint') from the small mound of debris dug from the quarry that twice served to pave St Mark's Square in Venice.

PIAZZA MAZZINI
In the lower town, on the east side of the Bisatto, is **Piazza Mazzini**, a wide square with the medieval Torre Civica on one side, with a fine loggia and crenellated parapet, next to a stretch of the original city walls. On the northeast corner of the square is the 16th-century Monte di Pietà, with a small loggia, and the **Museo San**

Paolo, with the archaeological and art collection of the town, along with excavations of a medieval church (*sanpaolomonselice.it*).

From here begins Via del Santuario, with the most interesting sights of the town.

CASTELLO CINI

At the foot of Via del Santuario, just off Piazza Mazzini, is Castello Cini (*castellodimonselice.it*), actually a network of buildings, the oldest of which are the 11th-century Casa Romanica and the 12th-century Castelletto. The complex was enlarged in subsequent centuries and restored by Count Vittorio Cini, an early adherent of Fascism who had been given the title Count of Monselice, later quarrelled with Mussolini and devoted himself instead to philanthropy and the arts. The interior houses a collection of paintings, sculpture, weapons, Renaissance furniture, tapestries, and in the Sala del Camino Vecchio, a monumental fireplace shaped like a tower. An antiquarium hosts five tombs with the bodies and funerary ornaments of seven Lombard warriors and children, dating from the mid-7th century, discovered on the hillside. There is also a small museum (Museo della Rarità) dedicated to the architect and designer Carlo Scarpa, with sculptures, drawings and glassware.

VIA DEL SANTUARIO

Continuing uphill along the cobbled Via del Santuario from Castello Cini, you soon come to the 16th- and 17th-century **Villa Nani-Mocenigo**, a private villa whose gateway reproduces a quotation from the 4th-century Roman poet Claudian: *Emeritam hic suspende togam*: 'Here hang up your toga of office'. In other words, this was intended as a place to relax. Beyond the gateway, the villa wall is notable for the curious 18th-century statues of dwarves that line its parapet, a nod to the original owners' name, *nani* meaning dwarves in Italian.

Just a little further on, round a bend in the road with wide views to the right over the town and the plain beyond, is the **Duomo Vecchio**, dedicated to St Justina. It is a Romanesque-Gothic church of 1256 with a 12th-century campanile and a three-part façade with a rose window, smaller mullioned windows, and a 15th-century porch. Inside, there is a single nave with three apses; the walls of the central apse have fragments of 13th-century frescoes, and there are various altarpieces by minor 15th–17th-century Venetian painters.

The road then leads through the **Porta Romana** (1651), marking the entrance to the grounds of the Villa Duodo and the pilgrimage route of the **Santuario delle Sette Chiese**, both founded by the Duodo family, granted permission from the papacy to build and name six chapels after the seven major basilicas of Rome (the chapel dedicated to both St Peter and St Paul serves as the sixth and seventh). The chapels, lining the road on the left, were designed by Vincenzo Scamozzi after 1605 and each contain a painting of their corresponding basilica in Rome, including five by Palma Giovane. The pilgrimage path ends with the octagonal **Oratorio di San Giorgio**, built by the Duodo family to house relics and the bodies of three martyrs sent from Rome.

The **Villa Duodo**, adjacent to the oratory, was also designed by Scamozzi (1593), though a new wing with the current façade was added by Andrea Tirali in 1740.

It now belongs to the University of Padua and can only be seen from the outside, though the formal garden and monumental staircase leading to the Exedra of St Francis are open to visitors.

To the left of the exedra, a stairway and then a path lead to the top of the hill (150m), with the imposing **Mastio Federiciano**, a keep built by Ezzelino da Romano, tyrant of Padua, for the Emperor Frederick II in 1239 and enlarged by Padua's subsequent ruling family the Carraresi. The fantastic views were remarked upon by both Ralph Waldo Emerson (who called Monselice the 'most picturesque town I have seen in Italy') and Mary Shelley, who mentions the panorama from the summit in the novel *Valperga*. Ongoing excavations here are uncovering early medieval material. There is a nature walk (**Percorso Naturalistico**; *at the time of writing open on Saturdays in spring and autumn; for details see castellodimonselice.it*).

ESTE

This little town, at the southern edge of the Euganean Hills (*map Veneto East A3*), was the chief settlement of the ancient Veneti before it became the Roman *Ateste*. The town later gave its name to the powerful House of Este, the dynasty that later became dukes of Ferrara and Modena. The Este family were displaced to Ferrara in 1240 by Ezzelino III da Romano, ushering in a tumultuous period for the town, before it settled under Venetian dominion in 1405.

THE CASTELLO AND MUSEO NAZIONALE

The huge battlemented **Castello Carrarese** dates mainly from 1339, and its impressive walls enclose a public garden.

The 16th-century Palazzo Mocenigo, built into the walls, is home to the **Museo Nazionale Atestino** (*closed Mon; atestino.cultura.gov.it*), founded in 1888 to house finds from excavations and opened here in 1902. The museum is notable for hosting the most significant collection of artefacts related to the ancient Venetic civilisation, reflecting Este's prominence in the period. The pre-Roman section has finds and grave goods from the Bronze Age and early Iron Age, collected across the Euganean Hills. The most important of these is the bronze Benvenuti situla (c. 600 BC), decorated with three bands of reliefs, a narrative sequence depicting scenes from the lives of the local aristocratic class. Artefacts from the pile dwellings of Laghetto della Costa, near Arquà (*see p. 46*), are also on display. Many of the finds from the Roman era date from the reign of Augustus, who founded a colony of veterans of the Battle of Actium (31 BC) in Este. The collection includes coins, mosaics, glassware and pottery (including the distinctive, so-called 'Aco beakers'), grave stelae and a fine bronze head of Medusa (1st century AD), with her hair tied under her chin. The last section is devoted to the medieval period onwards, with a *Madonna and Child* by Cima da Conegliano (1504).

THE VILLAS OF VIA CAPPUCCINI

Behind the castle are the lovely parks of several villas, including (at the junction of

Via Cappuccini and Via George Byron) the chalet-style **Villa Kunkler**, sometimes known as Villa Byron, having been occupied by Byron in 1817–18. Shelley also visited during this period, composing Lines Written Among the Euganean Hills while watching the sun rise and set from here. He also wrote 'to Mary', a poem longing for the arrival of his wife, which mentions the echo of the nearby castle. Mary herself mentions Este several times in the historical novel *Valperga*. On Via Cappuccini, through a gate, is the 18th-century **Villa Contarini degli Scrigni**, known also as the Vigna Contarena, with a richly frescoed interior. Though privately owned, the villa is sometimes open for guided tours, in conjunction with the Villa Kunkler. Also on Via Cappuccini, its entrance marked by the **Arco del Falconetto** archway (1525), is **Villa Benvenuti**, with a 19th-century park designed by Giuseppe Jappelli, from which many of the pre-Roman finds in the Museo Atestino were excavated. A path leads up the hill overlooking the castle to the 16th-century Palazzo del Principe, built for the Contarini family, possibly by Vincenzo Scamozzi.

THREE CHURCHES

On Via Garibaldi, close to the castle, is the **duomo**, dedicated to the early martyr St Tecla. The original medieval church was rebuilt in 1690–1720 by Antonio Francesco Gaspari and has an 18th-century campanile built on an 8th-century base. The unfinished façade of rough brick disguises a Baroque interior, with a large painting of *St Tecla Freeing Este from the Plague* over the high altar, by Giambattista Tiepolo (1759).

From here Via Garibaldi and Via Alessi bear southwest, over the canal, to the church of **Santa Maria delle Consolazioni** (or Santa Maria degli Zoccoli, 1504–10), with a campanile of 1598 and pretty cloister. The Cappella della Vergine contains a magnificent Roman mosaic pavement excavated nearby.

To the west, on the central island of a roundabout, is the octagonal church of the **Beata Vergine della Salute** (1639), with two octagonal campanili flanking the apse and three paintings by Este-born Antonio Zanchi inside.

ON AND AROUND PIAZZA MAGGIORE

Piazza Maggiore is the main square of the town, lined with attractive porticoed buildings, including the 14th-century Palazzo Scaligero and the Palazzo del Municipio, dating from the 17th century and still the seat of local government. To the east, on Via Principe Umberto, is the Romanesque church of **San Martino**, the oldest church in the town, with a campanile of 1293 that has been leaning outward since 1400. Inside is a 18th-century white Carrara marble altar with angel sculptures by Antonio Bonazza and, in the Cappella di San Lorenzo, a 14th-century fresco of the *Crucifixion*. Further along Via Umberto is the 15th-century basilica of **Santa Maria delle Grazie**, rebuilt in the 18th century, known for the early 15th-century Byzantine icon of the Madonna that gives the church its name, illuminated in the apse and venerated as miraculous. There are also two altarpieces by Zanchi.

About 5km southwest of Este, off the SP15, is the **Abbazia di Santa Maria delle Carceri** (*abbaziadicarceri.it*). Founded by Benedictine monks in the 11th century as a hospice for pilgrims, the monastery fell into decline before being transferred to the Camaldolese in 1408 by Pope Gregory XII. The complex includes an octagonal church of 1643, remains of a 12th-century Romanesque cloister and a larger 16th-century Renaissance cloister, with an ancient library decorated with frescoes.

MONTAGNANA

The magnificent medieval walls which surround the entire small town of Montagnana (*map Veneto East A3*) are among the best preserved in all Italy. They were built by the rulers of Padua, firstly the Ezzelino da Romano and then enlarged by the Carraresi in the 14th century, and are nearly two kilometres in circumference. They are particularly impressive since at their foot there is a park on the site of the moat, which in the days of Venetian domination (after 1405) was turned into grassy fields where hemp was grown (and 'spun' along the walls) for use in ships' riggings for Venice's great fleet. The walls are interspersed with twenty-four hexagonal towers and just four gates, the best preserved of which are the Rocca degli Alberi or Porta Legnano, dating from 1362, with a fortified bridge and tower, and the Porta Padova.

PORTA PADOVA AND THE CASTELLO DI SAN ZENO
Before crossing the moat to enter the town through Porta Padova, look right to see the **Villa Pisani Placco** (*in need of repair at the time of writing*), designed by Andrea Palladio. It was completed in 1555 for the Venetian nobleman Cardinal Francesco Pisani. The front and rear elevations both have a double central order of Ionic and Corinthian columns terminating in a pediment. At the back, the colonnades are open, giving onto shady loggias. Also noteworthy is the splendid frieze with bucranic metopes and the family coat of arms in the tympanum. There is also a harmonious ground-floor atrium, with statues of the *Four Seasons* by Alessandro Vittoria (1577).

Porta Padova is adjoined by the **Castello di San Zeno**, built by Ezzelino III da Romano in the 13th century. Its tall keep, the Mastio di Ezzelino, can be climbed. The castle is home to the **Museo Civico** (*closed Mon; comune.montagnana.pd.it*). The contents include Bronze and Iron Age finds (9th–8th centuries BC) from a local prehistoric site, and material from tombs and inscriptions dating from the 1st century AD when there was a Roman *vicus* (civilian settlement) here. There is also a collection of medieval ceramics and paintings, including a canvas by Antonio Zanchi, a native of nearby Este.

ON AND AROUND PIAZZA VITTORIO EMANUELE
The arcaded Via Carrarese leads towards the centre of the town, passing the **Palazzo del Municipio**, an austere building with rusticated portico, set back from the road, attributed to Michele Sanmicheli in 1553 (but later remodelled after a fire in 1593). The Sala del Consiglio has a coffered ceiling of 1605.

The street ends in the spacious main square, **Piazza Vittorio Emanuele**, with the **Duomo di Santa Maria Assunta**, built in a transitional Gothic-Renaissance style between 1431 and 1502 on the site of an 11th-century structure of which a few traces remain. There is no campanile; instead, three Gothic bell turrets crown the brick façade. The marble doorway was probably added in 1530 by Jacopo Sansovino, with a carved figure of the *Madonna* by Antonio Minello in the lunette. The tall, early Renaissance interior, a single aisle with barrel vaulting, has a large fresco of the *Assumption of the Virgin* in the apse, attributed to Giovanni Buonconsiglio, a protagonist of the Venetian school, who is known to have lived here from 1505 until 1513 (there is an altarpiece also by him on the south side). Other frescoes probably by his hand are on the west wall of the north transept and on the inside of the façade. On the high altar, in a stone frame, is a huge *Transfiguration* signed and dated 1556 by Veronese. On the west wall, on either side of the door, are frescoes of *David* and *Judith*, discovered in the 20th century, possibly the work of Giorgione. Though attribution is uncertain, we know Giorgione spent time in Montagnana, with a rare drawing of his depicting the city walls and castle of San Zeno on display in Rotterdam (the Boijmans museum).

From the bottom of the square opposite the duomo, an alley (Via San Francesco) runs south to the church of **San Francesco**, a 14th- and 15th-century edifice altered in the 17th century, with a tall 15th-century campanile next to the walls. It contains a *Transfiguration* by the school of Veronese (clearly inspired by the autograph work in the cathedral), and a *Madonna* by Palma Giovane.

EUGANEAN HILLS PRACTICAL TIPS

GETTING AROUND

- **By train**: There is a direct service of regional trains between Padua and Ferrara stopping at Terme Euganee-Abano–Montegrotto, Monselice and Rovigo, and services are fairly frequent. Less frequent slower trains also stop at Battaglia Terme. Este and Montagnana are also served by direct trains from Padua, and there is a more frequent service from Monselice.
- **By bus**: A network of regional buses operated by Busitalia Veneto links Padua to Abano Terme, Arquà Petrarca, Battaglia Terme, Due Carrare (for San Pelagio), Este, Luvigliano (for Villa dei Vescovi), Monselice, Montagnana, Praglia, Rovigo and Valsanzibio (*for timetables, see fsbusitalia.it*). During the summer, the Colli Euganei Link service is available, connecting the principle sites in the Euganean Hills.

WHERE TO STAY

ABANO TERME
€€€ **Trieste e Victoria**. A well-established, typical elegant spa hotel with lovely gardens and thermal pool. *Via Pietro d'Abano 1, hoteltriestevictoria. com.*

MONTAGNANA
€€ **Aldo Moro**. Family-run since 1940. Also has a restaurant. *Via Marconi 27, hotelaldomoro.com.*

WHERE TO EAT

ARQUÀ PETRARCA
Arquà is not short of places to eat.
€€ **La Montanella** (*montanella.it*) and
€€ **Al Guerriero** (*osteriaguerriero.com*) are well-established places in the old medieval centre, offering local cuisine.
€ **L'Enoteca di Arquà** offers wine and snacks (*lenotecadiarqua.it*).
MONSELICE
€€ **La Torre**. Well-established place serving traditional fare. The truffle ravioli is a speciality. *Piazza Mazzini 14, ristorantelatorremonselice.it.*
MONTAGNANA
€–€€ **Le Mura**. Bar-restaurant serving local hams and cheeses and known for its home-made pasta. The speciality is *bigoli al torcolo*, the traditional fat spaghetti of the Veneto. *Via Circonvallazaione 145, lemuramontagnana.it.*

LOCAL SPECIALITIES

Arquà Petrarca is known for its **olive oil and jujube fruits**. Este is a pottery town and has been known for its **ceramics** and tableware since the 18th century. Este Ceramiche revived the tradition in the 1950s and now have their manufactory and showroom at Via Sabina 31 (*esteceramiche.com*). The Euganean Hills as a whole are known for their **wines**. The Colli Euganei DOC was established in 1969, with both red and white wines produced. The red wine is made of mostly French grape varieties, including Merlot, Cabernet Sauvignon and Cabernet Franc, with up to ten percent Raboso, an ancient Venetian variety and one of the few native grapes to endure locally. The white wine is also a blend, made up of at least 30 percent Garganega, the grape most known for producing Soave, and 30 percent Glera (the Prosecco grape) or Sauvignon Blanc. Moscato Giallo, or yellow Muscat, is the basis for the only DOCG wine in the Colli Euganei, Fior d'Arancio (lit. 'Orange Blossom'). This is a sweet sparkling wine, with the volcanic soil adding a minerality that differentiates it from other yellow Muscat wines. Top producers include Maeli, near Baone, and Vignalta, near Arquà. The Abbazia di Praglia make a variety of wines, including classic method sparkling Pinot Noir and wines entirely made from the Raboso grape.

FESTIVALS AND EVENTS

Autumn is the time when most of the local festivals take place: the **Palio of Montagnana** is held on the first Sun in Sept, with a horse race between the ten districts of the town taking place along the grassy embankment round the city walls. The **Giostra della Rocca** (*giostradellarocca.it*) in Monselice is a similar event spread over three weekends in Sept, with nine different *contrade* (districts) of the town competing in five events: archery; a relay race; a chess tournament; the race of the mills and the centrepiece, the '*Quintana*', with two riders from each district facing off in a jousting tournament. On the first of Nov, the district with the highest score in the sum of the five sports competitions wins the *Palio dei Santi*.

ROVIGO & THE PO DELTA

The province of Rovigo, often referred to as the Polesine, is the stretch of land between the lower course of the Po and Adige rivers, the two longest rivers in Italy, and is the last alluvial plain of the former, created by the deposition of silt as it traverses from the Alps to the Adriatic. The character of the area is shaped by its relationship to water, especially in the delta of the Po, the largest wetland in Italy. The land here has been reclaimed from the sea over the course of centuries, creating a landscape quite unique for the country. Inland, most of the towns are situated along canals, whilst the charming city of Rovigo acts as the provincial capital.

ROVIGO

Rovigo (*map Veneto East A3–B3*) was founded at some point before 838, rising to local prominence in the centuries after flooding has devastated much of the area and the previous local capital of Adria. Rovigo was ruled by the House of Este until it was taken by the Venetians in 1482 as part of the War of Ferrara, and remained under their control until the fall of the Republic in 1797. Napoleon created a duchy here before it came under Austrian rule in 1815, where it remained until Austria was weakened by its defeat at Solferino (*see p. 162*) and later at Königgrätz (1866), after which Venice and its territory, including Rovigo, were joined to Italy.

A walled town in the 12th century, ruins of which are visible next to the two medieval towers, the Torre Grimani and the Torre Donà, evidence of the castle that once stood here. The latter is especially notable for its height and is open for visits. Though its main street is no longer paved with water (the River Adigetto was covered over to form the Corso del Popolo in the 1930s), the town still has a Venetian atmosphere around the pleasant *centro storico*.

Most of the cultural attractions of the city are focused around the central **Piazza Vittorio Emanuele II**, including the attractive 16th-century Palazzo del Municipio and the library of the Accademia dei Concordi, a cultural institute founded in 1580 and located in a palazzo built in 1814.

The **Pinacoteca dei Concordi** (*concordi.it and palazzoroverella.com*) is housed in the Palazzo Roverella, begun in 1474 on a design attributed to Biagio Rossetti, and located just off the Piazza. The fine permanent collection of over 400 paintings is focused on Venetian art from the 15th to 18th centuries, and includes most of the important artists of the period. Highlights include a *Madonna* by Bellini and a portrait of Antonio Riccobono by Tiepolo. The collection is particularly strong on the 18th century, with numerous portraits by Giovanni Battista Piazzetta and Alessandro Longhi. They also host temporary exhibitions, often focused on foreign artists. Opposite is **Palazzo Roncale**, a fine building by Sanmicheli (1555), which hosts exhibitions on local history and culture. At the other end of the piazza is the **Gran Guardia**, built in 1854 by Giambattista Meduna to accommodate Austrian soldiers.

Just to the east is the second square of the city, **Piazza Garibaldi**, with an equestrian statue of the hero himself by Ettore Ferrari, and the Caffè Borsa, there since 1902. The Camera di Commercio encloses the well-preserved Salone del Grano, built in 1934 and notable for a remarkable glass barrel vault — the facade of the building dates back to the 15th century. The Teatro Sociale has a Neoclassical façade dating from 1819 and hosts a well known opera season.

Via Silvestri leads out of the square past the large church of **San Francesco** (with sculptures by Tullio Lombardo) to Piazza XX Settembre, at the end of which is La Rotonda, or **Santa Maria del Soccorso**, a centrally-planned octagonal church surrounded by a portico, built in 1594 by the little-known architect Francesco Zamberlan. The campanile was designed by Baldassare Longhena in the 17th century. It is the Baroque interior decoration here that is especially striking, covered in 17th century '*teleri*', large canvases painted directly on to the walls. Paintings alternate between depictions of the life of the Virgin and celebrations of Venetian mayors : the lower band includes five by Francesco Maffei (*see below*) and others by Pietro Liberi. Above stucco statues (1627) is another cycle of paintings by various prominent Venetian artists of the era. The dome was painted in 1887 after the ceiling was collapsed by the explosion of local Austrian fortifications.

FRANCESCO MAFFEI

Often overlooked as an artist, Maffei's style is usually described as being fluidly, typically Baroque, with all the opulence that that implies, tempered by the recherché exaggeration of Mannerism. What critics often fail to pinpoint is the nervous, haunting quality that pervades all his work. In his own day he was called a painter 'not of dwarves but of giants…whose style stupefied everyone'. Maffei (1605–60) worked in Vicenza for most of his career, with occasional forays to other cities, of which Rovigo is a notable example. His best works are either religious or allegorical, particularly those that show the apotheosis or glorification of local dignitaries (such as his *Glorification of the Podestà Giovanni Cavalli* in La Rotonda in Rovigo). By dint of rapid, bird-like brushstrokes and an unpredictable use of colour, Maffei invests his works with a bizarre, other-worldly atmosphere. He died of plague in Padua.

THE POLESINE

This flat area west of Rovigo, between the Adige and Po rivers, is traversed by numerous canals. Its name, the Polesine, is derived from the Latin word for 'swamp' or 'marsh', reflecting the topography of the area. This is flat, agricultural country, prone to flooding. Rice is an important crop.

FRATTA POLESINE

At Fratta Polesine (*map Veneto East A3*), facing a bridge over a canal, is **Villa Badoer** (*open weekends and holidays*), built by Palladio in 1556 for the Venetian nobleman Francesco Badoer. It is enclosed by an attractive brick wall and preceded by a green lawn with two fountains and two 19th-century magnolia trees. The outbuildings are linked to the house by curving porticoes, and a wide flight of steps leads up to the villa with an Ionic portico and temple pediment. The empty interior is interesting for its remarkable plan (the service rooms and servants' quarters are on a lower level) and for the damaged contemporary frescoes in all the rooms of the villa, by the otherwise unknown Giallo Fiorentino, described by Palladio as 'grotesques of beautiful invention'. This is the only Palladian building entirely decorated in such a way, presumably at the behest of Badoer. Beside the villa is the **Villa Molin** (Grimani Avezzù), a fine building from the same period and in the Palladian style. The facade is slightly run down but the frescoed interior has been recently restored and is open for visits. There are several other interesting late 17th- or early 18th-century villas nearby.

Fratta Polesine was also the birthplace of Giacomo Matteotti (1885–1924), the Socialist politician and opponent of Mussolini who was kidnapped and assassinated by the Fascists in Rome. The house where he was born, which also has the family mausoleum with his tomb, is now the **Casa-Museo Giacomo Matteotti** (*casamuseogiacomomatteotti.it*). Matteotti has bequeathed his name to streets and squares in almost every Italian town.

LENDINARA

Lendinara (*map Veneto East A3*) has a few fine palaces and an exceptionally tall campanile beside its cathedral, built in 1797. There are numerous other churches here, including the Sanctuary of the **Madonna del Pilastrello**, built in 1579, a pilgrimage site attached to a Benedictine monastery. The pretty **Piazza Risorgimento** is overseen by the Palazzo Pretorio, a medieval fortress. Lendinara was the birthplace of a hero of the Italian Risorgimento Alberto Mario, who is commemorated in a monument here, while a plaque on his house records the exploits of his wife, the Englishwoman Jessie White, nicknamed 'Miss Uragano' ('Hurricane Jessie'). She devoted her life to the cause of Italian independence and to the amelioration of social conditions amongst the poor, notably the worker in Sicilian sulphur mines. Trained as a doctor, she later accompanied Garibaldi on many of his campaigns and got to know Giuseppe Mazzini in London and Genoa (where in 1857 she had been arrested and imprisoned for four months and where that she met her future husband, Alberto Mario). She died in Florence in 1906 and her ashes were brought to Lendinara to be buried in the cemetery beside her husband.

BADIA POLESINE

Badia Polesine (*map Veneto East A3*) lies between the Adige river and the Adigetto canal. The history of Badia is tied to the abbey that gave the town its name. Founded in the 10th century, the Benedictine **Abbey of Vangadizza** became an especially powerful monastery, granted feudal independence by Pope Sylvester II.

It began to decline in the 15th century, before being suppressed by Napoleon in 1797 and eventually abandoned. All that remains of the church is the drum of the domed chapel, which contains painted decoration attributed to Filippo Zaniberti and interesting stuccoes of the *Cardinal Virtues*. There is also a bell-tower and the picturesque 13th-centurye cloister is in excellent condition. Recent restoration has converted part of the abbey in to a civic library. The **Teatro Sociale** dates from 1813, with an interior similar to the larger La Fenice in Venice.

THE PO DELTA

The Po is the longest river in Italy (652km). Its source is at Piano del Re (2050m) in Piedmont, on the French border, and it is joined by numerous tributaries as it crosses northern Italy from west to east through Lombardy and the Veneto on its way to the Adriatic. The wide open plain—the largest in Italy—through which it runs and which separates the Alps from the Apennines, is known as the *Pianura padana*. In the late Middle Ages the Po was navigable, and one of the principal waterways of Europe. In 1599 the Venetian Republic carried out major works of canalisation in the delta area in order to deviate the course of the river south to prevent it silting up the Venetian lagoon. It now reaches the sea by seven different channels, with the delta formed by this operation the largest area of marshland in Italy. Circumstances here can be challenging: the waters of the Po are polluted and according to EU regulations, none of its waters should be used for drinking, swimming or irrigation. Drought in recent years is also threatening agriculture and ecology, especially in the Po Delta, as increased saltwater intrusion causes damage to soil. In the Polesine, land area able to be cultivated is rapidly decreasing.

However, the flat open landscape of the delta, with wide views over the reedy marshes and numerous wetlands (known as *valli*), is still remarkably beautiful, whether in typical misty weather or on clear autumnal days. It is a protected area, becoming a Regional Park in 1997, home to various delicate habitats created through the process of reclamation begun in Roman times, a battle still ongoing to this day as flooding and subsidence lower the land further below sea level. Rice and sugar beet were once intensely cultivated here, and some attractive old farmhouses survive, although most of them have been abandoned.

The marshes have interesting birdlife, counting over 370 species, including cormorants, herons, egrets, grebes and blackwinged stilts. Pila and the Po della Pila have important fisheries, and all over the delta area eels, bass, carp, tench, pike and grey mullet are caught. Clams (a new clam was imported into the delta in the early 1980s from the Philippines) and mussels are also cultivated here.

Much of the delta area consists of shallow channels and lagoons, dominated by thick reeds and rushes. Therefore, most of the activity is restricted to small boats operated by local fishermen with the knowledge required to navigate. A few characteristic bridges of boats and ferries survive. The whole Polesine area has been subject to floods since the 19th century.

ADRIA, LOREO AND ROSOLINA

Adria (*map Veneto East B3*), the ancient capital of the Polesine, gave its name to the Adriatic Sea (to which it is now joined only by canal). It was, along with Spina, the Etruscan port for Felsina (now Bologna). This past prominence is reflected in the excellent Museo Archeologico (*closed Mon*), which contains evidence of the city's Graeco-Etruscan origins. The core of the collection stems from the local Bocchi family, whose interest in antiquities led to the creation of a home museum in the 18th century. The earliest finds from the upper Polesine date from the 11th–9th centuries BC. There are also some very fine Greek red- and black-figure ceramics, and beautiful Roman glass from between the 1st century BC and the 1st century AD. Nearby is the 17th-century church of Santa Maria Assunta, which incorporates some Roman masonry. Across the Canal Bianco is the cathedral, which has a little 6th-century Coptic bas-relief and a crypt with remains of Byzantine frescoes.

Loreo (*map Veneto East B3*) is built on a canal and has a well preserved parish church, rebuilt in 1675 with a facade by Baldassare Longhena. **Rosolina**, further east (*map Veneto East C3*), is on the Via Romea, in parts a post-war revival of the long-decayed Roman Via Popilia, which ran down the Adriatic coast from Venice to Ravenna. Rosolina Mare and Isola Albarella are popular tourist destinations further to the northeast, on the delta itself.

PORTO TOLLE

Porto Tolle (*map Veneto East C3–C4*) is the part of the delta closest to the Adriatic, consisting of three islands, the most notable and largest of which is the **Isola della Donzella**. The island used to have *valli* with fisheries, but was reclaimed after a flood in 1966 and now is mostly home to rice fields, albeit at threat from increased salt content. The unique landscape here is characterised by marshland interspersed with modern rural hamlets. The southern part of the island is occupied by the **Sacca di Scardovari**, an attractive lagoon lined with fishermen's huts and boats. Mussels and clams are cultivated here, and it is inhabited by numerous birds. On its shores is a tiny protected area illustrating the typical vegetation of the wetlands that once covered this area.

The easternmost island on the delta, the **Isola di Batteria**, has been almost entirely engulfed by the sea, with ruins just about visible from land. At the end of the delta is a lighthouse built in 1949 on land only formed some hundred years ago.

PO DELTA PRACTICAL TIPS

GETTING AROUND

- **By train**: Rail links in the area are good. There are frequent trains from Rovigo to Badia Polesine (c. 30mins), calling at Fratta Polesine and Lendinara. Trains also link Rovigo with Rosolina (c. 45mins) via Adria and Loreo. From Rovigo there are also services to Padua and Chioggia

and there are some through trains to Verona.
• **By bus**: Buses operated by BusItalia (*fsbusitalia.it*) link Rovigo with Adria, Badia Polesine, Fratta Polesine, Lendinara, Porto Tolle, Rosolina and other regional centres.

WHERE TO STAY

ROVIGO
€€ **Villa Regina Margherita.** In an Art-Nouveau style building, fully modernised within, with restaurant. *Viale Regina Margherita 6, villareginamargherita.it.*

WHERE TO EAT

PORTO TOLLE
€€ **Ponte Molo**. In business since the early 1950s, serving local seafood. They also have simple rooms, if you want to stay. *Via Borgo Molo 5, pontemolo.it.*

ROVIGO
€€ **Tavernetta Dante**. Historic restaurant, proud of its traditional cuisine, reflecting the maritime heritage of the Veneto as well as the produce of its *terraferma*, from spaghetti vongole to rich duck ragouts. *Corso del Popolo 212, tavernettadanterovigo.it.*

VICENZA

Vicenza (*map Veneto West D2*) is an extremely beautiful and well preserved small town in a pleasant position beneath the foothills of the green Monti Berici. The architect Palladio, who settled here in 1523, practically rebuilt it in his distinctive classical style, and established its fame to such an extent that it has been greatly admired by travellers since the 18th century. His most important buildings here are the Basilica and the Teatro Olimpico, but there are also numerous fine palaces by him (or inspired by him). Vicenza is a particularly pleasant place to visit. It is very peaceful, has excellent railway links, and it is just a short walk from the station to the centre of town. From the centre it is also easy to reach (on foot) two of the most important villas in the entire Veneto: La Rotonda, Palladio's architectural masterpiece, and the Villa Valmarana, with its joyous frescoes carried out some two centuries later by Giambattista and Gian Domenico Tiepolo.

> **HISTORY OF VICENZA**
> The Roman municipium of *Vicetia*, the successor of a Gaulish town, was destroyed during the barbarian invasions, but traces of its theatre survived. It rose to importance again in the later Middle Ages and became a free *comune*. The Della Scala family, rulers of Verona, took control of the city after 1314, but from 1404 until the end of the Venetian Republic it placed itself firmly under the protection of the *Serenissima*. The Venetian dialect word *contrà* (or *contrada*) is still used instead of 'Via' for the streets in the older districts of the town, and a surprising number of grand Venetian-Gothic palaces survive. After a turbulent period in the early 19th century, together with the rest of the Veneto, Vicenza joined united Italy in 1866, but suffered much damage during the Second World War. Vicenza today is a busy town, home to numerous small companies (and some large ones), with a particular focus on textiles, leather and metalworking (including gold). The Colli Berici region, extending from Vicenza to the south, produces DOC wines.

ALONG CORSO PALLADIO

At the western entrance to the town centre stands the sturdy **Porta Castello** (*map Vicenza 3*), a fragment of a stronghold built by the Della Scala rulers of Verona but destroyed in 1819. In Piazza Castello, which opens out just inside the gate, look right to see the curious sight of a tall, narrow palace of just two bays, with three giant columns on massive plinths. This is **Palazzo Breganze**, designed by Palladio in the early 1570s but left incomplete. If finished, it would have been a palace on a colossal scale.

> ## ANDREA PALLADIO
>
> Andrea di Pietro della Gondola (1508–80), nicknamed Palladio (from Pallas Athena, the Greek goddess of wisdom) by his patron, the poet Giangiorgio Trissino (1478–1550), designed villas, palaces and churches throughout the Veneto in a Classical style that would profoundly change the face of the region and inspire numerous imitations. His *Quattro Libri*, or *Four Books on Architecture*, became a manual for later architects, especially in England and the United States. In the engraved illustrations for this treatise, Palladio noted the significant dimensions of his buildings, linking together their plan, section and elevation in a series of proportional relationships. The seemingly easy elegance that distinguishes Palladio's designs was, in fact, the result of his careful calculation of such proportional relationships. In applying these systems of numerical progression, which were often associated with contemporary musical harmonic theory, to the spatial relationships of a building, Palladio succeeded in creating the pleasing visual harmonies that characterise his architecture.

From Piazza Castello, the handsome Corso Palladio leads east. This is the principal street of Vicenza, with many fine palaces and fashionable clothes shops. At no. 13 on the left, with engaged Corinthian columns on two storeys, is **Palazzo Thiene Bonin Longare**, apparently designed by Palladio but probably continued by Vincenzo Scamozzi. It has a fine atrium and courtyard (and a garden beyond). Opposite is **Palazzo Capra**, transformed into shops but preserving its portal commissioned from Palladio in the 1540s: Ionic pilasters flank the doorway, and smaller Corinthian ones decorate the window above the balcony. Further on, the handsome Neoclassical façade on a high plinth of the church of **San Filippo Neri** was built in 1824 by Antonio Piovene on a design by Ottone Calderari. It contains a good 18th-century organ made by the Favorito brothers.

Beyond the Venetian-Gothic **Palazzo Thiene** (no. 47), in pink and peach pastel colours (once a 15th-century palace, it now has a modern interior), is the much better-preserved **Palazzo Brunello** (no. 67), painted in a deeper red, with its portico over the pavement and an interesting courtyard. It has two little balconies and roundels with reliefs of Roman emperors in profile over the central window on the *piano nobile*. Opposite, Contrà do Rode leads under **Palazzo Pojana**, also by Palladio, and beyond is the huge **Palazzo del Comune**, the Town Hall, with its flags, formerly a private palace, begun by Vincenzo Scamozzi in 1592 but only finished in 1662. It has a massive columned portico extending over the pavement, and classical columns in the courtyard.

Further up at no. 147 is **Palazzo da Schio**, known as the Ca' d'Oro since it resembles a 15th-century Venetian-Gothic palace. Its brick exterior has four little

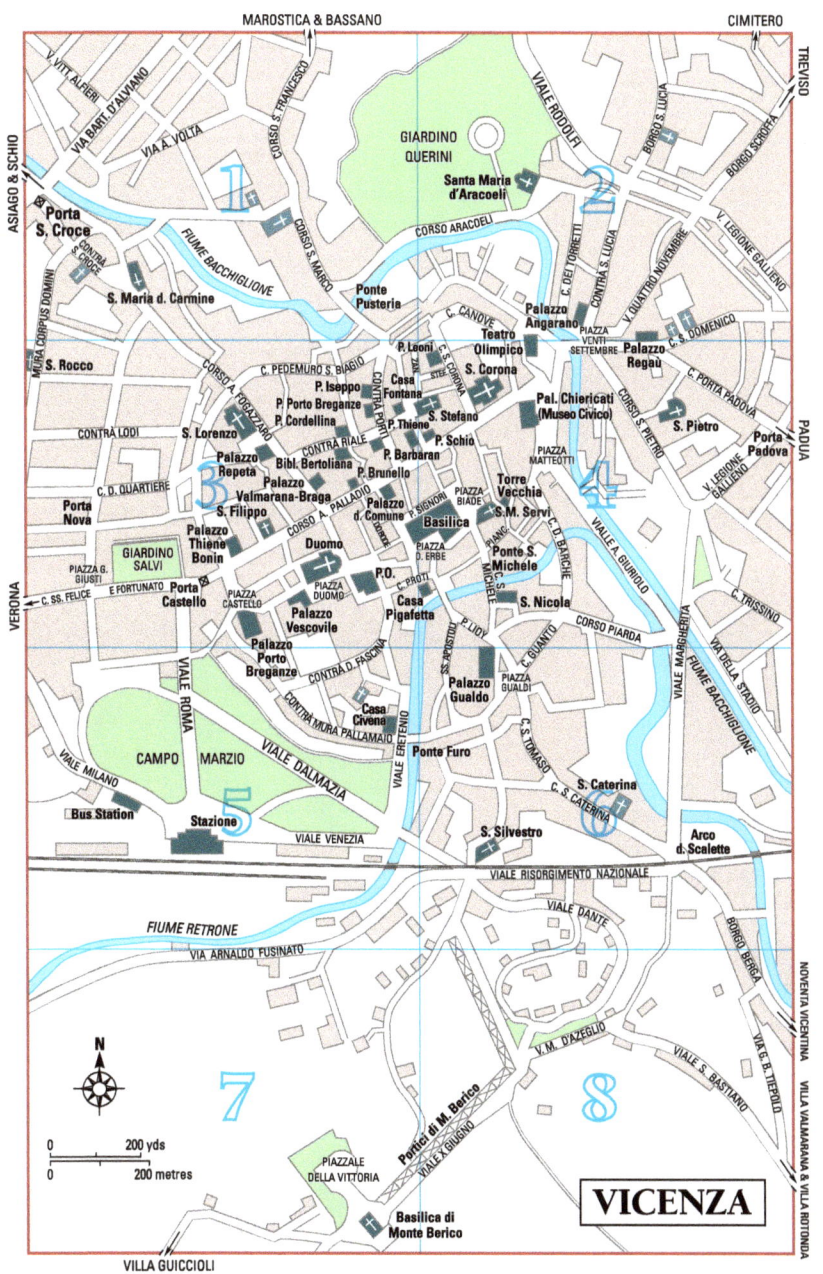

balconies and two grand windows on the *piano nobile* and floor above. It has a handsomely carved arch at its entrance, and archaeological fragments are preserved in the portico. Abutting it, above a shallow flight of steps, is the Neoclassical church façade of **San Gaetano**.

The Corso now begins to descend slightly and loses its pleasant paving. Beyond the raised garden railing of Santa Corona (*see p. 68*) is the narrow **Casa Cogollo**, which has two engaged Ionic columns beneath two Corinthian pilasters above. Above the entrance are two reliefs of winged figures. There is a well in the tiny courtyard. This was traditionally thought to have been built by Palladio for Pietro Cogollo, but is not now usually attributed to him.

TEATRO OLIMPICO

Map Vicenza 2–4. Closed Mon. Booking only necessary for groups. For opening times, see teatrolimpicovicenza.it.

In **Piazza Matteotti**, behind and to the right of the statue, is an imposing rusticated gateway into a walled garden belonging to Palazzo del Territorio, formerly part of a medieval castle, the rebuilt tower of which survives. The ticket office for the Teatro Olimpico is next to the entrance arch. Across the garden, which has a number of architectural fragments and ancient sculpture, an inconspicuous door gives access to the theatre.

The famous **Teatro Olimpico** was designed by Palladio for the Accademia Olimpica, an academy founded in 1555 for drama performances, of which Palladio was a distinguished member. Building only began the year of his death (1580) and so it fell to Vincenzo Scamozzi to complete it. The opening play, performed in 1585, was Sophocles' *Oedipus Rex*. Goethe saw the theatre in 1786 and found it 'inexpressibly beautiful'.

Beyond the room used by the Academy, and a vestibule where some of the tiny oil lamps designed by Scamozzi to light the scenery are displayed, visitors are directed downstairs where there is a gallery illustrating the history of the theatre, before emerging through a door onto the large stage. The shallow *cavea*, derived from Vitruvian models, is surmounted by a peristyle of Corinthian columns (which was the place from which the audience originally entered the theatre). It still has its tiered wooden seating and you can sit and admire the classical *frons scenae* or backdrop, built of wood and stucco, its architecture derived from ancient Roman buildings. In the niches are statues of distinguished academicians by Agostino Rubini and Domenico Fontana, and reliefs of the *Labours of Hercules* adorn the attic storey. Scamozzi designed the remarkable fixed scenery of three streets lined with noble palaces leading away from the stage in perfect perspective, towards a brilliant blue sky.

From the exit, keep left along the cobbled Stradella del Teatro Olimpico to return to Piazza Matteotti.

Fixed backdrop or *frons scenae*, designed by Palladio's follower Vincenzo Scamozzi, in the Teatro Olimpico.

Detail of the façade of Palladio's Loggia del Capitaniato, in central Vicenza.

MUSEO CIVICO

Map Vicenza 4. Closed Mon. For opening times, see museicivicivicenza.it.

The huge porticoed Palazzo Chiericati Valmarana is an excellent example of Palladio's early work, erected in the 1550s or 1560s, although the façade was only completed a century later. It is now home to the Civic Museum.

The atrium and entrance hall are handsome oval rooms with niches and apses beneath pronounced cornices. The room on the left has a very fine ceiling fresco of the *Chariot of the Sun* by Domenico Brusasorci. The chimneypiece has an ingenious (deliberately broken) stone frame. The adjoining room also has a good ceiling by Battista Zelotti and statues of Francesco Sforza and his wife, Bianca Maria Visconti, dating from around 1494. Here you can see a tiny Palladian spiral staircase.

A large room on the ground floor displays huge lunettes by Jacopo Bassano, Francesco Maffei and Giulio Carpioni, dating from the time when Vicenza was under Venetian domination and painted for the Council Chamber of the city magistrate.

Highlights of the display on the main floor include a *Transition of the Virgin*, signed and dated 1333 by Paolo Veneziano; *Calvary* by Hans Memling; paintings by Bartolomeo Montagna. A separate room recreates the interior of the church of San Bartolomeo, with precious altarpieces, including one by Cima da Conegliano.

Sixteenth-century works on the second floor include a stucco relief of the *Madonna and Child* by Jacopo Sansovino; *A Miracle of St Augustine* by Tintoretto; and works by

Veronese. Seventeenth- and 18th-century works in the Roi wing include the *Three Ages of Man* by Van Dyck and works by Giambattista Tiepolo and his son Gian Domenico as well as by Sebastiano and Marco Ricci.

Arranged on the top floor is a collection donated to the city by Giuseppe Roi (1924–2009). It consists mostly of small paintings, drawings and engravings of all periods, beautifully displayed.

The museum also owns 33 drawings by Palladio. These and other graphic works can be viewed on request.

The excavations which were carried out during restoration work are open in modernised underground rooms.

PAINTERS IN VICENZA

Vicenza's churches are full of interesting paintings by lesser-known artists influenced by the great Venetian school of painting. **Alessandro Maganza** (1556–c. 1630) was the son of an erudite painter Giovanni Battista, who was a close friend of Palladio and his patron Trissino. So it was natural that Alessandro was called in to work on the decoration of Palladio's Villa Rotonda here. Paintings by him can also be seen in Santa Corona, the Duomo, and the Basilica of Monte Berico. **Giulio Carpioni**, who died in Vicenza in 1678, carried out a number of paintings for Santi Felice e Fortunato, although he is best remembered for his genre paintings. **Giovanni Battista Pittoni** (1687–1767) was a well-known contemporary of Giambattista Tiepolo and his historical and mythological works were also popular outside Italy. There is an altarpiece by him in Santa Corona (and in the Duomo you can see a painting by an ancestor, Girolamo).

PIAZZA DEI SIGNORI & THE BASILICA

Piazza dei Signori (*map Vicenza 3–4*) is a dignified square graced by two huge columns standing on high, elaborate bases, one bearing the Redeemer (1640) and the other the Lion of St Mark (1520), a clear statement of Vicenza's loyalty to the Venetian Republic. At one corner of the piazza rises the unusually tall and slender **Torre di Piazza**, erected in the 12th century but heightened with additional storeys in 1311 and again in 1444.

Opposite the magnificent **Basilica** (*described below*) is the **Loggia del Capitaniato**, commissioned from Palladio in 1571 by the town council as part of the residence of the Venetian governors. Between the three arches on the façade are four giant semi-columns in brick which reach to the height of the attic storey. The stucco decoration by Lorenzo Rubini illustrates the Venetian victory at Lepanto in the same year. Beside it is the long façade of the **Monte di Pietà pawnbroker's**: the left wing dates from

1500 and the right wing from 1553–7, and they are separated by the church of **San Vincenzo**, by Paolo Bonin (1614–17).

The Basilica

The huge hall in the interior (*closed Mon*) is now used for exhibitions. The terraces at the top of the building can also usually be visited at the same time.

This splendid building is one of Palladio's masterpieces, and it was he who first called it a 'basilica' to illustrate his intention of creating a Classically-inspired public building for use as the town hall and law courts, in the tradition of an ancient Roman basilica. The nucleus of the building is the medieval Palazzo della Ragione, the *Palais de Justice*. In 1549 Palladio was called in to replace a double exterior loggia of 1494 which had partly collapsed. He had the ingenious idea of surrounding the building entirely with two open colonnaded galleries, Tuscan Doric below and Ionic above, crowned with a balcony terrace decorated with statues. The project was only completed in 1617, but Palladio's original design was adhered to nevertheless. Built in bright local limestone, the completed building shows Palladio's admiration for ancient Roman architecture and his skill in giving a new shell to an essentially Gothic core. Restoration of the building was completed in 2012.

Stairs lead up to the loggia and one of the three entrances to the huge Gothic hall of the Palazzo della Ragione, with a remarkable beamed ship's keel roof. The 13th-century building on this site was destroyed by fire in 1444 and this beautiful hall was rebuilt by Domenico da Venezia in 1460. When exhibitions are in progress it is unfortunately very difficult to appreciate the true grandeur of this huge space.

By a door off the loggia, a modern spiral staircase (or a lift) ascend to the terrace at the top of the building behind the statues. Here you can see from close up the lovely pink and white chequered exterior of the building with its round windows below the green roof (there are charming little empty niches at the corners). The view over the rooftops takes in the towers and campanili of the town, as well as Palladio's high green dome of the cathedral tribune, and his Villa La Rotonda on the hill of Monte Berico.

In the porticoes beneath the basilica, the quaint old wooden shop windows and shop signs have been preserved, even if today they don't always correspond to the merchandise for sale inside.

Piazza delle Erbe and Santa Maria dei Servi

The Basilica stands between Piazza dei Signori and **Piazza delle Erbe**, a market square with a medieval brick prison-tower connected to the Basilica, which is very well seen from here. On one side of the piazza is an interesting medley of houses with a portico supported on columns of all shapes and sizes. In the adjacent Piazza delle Biade, **Santa Maria dei Servi** has nine statues on its façade. It is a Gothic church of 1407 enlarged at the end of the century. On the first south altar, beside a pretty little carved doorway, is a lovely altarpiece of the *Madonna and Sts Sebastian and Roch* (with an angel musician below) by Benedetto Montagna. The second north altar is an early 16th-century Lombardesque work with statues and stone reliefs.

THE DUOMO & MUSEO DIOCESANO

The Duomo or Cattedrale (*map Vicenza 3; usually closed in the middle of the day*) was rebuilt after it had been all but destroyed in 1944, but the beautiful tall Renaissance tribune at the east end (begun in 1482), with a high dome (not visible in the interior) on a Palladian design added at the end of the 16th century, survived the bombs, and remains an extraordinary sight. The façade dates from the same century and the brickwork is patterned with pink lozenges and clover leaves on a white ground beneath a very unusual crowning frame at the top. The sturdy detached campanile was built in the 11th century on a ruined Roman building.

There is a raised sanctuary in the broad interior, and a pink balustrade in front of the side chapels. The third south chapel has 17th-century stuccoes and statues and paintings by Alessandro Maganza. In the fourth chapel (on the right wall) is a *Transfiguration* by Girolamo Pittoni. In the fifth chapel is a gold-ground polyptych of the *Dormition of the Virgin* by Lorenzo Veneziano (mid-14th century).

In the tribune, the high altar against the east wall is beautifully decorated with precious marbles and *pietre dure* by the local workshop of Pedemuro, where Palladio worked as a young man (some scholars believe he may have helped to make this altar, which would have been his very first work). On either side the twelve 17th-century paintings, in a pretty framework which follows the shape of the apse, are by local artists including Andrea Celesti, Pietro Liberi and Antonio Zanchi.

The chapel at the end of the north side has 16th-century funerary monuments with busts attributed to Alessandro Vittoria. The altarpiece and frescoes in the fourth chapel are the work of Bartolomeo Montagna. The crypt, with its four massive columns, also has a 15th-century polychrome relief and sarcophagi.

Museo Diocesano

The well displayed Diocesan Museum (*open Mon–Fri afternoons; Sat and Sun by appointment*) occupies the Bishop's Palace (Palazzo Vescovile), which also had to be rebuilt after 1944, although the charming courtyard-loggia of 1494 survived. The collection includes finds from the Roman city, including a 4th-century sarcophagus with a very early representation of the *Adoration of the Magi*. Medieval sculpture includes a very unusual 8th-century sarcophagus in the form of a trough with an inscription. There is a lovely cope with pairs of parrots dating from the early 13th century, probably derived from a Persian design and some fine 14th-century illuminated antiphonals and codices, Church silver, a gilded silver statuette of the *Madonna* dating from c. 1386, as well as the sword and spurs from a knight's tomb in the Duomo (1412). Alongside these treasures is an alabaster relief by the 15th-century English school, finds from excavations in the Hebrew city of Hebron, and a fascinating collection of Coptic crosses from Ethiopia.

At no. 6 Piazza del Duomo is the entrance to the **Criptoportico Romano** (*usually open Sat afternoon and Sun morning*). It was probably part of a 1st-century Roman residence.

SANTA CORONA

Map Vicenza 4. Entrance fee. Closed Mon.

Just out of Piazza Matteotti at the end of Corso Palladio, Contrà Santa Corona leads up past a garden to the important church of Santa Corona. It is early Gothic in style (1261) with a Renaissance east arm of 1489 and a lovely bright interior. It takes its name ('Holy Crown') from the story that in 1259, King Louis IX of France donated a thorn from Christ's Crown (which had come to France as booty from Constantinople) to the Blessed Bartolomeo da Breganze of Vicenza. This church was built specifically to house the precious relic.

North aisle: The **Porto Pagello Altarpiece (A)**, by Bartolomeo Montagna, has the unusual subject of *Mary Magdalene with Sts Jerome, Paula, Augustine and Monica*, with large predella scenes below; the third altarpiece of the **Charity of St Anthony (B)** is by Leandro Bassano; the fourth altar has the late Gothic **Madonna of the Stars (C)** by Lorenzo Veneziano, with an early 16th-century landscape view of Vicenza by Fogolino. The fifth altar was beautifully carved in 1501 by Girolamo Pittoni (on a design by Rocco da Vicenza) to contain a superb late work by Giovanni Bellini, the **Baptism of Christ (D)**. The group of three female figures on the left have wonderfully coloured robes, and an orange parrot assists from a rock. In the background is a wonderful mountainous landscape.

North transept: There is a late 14th-century painting by Tentorello of the **Mocking of Christ (E)**. The exquisite gold **reliquary of the Holy Thorn (F)** dating from the 14th century, is displayed in its own chapel.

Through a door in the north transept there is access to the **sacristy (G)**, with a pretty vaulted ceiling and fine cupboards. In the cloister you can see the **Chapter House**, which has 17th-century statues.

East end: In the **sanctuary (H)**, the beautiful high altar dates from 1669. It is inlaid with *pietre dure* with fruits and flowers and has three panels illustrating the *Last Supper*, *Resurrection*, and *Ascension* (with views of Vicenza and the Basilica below). Above is a marble tabernacle and on the balustrade is more exquisite marble inlay with birds and animals. You can also go behind the altar to see the choir stalls, which have fine wooden inlay dating from the end of the 16th century.

On the right of the sanctuary is the **Thiene Chapel (I)**, with two splendid Gothic family tombs and an altarpiece by Giovanni Battista Pittoni (1723). On the wall outside is a sculpted wood Crucifix dating from the 13th century.

A plaque on the nave pillar **(J)** records the **burial of Palladio** here in 1580; his remains were removed in the 19th century to the Cimitero Maggiore (*just beyond map Vicenza 2*).

South side: Off the crypt is the beautiful **Valmarana Chapel (K)**, designed by Palladio. It has a strikingly simple design with two lateral apses

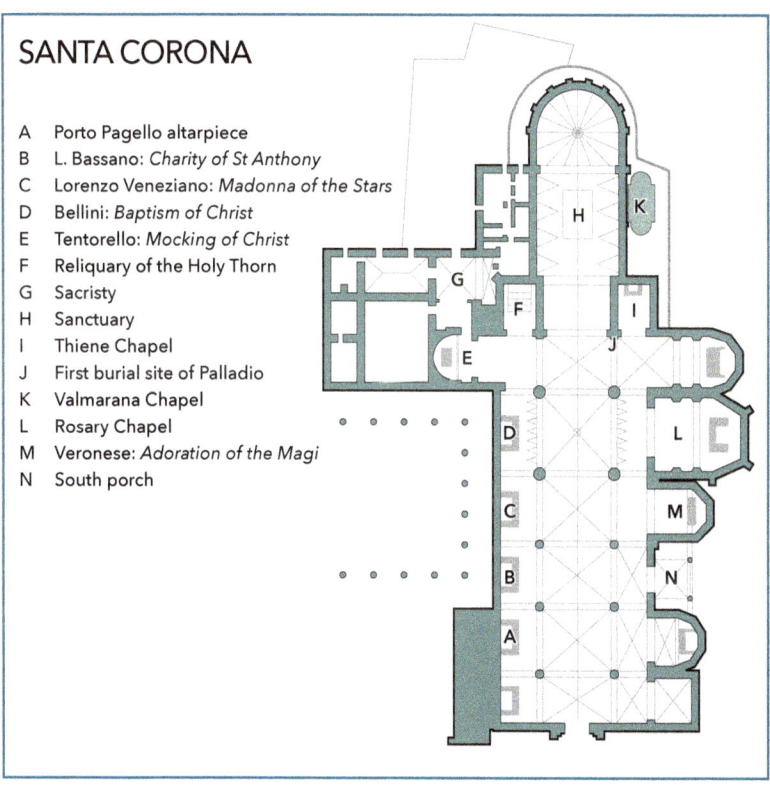

SANTA CORONA

A Porto Pagello altarpiece
B L. Bassano: *Charity of St Anthony*
C Lorenzo Veneziano: *Madonna of the Stars*
D Bellini: *Baptism of Christ*
E Tentorello: *Mocking of Christ*
F Reliquary of the Holy Thorn
G Sacristy
H Sanctuary
I Thiene Chapel
J First burial site of Palladio
K Valmarana Chapel
L Rosary Chapel
M Veronese: *Adoration of the Magi*
N South porch

with two roundels above for the windows and two Corinthian columns flanking the altar (and four Corinthian capitals in the four corners beneath the cornice)

The **Rosary Chapel (L)** was sumptuously decorated in the early 17th century by Giovanni Battista and Alessandro Maganza. In the third chapel there is a painting by Veronese, a very crowded ***Adoration of the Magi* (M)**. The eccentric dramatic scene includes the 'stable' supported by Veronese's familiar huge classical columns, and the kings are accompanied by a mounted soldier in shining armour. It was painted in 1573 at the same time as another similar work of the same subject now in the National Gallery in London.

In the **south porch (N)** there is an interesting tomb decorated with an elephant and pyramid, dating from around 1430.

Museo Naturalistico Archeologico

In the two cloisters of the former convent of Santa Corona, behind a Neoclassical façade of 1823, is the Museo Naturalistico Archeologico of the Museo Civico (*closed Mon; entrance at no. 4 Contrà Santa Corona*). Arranged in the monks' cells is the

Natural History collection, and geological material (with special reference to the Monti Berici). The museum also has finds from the site of the Roman theatre, Lombard material and Iron Age finds from the province, including reliefs of the 5th century BC.

NORTH OF CORSO PALLADIO

This lovely area of the old town has numerous interesting palaces in its quiet streets.

On the west side of Contrà Santa Corona is **Palazzo Leoni Montanari** (*map Vicenza 4*). Now owned by a bank, it is home to the Galleria d'Italia, with a collection of 18th-century Venetian art as well as Russian icons. The palace was remodelled in the late 17th century by two wealthy merchants, Giovanni Montanari and Nicolò Leoni, and has interesting architectural elements (some of which were added in 1808). Beyond the *androne*, with its carved dragons above the archway, is the lovely courtyard, and the staircase is decorated with elaborate stuccoes and statues by Angelo Marinali and paintings by Louis Dorigny. The huge hall on the *piano nobile*, with its five doors, has painted tapestries and stuccoes, and the Galleria della Verità has a very elaborate stucco ceiling with a painting by Giuseppe Alberti. The Loggia d'Ercole is also profusely decorated with stuccoes. The paintings include works by Canaletto and Pietro Longhi and two lovely small landscapes by Francesco Guardi. There are also paintings by Francesco Zuccarelli, Luca Carlevarijs, and a fine view of Venice's Grand Canal by Michele Marieschi. Among the icons are some pieces considered to be the most important in existence outside Russia.

Contrà Santo Stefano leads to Contrà Zanella, where the church of **Santo Stefano** (*map Vicenza 4; open only in the morning*) contains a painting by the great Venetian painter Palma Vecchio. Opposite is **Palazzo Negri de Salvi**, dating from the 12th century but altered in the 15th century, next to the brick Gothic **Casa Fontana**, with a balcony and two grand central windows on the two upper floors.

The huge **Palazzo Thiene** (*map Vicenza 3; open for exhibitions Thur–Sun*) was probably begun on a design by Giulio Romano in 1542 and may have been continued by Palladio after Giulio's death in 1546 (although it remained unfinished). The splendid entrance portico, with four delightful 'spongy' columns and architectural fragments displayed on the walls, leads into the cobbled courtyard. Here you can see the two sides attributed to Palladio and on the third side, a portico of four columns from the early Renaissance palace, which is incorporated into the structure. In the interior there is a very fine stuccoed ceiling by Alessandro Vittoria.

In the lovely peaceful **Contrà Porti**, you can see the Renaissance façade of Palazzo Thiene (no. 12), with rustication, and a fine portal with roundels in relief and remains of frescoes at the top, dating from 1489 by Lorenzo da Bologna. Opposite is **Palazzo Montano Barbaran**, with the **Palladio Museum** (*palladiomuseum.org*), which describes itself on its website as 'a research workshop open to the public'. The *palazzo* itself was, fittingly, designed by Palladio. The handsome entrance portico has paired columns and many of the rooms contain fine late 16th-century ceilings. The museum itself consists of models of the great architect's works and videos with experts describing his life and influence.

At no. 8 Contrà Porti (towards Corso Palladio) is the Gothic **Palazzo Cavallini**. In the other direction, at **no. 15**, a plaque records the death here in 1529 of Luigi da Porto, author of the story of 'Romeo and Juliet'. Next to it is **Palazzo Porto Breganze** (no. 17), a Venetian-Gothic building with a Renaissance doorway, and the magnificent 15th-century **Palazzo Colleoni Porto** (no. 19), with a loggia overlooking a little garden. Adjoining is **Palazzo Iseppo Da Porto** (no. 21), with a lovely *androne*, built by Palladio in 1548.

To San Lorenzo

On **Contrà Riale** (*map Vicenza 3*), in the former 17th-century monastery buildings of San Giacomo, is the historic **Biblioteca Bertoliniana**, left to the city in 1702 by Giovanni Maria Bertolo. On the right is **Palazzo Cordellina**, also owned by the library and used for exhibitions. Built by the Vicentine Ottone Calderari, it has a good *androne* in Palladian style.

Contrà Riale ends in the busier **Corso Fogazzaro**, with shops. To the right it leads past **Palazzo Repeta** (no. 49), built in the first decade of the 18th century by Francesco Muttoni. This palace stands on the corner of the piazza in front of the church of **San Lorenzo** (*usually closed in the middle of the day*). The splendid marble portal by Andriolo de Santi dates from the mid-14th century. The lovely interior has huge columns and a vaulted nave and aisles. The two stoups date from 1939. Above the west door is the very unusual 18th-century monument to Giovanni Battista da Porto, and at this end of the north aisle a monument to the architect Vincenzo Scamozzi, with his bust. At the east end of the south aisle, between the windows, is a *Deposition* by Luca Giordano. In the south transept, the altar of the Santissima Trinità, made for the Pojana family, has sculptures dating from 1456, and a fresco above painted at the end of the 15th century. In the sanctuary hangs a 15th-century wood Crucifix, and opposite two paintings by Francesco Pittoni there are two more monuments to members of the Da Porto family, one of them, recording the brothers Leonardo, Ludovico and Pietro, attributed to Palladio (1555). In the chapel to the left of the sanctuary are three statues signed by Antonino Veneziano in 1443, and an interesting large (but very ruined) detached fresco of the *Martyrdom of St Paul* attributed to Bartolomeo Montagna. There is yet another Da Porto monument here. The sacristy is entered through a door on either side of which are paintings attributed to Pittoni, and a door leads out to the 15th-century cloister, with its well dating from the previous century. At the end of the north aisle is a prettily carved altar thought to be by the workshop of Pedemuro, and in a niche in the centre of this aisle is a ruined 14th-century fresco of the Marys beneath the empty Cross.

Palazzo Valmarana-Braga

This *palazzo* (*Corso Fogazzaro 16; map Vicenza 3*), by Palladio (1565), has giant pilasters uniting two storeys and a handsome portico. It was badly damaged in WWII but has recently been restored by the family and now organises cultural events and offers apartments to rent (*palazzovalmaranabraga.it*). On the ground floor, the Studiolo has an exquisite ceiling with gilded stuccoes by Lorenzo Rubini and paintings by Giovanni Battista Zelotti (1567–8) and its original floor, and on the upper floor there are paintings by Giulio Carpioni and portals designed by Francesco Muttoni.

> **Goethe on Vicenza**
>
> Standing face to face with these magnificent buildings, which Palladio created, and seeing how already they are debased by men's mean and squalid requirements, one realises that most of them were conceptions that went far beyond the power of those who commissioned them to execute. How poorly adapted are these splendid products of a superior mind to the lives of ordinary men!
> *Italian Journey (19th September 1786)*

IN THE BEND OF THE RETRONE RIVER

The ornate, 15th-century **Casa Pigafetta** (*map Vicenza 3–4*), with three charming balconies on the top storey, a French motto on the façade, and a lovely old entrance arch, stands in the pedestrian lane of the same name. On the adjacent house, a plaque records Antonio Pigafetta (1491–1534), who was born in Vicenza and formed one of Magellan's company on his circumnavigation of the globe in 1519–22.

Further downhill, facing the river and with a portico over the pavement, the long white **Casa Civena** (*map Vicenza 5*) was probably the first palace to be built by Palladio (in 1540–6), and it still bears an inscription to his patron Trissino. Only the central bays are original, since it was altered in the 18th and 19th centuries.

Ponte Furo leads over the river, with a good view left of the green roof of the Basilica and the Torre di Piazza, and (right) of Monte Berico. In a widening of the road, in **Contrà Santi Apostoli**, the curve of the house fronts follows the shape of the Roman Theatre, the ruins of which once stood here and were drawn by Palladio.

From the castellated Porton del Luzo, a 13th-century gateway, continue along **Contrà Porton Luzo** past a very unusual house with brick columns above a rusticated ground floor, to an irregular piazza with a few trees and the huge long façade of the **Palazzi Gualdo**, dating from the 15th–16th centuries, decorated with square reliefs and with a good courtyard. Beside it, the Stradella del Pozzetto leads out of the piazza past the Contrà Paolo Lioy, where you can see the charming little Gothic **Casa Caola**. The river is recrossed over the lovely hump-backed **Ponte San Michele** (1620), its cobbled way only open to pedestrians. Just before the bridge, in this peaceful corner of the town, is the **Oratory of San Nicola** (*open by appointment; ask at the Museo Diocesano*). The 17th-century interior has canvases by Francesco Maffei, an artist often overlooked today, though in his own lifetime he was described as a painter 'not of dwarves but of giants...whose style stupefied everyone'. He worked mainly in Vicenza and died in Padua in 1660, of plague, aged 55. The ceiling paintings are the last work of Maffei's contemporary Giulio Carpioni. At the foot of the bridge, on the corner of Contrà Piancoli, is the **house where Goethe stayed** in 1786, when he came to Vicenza to admire the works of Palladio (plaque).

OUTSIDE PORTA CASTELLO

From outside Porta Castello (*map Vicenza 3*), Corso San Felice leads west, away from the centre of the town. It passes the railings and 17th century-entrance gate of the delightful **Giardino Salvi**, which was first laid out as a botanical garden. At one end of an L-shaped canal you can see the Loggia Valmarana, a villa in Palladian style built over the water in 1592. At the other end of the canal, here spanned by several bridges, is a loggia by Baldassare Longhena (1649).

Santi Felice e Fortunato

The first church of Santi Felice e Fortunato (*beyond map Vicenza 3, about 1km from Porta Castello, approached along a busy narrow road, but well worth visiting; if closed, ask at the Museo Diocesano*) was a Palaeochristian edifice, probably dating from the Constantinian era (4th century) and enlarged under Theodosius in the following century. The present structure dates from a reconstruction in the 10th century (and with 12th-century alterations).

In the little courtyard outside there are a number of ancient sarcophagi, including one with Palaeochristian symbols and an inscription. In front of the church façade stands a strange pillar called the ***Colonna di San Gallo***, with a carving of horsemen dating from 1300. The very curious fortified **campanile**, with a clock, dates from 1166. The church has an ancient **portal** with very early fresco fragments showing two angels of the Resurrection blowing their trumpets as the dead emerge from their tombs, dating from some time before 1154.

The **basilican interior** was restored in the 20th century, when the Baroque decorations were destroyed. In several places in the nave and aisle, 4th–5th-century mosaic pavements have been revealed beneath the modern floor. On the south wall are three large, framed 18th-century paintings and an altarpiece by Giulio Carpioni. At the end of the nave is a stone statue of the *Madonna della Misericordia* by Antonino Veneziano (c. 1452). In the raised sanctuary a 2nd-century sarcophagus serves as high altar and in the apse are good frescoes by Giulio Carpioni. At the end of the north wall is a finely carved 15th-century tabernacle. On this wall there are three more large paintings by Carpioni and an altarpiece by Alessandro Maganza.

Off the sacristy is an ancient domed cruciform chapel, or martyrium, probably dating from the 5th century, extremely interesting for its architecture, and with traces of mosaics, though it was sadly over restored a few years ago.

The charming little crypt has a curving wall, set up on which is an ancient 4th-century stele with an inscription relating to the two brothers Felix and Fortunatus (Felice e Fortunato) who were martyred in Aquileia during the persecutions of

Diocletian. Their relics, neatly tied up in small bundles, are displayed behind an old grate.

Outside the church is a little **Museo Lapidario** (*the walls are made of glass so if closed, you can see most of the contents from the outside*), which protects some of the Roman, Palaeochristian and Lombard carvings as well as sarcophagi from the church. One sarcophagus, complete with its lid, has symbolic pagan heads of the Four Seasons. The medieval sculpture includes a pair of 12th-century lions and there are six 18th-century wood busts of abbots.

SANCTUARY-BASILICA OF MONTE BERICO

Map Vicenza 7. For opening times and information about guided tours, see monteberico.it. To get there on foot (a pleasant walk talking approx. 90mins) take Viale Eretenio along the river from Ponte Furo (map Vicenza 5–6), then Viale X Giugno which crosses the railway and soon meets the long flight of steps which ascends the steep hillside beneath the Portici, a monumental portico with chapels was designed by Francesco Muttoni in the 18th century. There is a good view (east) of Villa La Rotonda (see below) from just below the basilica.

The green hillside of Monte Berico, conspicuous from all parts of the town with its sanctuary-basilica (*map Vicenza 7*) has been largely preserved from modern buildings. It stands on the site of a sanctuary, erected on the spot where two apparitions of the Virgin occurred in the 15th century. It is still a pilgrim shrine (with a festival on 8 Sept, the Nativity of the Blessed Virgin). It was rebuilt, apart from the campanile, by Carlo Borella in 1688–1703, although Lorenzo da Bologna's facade of 1476 was re-erected alongside the present south front. It contains a lovely *Pietà* by Bartolomeo Montagna (1500). In the refectory is the *Supper of St Gregory the Great*, a superb huge painting by Veronese dating from 1572. The great Venetian painter was clearly fascinated by the subject of festive repasts, and around this time he painted the subject many times, whether as a *Last Supper*, a *Marriage at Cana*, a *Supper in the House of Simon* or a *Supper in the House of Levi*. All the scenes are set in a majestic columned portico and include numerous figures of grandly-dressed Venetians, as well as servants and animals. This painting, over 8m by nearly 5m, was hacked into 32 pieces by Austrian soldiers in 1848, in retaliation for a rebellion of the Veronese against Austrian rule. It was restored at the expense of the emperor Franz Joseph. Also here is a *Baptism of Christ* by Alessandro Maganza.

Piazzale della Vittoria, beside the church, built as a memorial of WWI, commands a magnificent view of the mountains that once marked the front line. Viale X Giugno continues to the **Villa Guiccioli**, built at the end of the 18th century by Gianantonio Selva, with a beautiful park (*beyond map Vicenza 7; open 9–dusk except Mon*). The villa houses the **Museo del Risorgimento e della Resistenza** (*open Thur–Sun; closes at 2pm in July–Aug*).

VILLAS ON THE OUTSKIRTS

VILLA VALMARANA
Open daily 10–4, villavalmarana.com. From the Sanctuary Basilica of Monte Berico, Villa Valmarana can be reached on foot by following the Portici downhill, and (halfway down) taking Via Massimo d'Azeglio to the right, from which there is a good view of Vicenza. Just beyond a Carmelite monastery, the narrow cobbled Via San Bastiano (closed to through traffic) diverges right and leads downhill to the villa past a charming dovecote (15mins).
Villa Valmarana, called 'ai Nani' from the dwarves that decorate its garden wall, was purchased by Giustino Valmarana in 1715 and is still owned by the family. It is famous for the superb frescoes in the Palazzina by Giambattista Tiepolo, dating from 1757, with scenes from the *Iliad* and *Aeneid*, as well as from the epic poem *Gerusalemme Liberata* by Tiepolo's contemporary Torquato Tasso, and the romantic *Orlando Furioso*, published in 1532 by Ludovico Ariosto. The Foresteria was decorated with delightful pastoral scenes by Tiepolo's son Gian Domenico.

VILLA LA ROTONDA
Beyond map Vicenza 8. For opening times, prices and tours, see villalarotonda.it. A stony path (Stradella Valmarana) on the right beyond Villa Valmarana continues downhill to the villa.
The white Villa La Rotonda, also now a Valmarana home, was built as a belvedere for Paolo Almerico on this charming hilltop site. The villa has a central plan consisting of a circular core within a cube. The four classical porticoes complete its symmetry. Crowned with a remarkable low dome, its design is reminiscent of the Pantheon in Rome. Begun c. 1551 by Palladio, it was taken over at his death by Vincenzo Scamozzi and finished in 1606 for the Capra family. The Villa La Rotonda had a profound influence on the history of architecture and was copied in numerous buildings, including Chiswick House, London. The domed central hall was frescoed at the end of the 17th century by Louis Dorigny, and the *piano nobile* was painted by Anselmo Canera, Bernardino India and Alessandro Maganza. The *barchessa* was designed by Vincenzo Scamozzi.

CRICOLI
Beyond map Vicenza 1, Strada Marosticana 6.
The **Villa Trissino Trettenero** was designed (1531–8) by Palladio's first patron, Gian Giorgio Trissino. The architect himself worked here as a young man.

VICENZA PRACTICAL TIPS

VISITOR CARD

Free entry to selected sites comes with the Vicenza Silver Card or Vicenza Gold Card, available from the tourist office or museum ticket offices. For information, see the website: *teatrolimpicovicenza.it/en/info/facilities-2*

GETTING AROUND

- **By train**: Vicenza is within easy reach of Padua (trains take just over 15mins) and Verona (c. 25mins) and there are also services to Treviso. Regional stopping trains also run, taking longer between the main centres but connecting Vicenza to small places in its hinterland.

WHERE TO STAY

€€ **Due Mori.** The oldest hotel in Vicenza, opened in 1854 and now offering a comfortable blend of old and new, in an excellent position right in the centre of town. *Contrà Do Rode 24, albergoduemori.it. Map Vicenza 3.*

WHERE TO EAT

€ **Righetti.** A very inconspicuous restaurant, though right in the centre of town, frequented by locals. Excellent quality and reasonably priced regional dishes. You set your own table, and go to the counter to order, and pay at the desk at the end. There is also seating outside in the piazza in good weather. *Piazza Duomo 3, selfrighetti.it. Map Vicenza 3.*

There are numerous wine bars in Vicenza. **La Meneghina** (*Contrà Cavour 18; champagneforbreakfast.wine*) first opened in 1791 (*the street leads down to Piazza dei Signori past the flank of the Palazzo del Comune; map Vicenza 3*). **Ostaria il Grottino**, in Piazza delle Erbe, is a good place for drinks, snacks, sandwiches and small plates (*map Vicenza 4*). **Pasticceria Sorarù**, in Piazza dei Signori, has plenty of seating outside (*map Vicenza 4*).

LOCAL SPECIALITIES

The vineyards on the Colli Berici produce renowned wines.

A symbol of the town is dried stockfish, *bacalà alla vicentina*, cooked in various ways (and spelt thus, instead of with two 'c's as in Venice. There is even a local confraternity which celebrates the fish, which was introduced from Norway into the region when fresh fish was hard to come by (*see baccalaallavicentina.it*).

FESTIVALS AND EVENTS

Festival of the Madonna di Monte Berico, Sept 8.

THE VENETO VILLAS

Most of Palladio's villas in the Veneto (and many from later periods) are to be found in the province of Vicenza. The names of the villas tend to change with each new owner (and can end up as long as a DNA string), but they generally also carry the name of the original proprietor. They are scattered widely over the province, often in remote areas outside small towns, having been designed as retreats from the hustle and bustle. Many of them are still privately owned and by no means all are open to the public. In some cases, the exteriors and gardens are often their most important features, some being surrounded by extensive parks. Opening times change frequently and accessibility varies. The best way to visit the villas, since some are quite a distance off the beaten track, is by car.

THE VILLAS OF THE VENETO

The province of Vicenza is particularly rich in villas of the famous 'Veneto Villa' type. These were built from the 15th century onwards by rich noble Venetian families who were anxious to invest in land on the *terraferma* and contribute to its fertility by the construction of canals and irrigation systems. The names of the villas typically changed with each new owner, but they generally also carry the name of the original proprietor: sometimes the official name forms a long string. In the early 16th century Palladio invented an architecture peculiarly fitted to these prestigious villas, which he saw both as places of repose and as working farms: many still preserve their extensive outbuildings. Palladio derived their design in part from the villas of the ancient Romans and used Classical features in their construction. He took particular care in the siting of his villas, sometimes on low hills or near canals, and almost always surrounded by gardens and farmland. The distinctive service wings are known as *barchesse*. The name comes from the boat houses which were provided for the earliest villas on the Brenta Canal.

Numerous villas by Palladio survive in the province. In the 17th and 18th centuries many more villas were constructed, some of these particularly interesting for their interiors and frescoes (including some by Tiepolo and his son Gian Domenico). Architects of importance who succeeded Palladio include Vincenzo Scamozzi (1552–1616), who was born in Vicenza and who completed a number of Palladio's buildings here, although he also worked extensively in Venice and other parts of the Veneto. Other architects influenced by Palladio were Antonio Pizzocaro, Francesco Muttoni and Giorgio Massari. Orazio Marinali was responsible for the statuary in many of the gardens.

A selection of the villas is given below, in alphabetical order by the closest town. There is no comprehensive website listing all of them, since many are still private residences. Useful resources include *villevenetetour.com/en*, *vicenza-unesco.com* and *palladianroutes.com*. For lovers of Palladio who want to see as many of his villas as possible, others in the region, apart from those listed below, are: Villa Badoer at Fratta Polesine (*p. 55*), Villa Barbaro at Maser (*p. 144*), Villa Emo at Fanzolo di Vedelago (*pp. 134–5*), Villa Foscari on the Brenta (*pp. 40–1*), Villa Pisani Placco at Montagnana (*p. 50*) and Villa Cornaro at Piombino Dese (*p. 135*).

AGUGLIARO (*map Veneto West D3*)
Villa Saraceno. Begun by Palladio between 1545 and 1555 and surrounded by farm buildings, in the hamlet of Finale, south of Agugliaro. Owned and very well restored by the Landmark Trust of Great Britain (*landmarktrust.org.uk*). **Villa Saraceno delle Trombe Bettanin**, a little further west (*Via Finale 10*), was designed in 1550 by Sanmicheli.

ALTAVILLA VICENTINA (*map Veneto West C2*)
Villa Valmarana Morosini. Built by Francesco Muttoni in 1724, now a college, with its service wings renovated in a modern style as a hotel (*valmaranamorosinihotel.it*).

BAGNOLO (*map Veneto West C3*)
Villa Pisani Bonetti. One of Palladio's most beautiful villas, begun in 1540 (the loggia was added around 1560). The main entrance has rusticated arches beneath a pediment, and the villa is surrounded by farm buildings. The piano nobile, cellars, and garden can be visited by appointment (*Via Risaie 1; villapisani.net*).

BERTESINA (*map Veneto West D2*)
Villa Gazzotti Grimani Curti. An early work by Palladio (1542–3), interesting for its façade. The interior is not open, though only the central hall and loggia remain from the original design (*Via San Cristoforo 23*). On the estate, surrounded by a huge park, is **Villa Ghislanzoni Curti**, built in 1764, and now offering holiday apartments (*villaghislanzoni.it*).

BOLZANO VICENTINO (*map Veneto West D2*)
Villa Valmarana Scagnolari Zen. Designed around 1563 by Palladio for Giovanni Francesco Valmarana, but left unfinished and altered later (and seriously damaged in WWII). The pretty little chapel was added in 1615. In the garden are numerous 18th-century statues by Francesco Marinali the Younger (*Via Ponte 3, Località Lisiera; no admission*).

BREGANZE (*map Veneto West D1–D2*)
Villa Diedo Malvezzi Basso. Built in 1664–84, with later additions (*Via Montegoggio 29; no admission*). Breganze is known for its wines, which can be purchased at the **Maculan Winery** in the village (*maculan.net*). Wines include Fratta, a red made from Cabernet and Merlot grapes grown on the sunny slopes to the north, as well as Torcolato, a sweet wine made from grapes specially dried in long, hanging skeins.

CALDOGNO (*map Veneto West C2*)
Villa Caldogno Nordera. Built around 1545, and generally attributed to

Palladio, with frescoes dating from the same century by Gianantonio Fasolo and Battista Zelotti. The main salon can be visited, as well as the reinforced concrete bunker in the grounds, built when the German army requisitioned the villa towards the end of WWII. *Via Zanella 3; villacaldogno.it.*

CASTELGOMBERTO (*map Veneto West C2*)
Villa da Schio Piovene. Built in 1666, probably by Antonio Pizzocaro. It has 18th-century additions and its garden has statues by the workshop of Orazio Marinali. Inside are three early works by Giambattista Tiepolo. The chapel dates from 1614. Today it is used as an events venue and there are also holiday lets in the grounds. *Via Villa 147; villadaschio.com.*

COLZÈ (*map Veneto West D2*)
Villa Feriani. Rebuilt in the 17th century, with a chapel containing sculptures by Orazio Marinali. There is pleasant but simple *agriturismo* accommodation on the estate (*villaferiani.it*).

COSTOZZA, NEAR LONGARE (*map Veneto West D2*)
Villa da Schio. Three buildings on a hillside, surrounded by a lovely garden which features sculptures by Orazio Marinali. He worked in the stone quarries of Costozza, which had supplied building stone to the Romans as well as to Palladio. The **Villino Garzadori**, built in 1690, has frescoes by Louis Dorigny (*Piazza da Schio 2; costozza-villadaschio.it*).

DUEVILLE (*map Veneto West C2–D2*)
There are two villas here, **Villa Porto** (1554) and **Villa Da Porto Casarotto**, built by Ottone Calderari in 1770–6.

GRISIGNANO DI ZOCCO (*map Veneto West D2–D3*)
Villa Ferramosca-Beggiato. Designed by Gian Domenico, the father of the more famous Vincenzo Scamozzi, around 1568, with a Palladian style loggia and pediment. *Via Vittorio Veneto, Località Barbano; occasionally open in the mornings.*

LONGA (*map Veneto West D2*)
Villa Chiericati Lambert. Built in 1590 (but altered in the 19th century), with 16th-century frescoes attributed to Pozzoserrato, and surrounded by a park. It is now the seat of Showa, a Japanese musical academy. *Not open to the public.*

LONIGO (*map Veneto West C3*)
Palazzo Pisani, a grand mansion of 1557 with an elaborate double outdoor stairway, is now the Town Hall (*visits by appointment at the Tourist Office*). On the outskirts stands the **Rocca Pisana** (1576), a charming work by Vincenzo Scamozzi, recalling Palladio's Villa Rotonda, built for the Venetian nobleman Vettor Pisani. It is now an events venue and can also be rented (*roccapisana.com*).

LUGO DI VICENZA (*map Veneto West C1–D1*)
Villa Godi Malinverni. One of the earliest known works by Palladio (1540–2). The *piano nobile* was frescoed in the 16th century by Giovanni Battista Zelotti. One wing has a representative collection of 19th-century Italian paintings (*Via Palladio 44; villagodi.com*). **Villa Piovene Porto Godi** is also

at Lugo. Palladio is thought to have built the central core in around 1539, with an Ionic pronaos, and in the 18th century Francesco Muttoni added the two porticoes on either side and the long central flight of steps up through the garden, which has statues by Orazio Marinali or his workshop. It is surrounded by a large park (*Via Palladio 51; vicenza-unesco.com*).

MONTECCHIO MAGGIORE (*map Veneto West C2*)
This picturesque village and legendary stronghold of the 'Montagues' of *Romeo and Juliet*, has two restored castles of the Scaligeri, lords of Verona. Just outside is the **Villa Cordellina Lombardi** (*Via Lovara 36*). Built by Giorgio Massari (1735), it has very fine frescoes (1743) by Giambattista Tiepolo in the central hall. Now the property of the Province of Vicenza, it is used for concerts, conferences and other events.

MONTEGALDA (*map Veneto West D3*)
Castello Grimani Sorlini. A 12th-century castle adapted as a villa in the 18th century, with a fine park decorated with statues by the workshop of Orazio Marinali. *Via Castello 21; castellodimontegalda.it*.

MONTEVIALE (*map Veneto West C2*)
Villa Loschi Zileri Motterle. Attributed to Francesco Muttoni and Muttonio Massari, surrounded by a fine park with exotic trees. The staircase and *salone* have the earliest frescoes by Tiepolo (1734) outside Venice. The villa complex has now been repurposed for mixed use as apartments and office, and can be visited. *Via Zileri 1, Località Biron; villazileri.com*.

ORGIANO (*map Veneto West C3*)
Villa Fracanzan Piovene. Built in 1710 and attributed to Francesco Muttoni, with an interesting garden (and *barchessa*). *Via San Francesco 2; visits possible on Sun and holidays; villafracanzanpiovene.it*.

POIANA MAGGIORE (*map Veneto West C3*)
Villa Poiana (or Pojana). Built in 1555 by Palladio, with a typical Palladian arch over the entrance. It has contemporary frescoes by Bernardino India and Anselmo Canera and stuccoes by Bartolomeo Ridolfi. The frescoes in the atrium are attributed to Giovanni Battista Zelotti. It is one of the architect's very best works and is still in a rural setting. *Via Castello, vicenza-unesco.com*.

QUINTO VICENTINO (*map Veneto West D2*)
Villa Thiene. Dated around 1545, this villa was left unfinished by Palladio. *Via IV Novembre 4; vicenza-unesco.com*.

SANDRIGO (*map Veneto West D2*)
Villa Sesso Schiavo Nardone. Built by a follower of Palladio in 1570, with contemporary frescoes by Giovanni Antonio Fasolo (*Via San Lorenzo 5; visits by appointment; villasessoschiavo.it*). Sandrigo is also the birthplace of the 'Venerable Confraternity of *bacalà alla vicentina*' (a dish of salt cod simmered in milk) and celebrates it with a festival in Sept. €€ **La Trattoria di Palmerino** is a long-established family-run restaurant specialising in *bacalà* (*palmerino.eu*).

SAREGO (*map Veneto West C3*)
Villa da Porto 'La Favorita'. Built by

Francesco Muttoni in 1714–15. *Località Monticello di Fara; Via Conte da Porto 7.*

THIENE (*map Veneto West C1–C2*)
Villa Beregan Cunico (Ca' Beregane). Built in 1639 by Antonio Pizzocaro, on the road between Thiene and Vicenza, it has an exceptionally long low façade with numerous windows (*only open by appointment, T: 0445 360923*). **Castello di Thiene** (also known as Palazzo Porto-Colleoni) is a late Gothic Venetian castle which was the residence of the Porto family. It may have been begun by Domenico da Venezia and was completed in 1476. It is fully furnished and was frescoed around 1570 by Giovanni Antonio Fasolo and Giovanni Battista Zelotti, who together decorated many other villas in the Veneto. It has a charming chapel and a magnificent stable block dating from the late 17th or early 18th century, attributed to Francesco Muttoni. It is surrounded by a public park (*Via Garibaldi 2; to visit, see castellodithiene.com*).

VANCIMUGLIO (*map Veneto West D2*)
Villa Chiericati Porto Rigo. Built in 1554, almost certainly by Palladio (but left unfinished), with an Ionic portico. *Via Nazionale 1.*

VIGARDOLO DI MONTICELLO CONTE OTTO (*map Veneto West D2*)
There is no evidence that this village directly influenced Jefferson's choice of the name Monticello for his home in Virginia, but Jefferson certainly owned Palladio's *Four Books on Architecture*, and considered it his 'Bible'. The **Villa Valmarana Bressan** was begun in 1541 by Palladio. It is an austere building with a typical entrance. Recent restoration work has revealed remains of frescoes. It is now used for events and banquets and can be visited by appointment. *Via Vigardoletto 33; villavalmaranabressan.it.*

VILLAVERLA (*map Veneto West C2*)
Villa Verlato Putin. Built in 1576 by Vincenzo Scamozzi, it has the appearance of a *palazzo* and contains frescoes by the little-known Girolamo Pisani and Giovanni Battista Maganza. Now cared for by the FAI, Italy's environmental fund, it is open on certain days (*Piazza del Popolo 1; fondoambiente.it*). **Villa Ghellini**, built in 1664–79, is the most important work of Antonio Pizzocaro (*Via Sant'Antonio 4; occasionally open*).

Bassano del Grappa: the Ponte degli Alpini, always known as the 'Palladian Bridge', over the River Brenta.

BASSANO DEL GRAPPA & MAROSTICA

BASSANO DEL GRAPPA

Situated where the Brenta River emerges from the foothills of the Venetian prealps, Bassano del Grappa (*map Veneto West D1*) is a pleasant town of arcaded streets and old houses, many of which still have faded frescoes on their façades. The town is famous as the home of a family of well-known painters—the da Ponte (*see below*), called Bassano after this, their birthplace. It is also known for its famous wooden bridge across the Brenta, designed by Palladio. The town's name comes from the nearby Monte Grappa (1775 m), where the Italian and Austro-Hungarian armies clashed in a series of terrible battles in 1917–18, now the site of a striking war memorial (*see p. 86*). Ernest Hemingway came to Bassano as a Red Cross volunteer in October 1918, during the final days of the Grappa campaign, an experience which provided much of the inspiration for *A Farewell to Arms*. Bassano is also known, coincidentally, as the birthplace of grappa, the spirit distilled from grape skins (though the name of the spirit has no etymological link with that of the mountain). Grappa can be sampled across the city.

THE BASSANO FAMILY

There were four main members in this prominent family of Venetian painters. Francesco da Ponte the Elder (c. 1475–1539) worked in Bassano and painted in a rustic style, using soft colours like those of the Bellini. His son Jacopo (c. 1510/18–92) the most famous of the family, rose to prominence in late-Renaissance and early-Baroque Venice. His religious paintings, lush landscapes, and scenes of everyday life show the influence of fashionable contemporaries such as Parmigianino. A pioneer of the genre scene and one of the first painters to be interested in peasants and animals, his Biblical characters are represented as real yokels, and he often pays more loving attention to the ox and the ass than to the human characters. Jacopo had four painter sons: Francesco, Gerolamo, Giovanni Battista and Leandro. Leandro and Francesco achieved fame and some fortune in Venice. Leandro was even given a noble title by the doge. Francesco worked a lot with his father, but his life ended in tragedy: he threw himself to his death from a top floor window at the age of 44.

EXPLORING BASSANO

Castello degli Ezzelini

The oldest part of the town is in the northernmost part of the historic centre, and consists of the walled complex of the **Castello degli Ezzelini**, named after the local overlords and which dates to 900–950 but was enlarged and fortified in the 13th, 14th and subsequent centuries, when the town was successively under the rule of the Ezzelini (also known as the Da Romano), the Visconti of Milan, and, after 1404, of Venice. A tower of the old fortress serves as the base of the campanile. There is a walk along the walls of the ruined castle, ending with a panoramic view including the Brenta river and the Palladian bridge (*see below*). Also inside the complex is the **duomo (Santa Maria Assunta)**, with altarpieces by Leandro Bassano. There has been a church on the site since at least 998, with the current structure dating to the 15th century (the facade was rebuilt in 1641). The area to the south of this developed around three adjacent squares: Piazzetta Monte Vecchio and the more recently renamed Piazza Garibaldi and Piazza Libertà.

San Francesco and the Museo Civico

Piazza Garibaldi is a long, oblong square overlooked by the 14th-century Torre Civica and closed on the opposite side by the church of **San Francesco**, founded in the 12th century by a member of the Ezzelini family on his safe return from the Holy Land. It is a Romanesque-Gothic building with an elegant vestibule of 1306, a graceful campanile, remains of 15th-century frescoes and, in the apse, a painted wooden Crucifix of the 14th century. A door on the right of the porch leads to the **Museo Civico** (*museibassano.it*), housed in the former Franciscan friary with its beautiful 17th-century cloister. The museum is large for a town of its size, with sections on natural history, archaeology and an art gallery of over 250 paintings. Of particular note is the collection of works by Jacopo Bassano and his workshop, the most comprehensive overview of his work anywhere in the world, and the large space dedicated to the sculptor Canova (*see Possagno, p. 144*). The diverse collection also includes: a collection of ancient Greek and Italic vases (with some very fine volute kraters); a Crucifix by Guariento and works by the Vivarini and Tiepolo.

Piazza Libertà

The arcaded **Piazza Libertà** is the heart of historic Bassano. Formerly Piazza San Giovanni, after the imposing church of San Giovanni Battista, which occupies the southern side (its present appearance dating to 1782), it was renamed 'Freedom Square' after the Veneto's accession to the Kingdom of Italy in 1866. On the side opposite the church is the Palazzo del Municipio, with a large clock and a fresco of St Christopher by Francesco Bassano the Elder. At the other end of the square are two columns, topped by a Lion of St Mark and a statue of the patron saint of the city, San Bassiano. They are the work of Orazio Marinali, a Baroque-era sculptor whose works can be seen in many of the villas of the region.

Piazzotto Monte Vecchio was the main square of the city in the Middle Ages, and retains a medieval character, lined with fine old palaces, most notably the

15th-century Palazzetto del Monte di Pietà, with inscriptions and coats of arms on the façade. Following either street northwest from the square takes you to Via Bartolomeo Gamba, which leads downhill to the river.

Via Gamba and Palladio's bridge

Ponte degli Alpini, the famous covered wooden bridge across the River Brenta, was originally built in 1209. After being destroyed by a flood in 1567, it was redesigned by Palladio in 1569. Initially he submitted plans for a new stone bridge, but this was rejected by the city for differing too much from its predecessor. He then designed the bridge as we see it today: It has been destroyed three times since, most recently by the Allies in 1945, but always rebuilt in the Palladian style. The bridge takes its current name from the Alpini regiment, Italy's mountain infantry force, who crossed it numerous times during the campaigns on Monte Grappa in the First World War. The regiment was also responsible for rebuilding the bridge after the Second World War. The view upstream is extremely picturesque, with the wooded mountains rising above the clustering red roofs of the town, the foaming water of the river and the houses on the riverfront, all well preserved. The best view of the bridge itself is from the far side, from a lane which leads left beside a little garden on the banks of the river.

Just as you enter the bridge from Via Gamba, on the left, is **Nardini**, a characteristic little bar, with a grappa distillery of 1779, the oldest distillery in Italy and its eponymous grappa still one of the leading brands in the country. You can sample grappa here, and buy bottles to take home. They will tell you that Hemingway often popped in for a shot. Back on Via Gamba, in the old Palazzo Delle Teste, is the **Poli Museo del Grappa**, illustrating the history of grappa and its production whilst also offering the chance to taste and buy some Poli grappa (*open daily 9–7.30; poligrappa.com*). Their distillery, and another museum, is located in the town of Schiavon, 12km to the southwest of Bassano. At the far (west) end of the bridge, entered through the Taverna al Ponte, is the **Museo degli Alpini**, a small war museum focused on the Alpini, with a range of memorabilia (*Via Angarano 2; open Tues–Sun 9–8*).

Palazzo Sturm

South of the Palladian bridge is the lovely 18th-century Palazzo Sturm (*Vicolo Schiavonetti; museibassano.it*), which houses two museums. The entrance is through the Neoclassical courtyard overlooking the river. The **entrance hall** (1765) has frescoes by Giorgio Anselmi in Bolognese Baroque style, including a *Fall of the Giants* and other allegories. The **Museo della Ceramica** exhibits local ceramics from the 16th century onwards illustrating the production of Italian manufactories, with a particular focus on the Antonibon family, based in the nearby town of Nove (*see p. 88*). Beyond a belvedere (now enclosed) overlooking the river is the delightful little **Sala dell'Alcova**, which preserves its original 18th-century Rococo decoration, including exquisite inlaid woodwork and painted Old Testament scenes by the Treviso-born artist Gaetano Zompini. The **Museo Remondini** (named after a family of local printers) is on the ground floor and illustrates the history of typography and chalcography. Its highlights include drawings, prints and engravings by a variety of artists, including Mantegna and Dürer. They are shown in rotation because of their fragility.

Villa Ca' Erizzo Luca

In the northern part of town, close to the river, is Villa Ca' Erizzo Luca, a beautiful frescoed villa which was used as the headquarters of the Red Cross during the First World War. Hemingway stayed here in 1918 together with his fellow volunteers, including John Dos Passos, inspiring a never-published short story 'The Woppian Way'. Five rooms of the villa have been turned in to a museum dedicated to Hemingway and the First World War, whilst the rest of the villa can be visited on the second Sun of every month. There is also a taxidermy museum in the complex, The Wild Life museum. (*Via Ca' Erizzo 35; at the top of Via Gamba turn left, keep straight along Via Margnan and Via San Sebastiano, which turns into Via Ca' Erizzo; museohemingway.it, villacaerizzoluca.it.*)

OUTSKIRTS AND ENVIRONS OF BASSANO

On the western outskirts of Bassano, at Sant'Eusebio, is the **Villa Angarano**. The villa was originally conceived by Palladio at the behest of his close friend, nobleman Giacomo Angarano, but only the two *barchesse* were built. The central body was not built until the late 17th century, by Domenico Margutti, a pupil of Longhena, the great Venetian Baroque architect. It belongs to the five Bianchi-Michiel sisters, who make wine and olive oil here (*visits by appointment villaangarano.com*).

In the southern outskirts of Bassano, east of the river, is the **Villa Rezzonico**, its corner towers reminiscent of a medieval castle, though it was built in the early 18th century for the father of the future Pope Clement XIII. The architect is unknown: At one point it was attributed to Longhena, and then Massari. It has a fine park and garden. Napoleon stayed here in 1796, at the time that his troops, under Massena, defeated the Austrians near Bassano. It is now used for weddings and events (*Via Ca' Rezzonico 68, villacarezzonico.it*).

North of Bassano is **Romano d'Ezzelino** (*map Veneto West D1*), once a stronghold of the Ezzelini, whose other name, Da Romano, also comes from here. South of the town centre is the 18th-century **Villa Cornaro** which has an orangery by Vincenzo Scamozzi (*used for events; not regularly open*). Close by is the Museo Bonfanti-Vimar, a museum of the automobile which offers thematic displays (*museobonfanti.veneto.it*).

East of Bassano is **Mussolente**, with the **Villa Negri Piovene** on a low hill approached by a long flight of steps from the Asolo road, and flanked by two porticoed outbuildings (*recently restored and privately owned, guesthouses to rent; villanegripiovene.com*).

North of Bassano, on the summit of Monte Grappa (1776m), is the war memorial known as the **Sacrario Militare di Cima Grappa** (*open daily 9–5, with a break for lunch*), an enormous Rationalist ziggurat, opened in 1935 and containing (in two separate ossuaries) the remains of over 22,000 soldiers from the Italian and Austro-Hungarian armies, who bitterly contested this summit during WWI, in the course of three desperate battles fought in 1917 and 1918. The architect, Giovanni Greppi, also designed the memorial on the battlefield of Caporetto (now in Slovenia), in a similar stepped formation. (*For more on the Veneto in WWI, see p. 147.*)

MAROSTICA

Marostica (*map Veneto West D1*), a stronghold of the Ezzelini in the 12th–13th centuries, was rebuilt in 1311–86 by the Scaligeri. It came under Venetian control in 1404 and remained faithful to the Republic from then onwards. Today it is a charming old fortified townlet preserving its medieval ramparts, which connect the lower castle on the piazza with the upper castle on the green hillside above. It has a particularly pleasant climate, and excellent cherries are grown in the surroundings. A cherry festival (*Festa delle Ciliegie*) is held in late May. Marostica is also famous for its biennial chess game with human combatants, a spectacle somewhere between sport and theatre.

MAROSTICA'S HUMAN CHESS GAME

The famous *Partita a Scacchi*, in which the whole town participates, takes place in Marostica every two years (even years) in early September. The tradition commemorates a duel fought in 1454 between Rinaldo d'Angarano (black) and Vieri da Vallonara (white) for the hand of Lionora, daughter of Taddeo Parisio, the local Venetian governor. Vieri won the first match (whether to Lionora's delight or consternation is not recorded), and white still wins every game today, although a different game from the history of chess is chosen to be re-enacted each year. The herald who conducts the event speaks in Venetian dialect. At the end of the game the wedding takes place, with some 500 participants in 15th-century costume—flag-throwers, drummers, medieval musicians and a host of attendants. In odd years, when the 'players' are sent abroad to perform the game, an international chess festival is held in the town. (*For more information and tickets—book early—see marosticascacchi.it.*)

PIAZZA CASTELLO TO THE CASTELLO SUPERIORE

The delightful **Piazza Castello**, with the stone chessboard on which the game (*see above*) is played, has a superb view of the ramparts climbing the green hillside to the upper castle. The battlemented **Castello Inferiore** was built by the Scaligeri in the early 14th century. There are a beautiful well and an ancient ivy in the courtyard; stairs lead up to the loggia of the piano nobile, with a catapult reconstructed in 1923. All the rooms on this floor are frescoed, most notably the Sala del Consiglio, which hosts cultural events and a small exhibition on the chess match. In the keep is the Sala del Capitano with an original cross vaulted ceiling. Chessboards are provided for the public at the other end of the piazza, in a loggia beneath a bank building (matches are often played here at weekends).

Via Sant'Antonio leads to the large 17th-century church of the Carmine, at the top of a flight of steps, with views of the Castello Superiore rising above it. The street passes the church of **Sant'Antonio**, with a high altarpiece of *St Paul Preaching to the*

Athenians by Jacopo Bassano and his son Francesco (1574). Opposite is the small **Cappella del Santissimo Sacramento** (1486), open for exhibitions, with scant traces of a fresco by Jacopo Bassano in the lunette over the entrance.

From the top of the street, a path leads up the green hillside to the **Castello Superiore** (*it can also be reached by road*), enjoying views across the Venetian plain. The castle was also built by the Scaligeri, slightly after the Castello Inferiore, but ruined by the Venetians in the 16th century.

The oldest church in Marostica is **Santa Maria Assunta**, though its present appearance dates from the 18th century. In the choir are two canvases by Andrea Celesti (*see p. 167*). In the north aisle is a marble relief of the *Madonna and Child*, a votive offering by the 16th-century botanist Prospero Alpini (1553–1617), after returning home safely from Egypt. Alpini (who gives his name to the street in which the church is located) is credited with introducing coffee to the Venetian Republic. The red villa behind railings, at the beginning of the street, with the wooded hillside rising behind it, is his birthplace.

ENVIRONS OF MAROSTICA

NOVE AND CARTIGLIANO

Southeast of Marostica is **Nove**, known for its ceramics. The Antonibon family were active here from 1727 producing majolica and porcelain, examples of which can be seen in the Museo Civico in Palazzo de Fabris, which also has an extensive 20th century collection, including a vase by Picasso (*museonove.it*).

On the other side of the Brenta at **Cartigliano** is the eccentric, unfinished Villa Morosini Cappello on Piazza della Concordia, truly an extraordinary sight. It was begun in 1560 probably by the engineer Francesco Zamberlan, who was a friend and collaborator of Palladio, and is best known for La Rotonda at Rovigo. The remarkable trabeated Ionic colonnade that surrounds the *piano nobile* may have been added in the 17th century. The interior is used by the municipal government. In the parish church, the Chapel of the Rosary is decorated with frescoes (1575) by Jacopo Bassano and his son Francesco, and has an altarpiece by Bartolomeo Montagna.

THE ALTOPIANO DEI SETTE COMUNI

Bassano and Marostica lie at the foot of the Altopiano dei Sette Comuni—a plateau c. 1000m above sea level that takes its name from seven townships (Asiago, Enego, Foza, Gallio, Lusiana Conco, Roana and Rotzo; *map Veneto West C1–D1*), united from 1310–1807 in an autonomous federation. The inhabitants of the plateau are of Germanic origin (the Cimbri) and the area is both a winter and summer resort. **Asiago**, near the centre of the plateau, is the main township and was the scene of bitter fighting in the First World War, including a major battle between Italian and Austro-Hungarian forces in 1916 (*for more on WWI in the Veneto, see p. 147*).

Recoaro Terme, in the far west of the province of Vicenza (*map Veneto West C1*) is a well-known spa with ferruginous springs.

BASSANO AND MAROSTICA PRACTICAL TIPS

GETTING AROUND

- **By train**: There are direct services to Bassano del Grappa from Padua (65mins) and Venice (90mins); other routes involve a change at Cittadella or Castelfranco Veneto.
- **By bus**: There are frequent services between Bassano del Grappa and Marostica (15mins). Buses from Bassano bus station, just west of the railway station, also serve Cartigliano via Nove, and there are services for Asiago too (90mins), though these often require a change at Thiene. For Recoaro Terme, the best solution is to take a bus from Vicenza main bus station (c. 80mins). There are buses roughly every hour between Bassano del Grappa and Vicenza (journey time c. 1hr) and frequent direct services between Marostica and Vicenza. These are all run by Società Vicentina Trasporti (*svt.vi.it*).

WHERE TO STAY

BASSANO DEL GRAPPA
€–€€ **Hotel Al Castello**. At the top of the old town, a simple, old-fashioned place with basic comfort, good prices and a warm welcome. *Via Bonamigo 19 (Piazza Terraglio), hotelalcastello.it.*

WHERE TO EAT

BASSANO DEL GRAPPA
€€ **Trattoria El Piron**. A family restaurant in business for many years, serving Veneto cuisine right in the heart of town. *Via Zaccaria Bricito 12 (off Via Gamba), elpiron.it.*
€€ **Nuovo Borgo Bassano**. Local dishes made with local ingredients, including (in season) the famous asparagus. *Via Margnan 7, nuovoborgobassano.it.*
MAROSTICA
€ **Osteria Madonnetta**. Wine bar popular since 1904, serving good food and local wines. *Via Vajenti 21, osteriamadonnetta.it.*

LOCAL SPECIALITIES

Bassano is particularly known for its **white asparagus** (Asparago Bianco di Bassano DOP), which has its own festival in April. **Grappa** is for sale all over Bassano, and can be tasted at the historic Poli and Nardini distilleries. **White wine** made from the Vespaiolo grape, grown in the Breganze region southwest of Marostica, is also a local speciality. The Torcolato sweet wine is famous. Nove is well known for its **ceramics**, and Marostica for its **cherries** (festival in late May). Rotzo, in the Altopiano dei Sette Comuni, is famed for its **potatoes**, which are said to be especially good for making gnocchi.

VERONA

'Fair Verona' (*map Veneto West B3*) is the city which Shakespeare chooses as the scene for his *Romeo and Juliet*. And Verona is indeed one of the most attractive large towns in northern Italy. The wide pavements of its pleasant streets, made out of huge blocks of the local red marble, give the town an air of opulence. The birthplace of Catullus and perhaps Vitruvius in the 1st century BC, Verona has impressive Roman remains, including the famous amphitheatre known as the Arena (which is extremely well preserved) and its ancient theatre on the hillside above the river. It has an unusually high number of very beautiful large Romanesque and Gothic churches, the finest of which is the basilica of San Zeno. Many of them have very colourful frescoes and their lovely works of art are mostly by skilled local artists.

The Della Scala family, who ruled the town from the late 13th century, are commemorated by sumptuous tombs and in their former castle, Castelvecchio, now a museum. Piazza dei Signori and the adjoining Piazza delle Erbe are two of the finest squares in Italy, and nearby, peaceful narrow streets occupy a loop of the river Adige, which is an important feature of the town. Verona's historic prosperity is derived from the fact that it stands at the junction of two main traffic arteries: from Germany and Austria to central Italy, and from Piedmont and Lombardy to the Veneto and Friuli-Venezia Giulia. It is well equipped to receive hundreds of thousands of visitors every year and is especially crowded in summer, when opera is performed in the Arena.

Porta dei Borsari, the main entrance gate to the ancient Roman city.

HISTORY OF VERONA

Originally a Bronze Age settlement, Verona became a Roman colony in 89 BC and flourished under the Roman emperors. In the early Middle Ages a succession of Ostrogoths, Lombards and Franks chose Verona as their seat, before it became an independent *comune* in 1107. Family feuds within the city (on which the story of Romeo and Juliet is based) were settled by the tyrant Ezzelino da Romano, who ruled the city (at times together with Padua) from 1231 until his death in battle in 1259. A year later Mastino Della Scala transformed his office of *podestà* into a more powerful role and his family retained exclusive control of the government of the city as a *signoria* for the next 120 years. Their reigns, especially that of Cangrande I, from 1311 to 1329, saw the power of Verona greatly increase in the Veneto. The splendid Castelvecchio, with its bridge over the Adige, was built by the Della Scala, and they are also recorded in their elaborate monuments grouped together in a grand enclosure beside their palace in Piazza dei Signori. For a few years after the Della Scala, Gian Galeazzo Visconti of Milan took control of the city, but by 1405 Verona had chosen to become part of the Venetian Republic; it remained under her protection until the downfall of the *Serenissima* in 1797. Just one year later, armed rebellion against the French (the '*Pasque Veronesi*') brought retaliation in which much of the city was destroyed. In the 19th century the city passed back and forth between the hands of the French and the Austrians before it was ceded to Austria at the Congress of Vienna and so was forced to become an Austrian stronghold during the Italian wars of independence. In 1866 it finally joined united Italy.

During the Second World War the city suffered considerably from bombing, and the bridges were all blown up. In the Castelvecchio in 1944, Mussolini's puppet Republican government staged the trial of Count Galeazzo Ciano, Mussolini's son-in-law, who had been a Fascist minister but later became a leading opponent of the *Duce* (the court ordered Ciano's execution).

PIAZZA BRÀ & THE ARENA

The huge Piazza Brà (*map Verona 11*), mostly closed to traffic and with a garden in the centre, takes its name from the Veronese dialect word *braida*, from the German *breit*, meaning 'wide'; and it is indeed particularly spacious. Three of its sides are occupied by monumental buildings, one dating from ancient Roman times (the amphitheatre) and the other two from the Neoclassical period. On the fourth side is an exceptionally wide pavement called the **Liston**, lined with cafés and restaurants, popular and lively almost all day long, and, in the centre, Palazzo Malfatti, with a high rusticated portico and a balcony on the first floor. It was built by Verona's greatest native architect, Michele Sanmicheli, towards the end of his life in 1555.

92 BLUE GUIDE THE VENETO

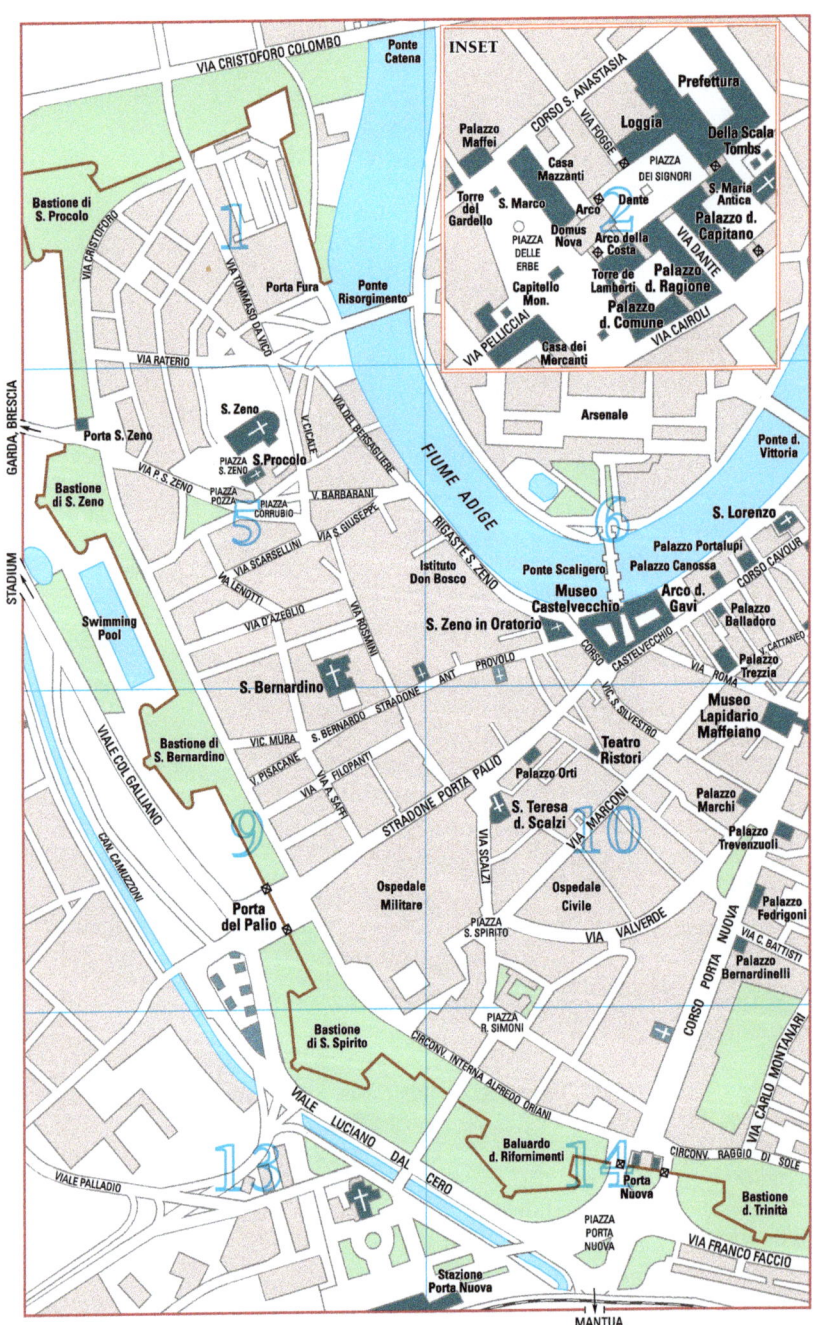

VERONA 93

The **Portoni della Brà**, a battlemented archway of 1389, stands astride the busy Via Porta Nuova, the entrance to the city from the south (and the railway station). The line of the medieval walls was here, and the Portoni archway fittingly bears an inscription with Romeo's desperate affirmation: 'There is no world without Verona walls', spoken after he finds himself banished from the city.

The archway adjoins the huge Doric **Palazzo della Gran Guardia**, begun in 1609 by Domenico Curtoni for military use (and completed some two centuries later by Giuseppe Barbieri). It is now an exhibition venue. Even more imposing is the huge Neoclassical **Palazzo Municipale**, also by Barbieri, the Town Hall of Verona.

The **Arena**, the great Roman amphitheatre (*map Verona 7*) was built c. AD 100 and is very well preserved: it is the third largest Roman amphitheatre to survive, after Rome and Capua. An earthquake in 1183 destroyed all but four arches of the outermost arcade, but the inner arcade of two orders superimposed is almost complete with its 74 arches (the Colosseum has 80). Splendid vaulted passageways open into the cavea, where the 44 tiers of seats can accommodate some 22,000 spectators (they were restored in the 16th century after the stone had been pillaged for building material in the Middle Ages). The performance here of *Aida* in 1913 set a new standard for the production of operatic spectacle, and the Arena still hosts a popular opera festival in the summer.

ROMAN GATES AND ARCHES

Apart from the famous Arena and the Roman Theatre, a number of gates survive from Roman Verona. The main entrance to the city was the splendid **Porta dei Borsari** (*map Verona 7*), the outer front of which is now in the centre of town. It was built in the mid-1st century AD with a double archway surmounted by two stages of windows and niches. It was here that the Via Postumia arrived and the *decumanus maximus* began. As the inscription states, it was restored by Gallienus in AD 265. Roman masonry can be seen in some of the adjoining houses. At the other end of Corso Cavour is the **Arco di Gavi** (*map Verona 6*), also dating from the 1st century AD, erected astride the Via Postumia in honour of the Gavii family. Although demolished in 1805, it was reconstructed in 1932 and was recently restored. Via Leoni (*map Verona 7–8*) is named after the Roman **Porta dei Leoni**, dating from the same century, which survives in a damaged state.

Museo Lapidario Maffeiano

Founded in 1716 by the dramatist Scipione Maffei (1675–1755), the Maffeiano (*map Verona 10; closed Mon; museomaffeiano.comune.verona.it*) was one of the first public museums in Italy. It is housed around a courtyard with a magnificent porch at one end, with six huge Ionic columns, built in 1604 by Domenico Curtoni (who was clearly influenced by Palladio). He designed this building to be seen in conjunction with his Palazzo della Gran Guardia, on the other side of the Portoni archway.

The courtyard was used in Maffei's day to display ancient inscriptions and the low Roman Doric porticoes on either side it were added in 1745 to display the lapidary collection. The collection today, ranging over three floors, includes some 100 Greek inscriptions from Smyrna, the Cyclades, Attica and the Peloponnese, dating from the 5th century BC to the 5th century AD and constituting the best collection of its kind in Italy. There is also Roman material from the Veneto and some Etruscan cinerary urns. In fact, in the courtyard, there are Etruscan urns set into the wall of the entrance porch by Maffei in the 18th century.

PIAZZA DELLE ERBE & PIAZZA DEI SIGNORI

Piazza delle Erbe

This delightful piazza (*map Verona Inset*) occupies the site of the Roman forum. In the centre, paved with huge square blocks of red Verona marble, is a Gothic column with a stone lantern, as well as a monument made up of a group of four columns and an ingenious fountain dating from 1368 with a Roman statue known as the '*Madonna Verona*'; and a tall column set up in 1523 bearing the Lion of St Mark (a replacement made in 1886 after the original had been destroyed at the fall of the Venetian Republic). The square is always busy (it is still used as a market place) and there are a number of cafés and restaurants. The brick, battlemented **Casa dei Mercanti**, the merchants' headquarters, was founded by Alberto della Scala in 1301. The *Madonna and Child* in the niche is by Girolamo Campagna (1595). A bronze statue commemorates the victims of an Austrian bomb that fell on this site in 1915. By the Torre del Gardello (1370)

'Letter box' for public denunciations, in this case against usurers, in Piazza delle Erbe. These were common in the Venetian Republic and its associated territories.

is the handsome **Palazzo Maffei** (1668), crowned with a balustrade bearing six statues. The **Casa Mazzanti**, once a palace of the ruling Della Scala family, has a 16th-century frescoed façade and a terrace running the whole of its length. The **Arco della Costa**, named from the whale's rib (*costa*) that hangs suspended beneath the vault, leads through into Piazza dei Signori, past the long flank of **Palazzo della Ragione** (*see below*).

Piazza dei Signori

Piazza dei Signori (*map Verona Inset*), entered beneath archways spanning a number of old streets, was the centre of medieval civic life. It is overlooked on its southeast

Palazzo della Ragione in Piazza dei Signori, with its once-proud Lion of St Mark, a symbol of Venice that was defaced by Napoleonic troops.

side by the great Palazzo della Ragione, from whose tall tower, the 12th-century **Torre dei Lamberti** (84m high; stairs or lift), there is a fine view. The *palazzo* was founded before 1193 but much altered in the 19th century. One wing of it is now home to the modern art gallery, GAM Achille Forti (*gam.comune.verona.it*). The wing overlooking Piazza dei Signori bears a huge, defaced Lion of St Mark, a victim of the systematic Napoleonic vandalism of all symbols of the power of Venice. The marble-faced **Palazzo del Capitano** has a crenellated tower and a portal by Sanmicheli. Opposite it stands the elegant Renaissance **Loggia del Consiglio**, dating from 1493, with arcades, a pretty balustrade, and twin windows. The statues depict famous Romans born in Verona and the inscription records Verona's faithfulness to Venice and their mutual affection. The **Palazzo degli Scaligeri** (now provincial government offices), has been restored to its original 14th-century appearance with a brick front and spiky swallowtail crenellations. It faces the handsome **Domus Nova**, reconstructed in 1659, which stands beside an archway crowned with a statue of the dramatist Scipione Maffei (1756). In the centre of the square is a statue of Dante (who lived in Verona in exile, after being sentenced to death in his native Florence), set up in 1865. The **Caffè Dante** is named after him. Beneath the level of the piazza and in Via Dante, Roman paving has been revealed.

The Della Scala Tombs (or Arche Scaligere)

From the northeast corner of Piazza dei Signori, an archway leads to a little square with the church of Santa Maria Antica beside a railing which, ever since the 14th century, has protected the tombs of the Della Scala family, or Scaligeri (pron: scaLEEjeri).

THE DELLA SCALA DYNASTY

The Della Scala family, or Scaligeri, ruled Verona during the 13th and 14th centuries. The founder of the dynasty was Mastino I, 'the Mastiff', who became *podestà* (chief magistrate) after the death of the tyrant Ezzelino da Romano in 1259. He converted the position into a hereditary one and named himself *capitano del popolo*. A faction of disaffected nobles plotted his downfall, and in 1277 he was assassinated in the Piazza dei Signori. The greatest of the Scaligeri was Mastino's grandson, Cangrande I, the 'Great Dog', who inherited the title in 1311. Cangrande was the archetypal medieval Italian ruler: ruthless warrior and tyrannical overlord, yet at the same time a cultured patron of the arts. He supported the Ghibelline faction (the imperial party) against the Guelphs (the papal party), and harboured Dante, who had been exiled from Florence for his political views. Cangrande conquered Padua, Treviso and Vicenza. His nephew Mastino II brought Verona to the zenith of her power, capturing Brescia and Parma. But he was cursed with a line of cruel and murderous heirs. Their lust for conquest led the powerful city states of Florence and Venice to make a pact against them, and gradually much of Verona's territory was lost again. When Gian Galeazzo Visconti, Duke of Milan, made an assault on Verona, the last of the Della Scala fled the town under cover of darkness, on 19th October 1387. They were never to rule in Verona again. Their great castle remains, however, filled with extraordinary works of art. And around the ceiling cornices of many of the rooms, you can still see frescoes of the family emblems: the ladder (*scala*) and the spotted dog (*can* or *mastino*).

The emblem of the Della Scala family, a ladder (*scala*) borne by a spotted dog (*can* or *mastino*) on either side.

This 'royal enclosure' celebrates the great ruling dynasty and was a statement of its power. The magnificent wrought-iron work is decorated with the repeated motif of a ladder (*scala*), their emblem. All the tombs date from the same century, when the Della Scala were the *signori* (lords) of Verona: they dominated much of the Veneto *terraferma*, and for a brief time even ruled as far away as Parma and Lucca. The two most elaborate monuments, by Bonino da Campione, are those of Mastino II (d. 1351) and, in the opposite corner, that of Cansignorio (d. 1375), his son. The very fine Gothic tabernacles decorated with numerous statues and columns protect the tombs with recumbent effigies, but the two rulers are also shown as proud figures on horseback crowning the summits. The carving on the tomb of Cansignorio is particularly fine. Against the wall of the church is the plain tomb of Mastino I, the first of the Della Scala dynasty, assassinated a few steps away in Piazza dei Signori in 1277. Protected by a low roof is the tomb of Giovanni (d. 1359) by Andreolo de' Santi. Nearby is the sarcophagus with bas reliefs of Bartolomeo, Mastino's nephew.

He gave refuge to Dante after a faction of the Guelph party in Florence had accused him of fraud and corruption, at a time when he was away in Rome. When he failed to return to defend himself he was sentenced death. Opting never to return to his native city, he stayed in Verona under Bartolomeo's protection and in his *Paradiso*, he praises Bartolomeo for this courtesy.

Over the side door of the church is the tomb of Cangrande I (d. 1329), also by Bonino da Campione (with a copy of the original equestrian statue now in Castelvecchio). Cangrande I was the most famous member of the family because of his significant conquests in northern Italy. He, too, features in Dante's *Paradiso* since he also gave hospitality to the exiled poet between 1312 and 1318.

The church of **Santa Maria Antica** (*map Verona Inset*) has a 12th-century campanile and a lovely early Romanesque interior with a red marble bishop's throne on the right wall of the sanctuary.

The 'House of Juliet'

South of Piazza delle Erbe, at Via Cappello 23, is the so-called Casa di Giulietta (*map Verona 7; closed Mon morning*), one of the most visited places in Verona because of its (spurious) associations with Juliet Capulet. Shakespeare's *Romeo and Juliet* tells the story of Juliet Capulet (the anglicisation of Cappelletti) and Romeo Montague (Montecchi), an adaptation of a tale by the 16th-century novelist Luigi da Porto. The legend of a feud between the two families is apocryphal; in fact, it is probable that the clans were in close alliance. The romantic balcony (which only dates from 1935) overlooks the courtyard, and an entire wall at the entrance has been provided for visitors' signatures. The interior of this restored 13th-century house has fine wooden ceilings on the top floor, where there is a ship's keel roof. There is also a bronze statue of the fictional heroine (touching its breast will supposedly bring you a new lover). The house infuriated Arnold Bennet: 'I am [determined] somehow to vent my rage at being shown Juliet's house, a picturesque and untidy tenement, with balconies certainly too high for love, unless Juliet was a trapeze acrobat...This was not Juliet's house, for the sufficient reason that so far as authentic history knows, there never was any Juliet.'

SANT'ANASTASIA

Map Verona 3–4. For opening times and visitor information, see chieseverona.it.

The fine Gothic basilica of Sant'Anastasia is the largest church in Verona. It was begun in 1290 but work continued on it throughout the following two centuries and the façade, with its stripes of pink, white and grey, is still unfinished. The quaint relief over the double doors bears six scenes from the *Annunciation* to the *Resurrection*. Two **sculptured panels on the right of the door** have episodes from the life of St Peter Martyr. Born in Verona, he became a Dominican in 1221 and was famous as

SANT'ANASTASIA

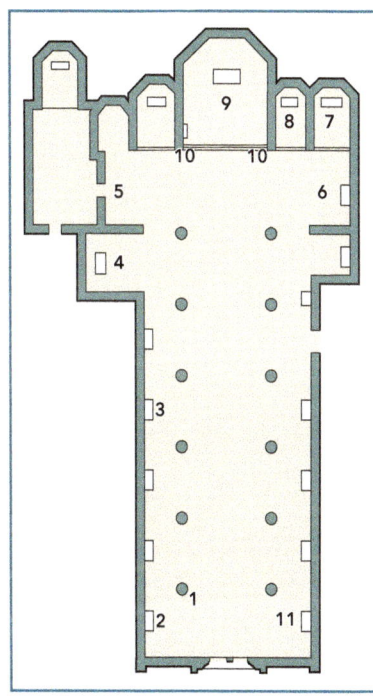

1. Stoup by Gabriele Caliari
2. Frescoes by Francesco Morone
3. Altarpiece by Giolfino
4. Fresco attributed to Lorenzo Veneziano
5. North transept
6. South transept
7. Fresco by Altichiero
8. Pellegrini Chapel
9. Sanctuary
10. Sanctuary arch (fresco by Pisanello)
11. Screen by Sanmicheli

a preacher (one of the scenes shows him addressing a crowd of worshippers). He was stabbed to death by heretics on the road between Como and Milan in 1252 (the other scene records his martyrdom) and the following year he became the first Dominican saint. This church, despite always being known as Sant'Anastasia, is dedicated to him.

Interior of Sant'Anastasia

The huge interior is unusually bright and the vaults of the nave and aisles covered with very colourful frescoes against a white ground. The splendid pink, white and grey pavement dates from 1462. The massive columns are made of red Veronese marble.

North side: Both **stoups** are supported by two life-like crouching figures: that on the left (**1**) carved in 1495 by Gabriele Caliari, father of the great Venetian painter Paolo Veronese. The the first chapel (**2**) has **frescoes by Francesco Morone**. At the sumptuous fourth altar (**3**) is the *Descent of the Holy Spirit* by Nicolò Giolfino (1518), a pupil of Liberale da Verona, surrounded by statues of saints and the *Redeemer* (above is a fresco by Francesco Morone). The fifth north chapel (**4**) dates from 1596 and has a detached **fresco attributed to Lorenzo Veneziano**, and paintings by the 17th century Veronese school.

Stoup in Sant'Anastasia, borne by a crouching figure carved by Gabriele Caliari, father of the great painter Veronese.

Transepts: In the **north transept (5)** are early 15th–16th century frescoes attributed to Bonaventura Boninsegna. Above them are three framed paintings dating from the 15th/16th century by Paolo Farinati, Alessandro Turchi, and Liberale da Verona, and on the left, also in a frame, *Three Saints* by Francesco Morone. The **south transept (6)** has a wonderful altarpiece by the Veronese painter Girolamo dai Libri of the *Madonna and Child Enthroned between St Thomas Aquinas and St Augustine.*

East end: On the right wall of the second chapel **(7)** is a superb large **fresco by Altichiero**, dating from the last decade of the 14th century which shows three members of the Cavalli family presented by their patron saints to the Madonna (a fragment). The tomb of Federico Cavalli has a fresco by Stefano da Zevio.

The **Pellegrini chapel (8)**, to the right of the sanctuary, has four apostles painted on either side of the entrance arch attributed to the school of Mantegna. The good Gothic family tombs here incorporate fine frescoes dating from the late 14th century. Wilhelm von Bibra, ambassador of Cologne to the Vatican, who died in 1490, is shown in an effigy, fully armed. The altarpiece of the *Madonna and Child with Saints* is by Lorenzo Veneziano, and includes portraits of the two donors Mastino II Della Scala and his wife Taddea. The terracotta reliefs of the life of Christ are by Michele da Firenze (1435).

The **Sanctuary (9)** has a *Last Judgement* dating from around 1360 by Turone on the right wall and on the left wall 15th-century frescoes (difficult to see) by Michele Giambono around to the tomb of Cortesia Serego, a general who served under Antonio della Scala, who is shown in an equestrian statue of 1429 by the Florentine sculptor Nanni di Bartolo. Nanni was a pupil and collaborator of Donatello's and first introduced the vogue for works in terracotta in the Veneto (he also produced a sculpture for a tomb in San Fermo).

Very high up on two sides of the entrance arch is a very damaged but famous **fresco by Pisanello (10)**, a delightful scene of St George at Trebizond. The saint is about to mount his grey charger (memorably seen from behind, while his attendant's horse is shown full face to the viewer) and the princess appears between them in profile. As Berenson lamented, this work was carried out 'with no thought for the spectator on the floor of the church'!

South side: The first altar **(11)** has a marble screen designed by Michele Sanmicheli.

THE CATHEDRAL COMPLEX (DUOMO)

Map Verona 3. For opening times and visitor information, see chieseverona.it.

The Romanesque exterior of the Duomo, the cathedral of Verona, survives from its rebuilding around 1120, notably the two porches and apse. At the main entrance, two griffins support the columns and the carving is signed by Maestro Nicolò, the sculptor who also worked at the church of San Zeno in the 1130s. In the lunette are polychrome *Nativity* scenes, and the two statues on either side of the door represent the paladins Roland (identified by the name carved on his sword) and Oliver. The south porch has a double order of ancient Roman columns with finely carved capitals, between which are reliefs of the story of Jonah and the Whale, and a lion. The magnificent apse, with delicate carving high up above the pilasters, also survives (it can be seen from Piazza Vescovile). The campanile was continued above its Romanesque base by Michele Sanmicheli (and the bell chamber only added in 1927).

Interior of the Duomo

The huge interior was covered with colourful frescoes in the 15th and 16th centuries, when the side chapels were constructed. The clustered pillars have interesting capitals. Round each chapel is a charming framework of sculptured pilasters and architectural fretwork. The walls around the first three chapels on either side were decorated with architectural frescoes by Giovanni Maria Falconetto in 1503.

South side: The second chapel contains a small, crowded *Adoration of the Magi* by Liberale da Verona surrounded by 16th-century paintings of four saints and the *Deposition* by Nicolò Giolfino, his pupil. The fourth domed chapel has extravagant Baroque decorations with six huge columns and stuccoes, ingeniously lit by two windows. The magnificent organ survives from the 16th century. At the end of this aisle is the lovely Cappella Mazzanti, with sculptured pilasters by Domenico da Lugo (1508): it protects the beautiful tomb of St Agatha, carved by a Campionese master (from Lake Lugano) in 1353. On the wall just to the right is the red tomb slab of Pope Lucius III, who died in Verona in 1185.

East end: The graceful curved choir-screen, in pink and grey marble, was designed by Michele Sanmicheli in 1534. At the same time the dramatic frescoes in the choir were carried out by Francesco Torbido, thought to be on cartoons by Giulio Romano.

North aisle: The Cappella Maffei has frescoes high up outside over the entrance and in the lunette by Giovanni Maria Falconetto, and sculptured pilasters (as in the chapel opposite). The lovely predella here is by Michele da Verona. Outside the first north chapel is the tomb of Bishop Galesio Nichesola (d. 1527), a fine work attributed to Jacopo Sansovino, who also designed the altar-frame in the chapel which encloses an ***Assumption*** **by Titian**, painted some 17 years after his much more famous painting of the same subject in the Frari in Venice.

The cathedral complex

Off the north side of the Duomo is the entrance to a 12th-century vestibule with ancient columns, and part of the foundations of an early Christian basilica of the 4th century. **San Giovanni in Fonte** was built in the early 12th century, and the huge octagonal font hewn in the same century from a single block of marble has finely carved panels attributed to Brioloto. The fragmentary frescoes date from the 13th and 14th centuries, the painted Cross from the 15th century (attributed to Giovanni Badile), and the painting of the *Baptism of Christ* is by Paolo Farinati (1568).

From the vestibule, steps lead up to the church of **Sant'Elena**, dating from the 9th century but restored in the 12th century, beneath which excavations have revealed remains of two early Christian basilicas (4th and 5th centuries), with fragments of mosaic pavements. The tombs of two early bishops have also been found here. The finely carved narrow stalls date from the 16th century.

To the left of the Duomo façade, a passageway leads to the exterior portico of Sant'Elena and the charming **Romanesque cloister** with twin columns (in a two-storey arcade above one walk), also partly on the site of the 5th-century basilica, with remains in two places of a 6th-century mosaic pavement, one of which is polychrome.

In Piazza del Duomo an archway leads to the **Chapter Library**, founded by Archdeacon Pacificus (778–846), which has many precious texts and illuminated choirbooks dating from around 1368 and attributed to Turone.

Opposite the south door of the Duomo, a seated 14th-century figure of *St Peter* surmounts the doorway of **San Pietro in Archivolto**. Via Pietà Vecchia leads to **Piazza Vescovile** with the magnificent Romanesque east end of the Duomo. The **Bishop's Palace** has an unusual exterior of 1502 with Venetian crenellations and a lovely portal decorated with statues including a delightful *Madonna and Child* attributed to Fra' Giovanni da Verona. The striped wall belongs to San Giovanni in Fonte (*described above*).

ON THE LEFT BANK OF THE ADIGE

Much busier with traffic than the part of town on the right bank of the river (many of whose streets are pedestrianised), the left bank has some very interesting monuments and churches. A good way to cross is by the fine **Ponte della Pietra** (only open to pedestrians) is guarded by a picturesque tower. It was reconstructed after WWII using part of the Roman and medieval masonry dredged up from the river.

Teatro Romano and the Museo Archeologico

Verona's **Roman theatre** (*map Verona 4; entrance at Regaste Ridentore 2; museoarcheologico.comune.verona.it*) occupies a superb position, dug into a steep hillside on the bend of the river. It was founded under Augustus and later enlarged. During the Middle Ages, houses and churches were built on the ruins (and to this day the little church of Santi Siro e Libera, dating from 920 but altered in the 14th century, survives). After excavations begun in 1834, the two entrances, the arches that supported the cavea, and the *scaena* itself (now a third of its original height) were all exposed. The seats have been restored and the theatre is still usually used for a summer drama season. The huge blocks of tufa that supported the *scaena* remain, and a few statues found in the theatre are on display. Here will also see some lead

View across the Adige, on a day of leaden skies, to Castel San Pietro amid its mournful cypresses.

pipes which were part of the aqueduct the Romans built to supply water to the city.

The 15th-century convent building above the theatre, with its refectory, cloister and chapel (frescoed in 1508 by Giovan Francesco Caroto), houses the **Museo Archeologico**, founded in 1857. The interesting little collection of Roman finds from Verona and its environs includes Hellenistic bronzes, well-preserved glass, sculpture, mosaic fragments, inscriptions and sepulchral monuments. From the windows are splendid views of the theatre and the city beyond.

On the hillside high above the theatre can be seen **Castel San Pietro**, where the Austrians built their barracks on the foundations of a Visconti castle destroyed by the French in 1801.

Santo Stefano and San Giorgio in Braida

In the venerable church of **Santo Stefano** (*map Verona 4; usually closed in the middle of the day*), high up on the arches of both transepts, are charming frescoes of angel musicians by Domenico Brusasorci. Further west, the large church of **San Giorgio in Braida** (*map Verona 4; usually closed in the middle of the day*) was begun in 1477 on the site of a 12th-century church and completed on a design by Michele Sanmicheli, who added the cupola and who also began the unfinished campanile. It contains numerous fine paintings, including a very darkened *Baptism of Christ* by Tintoretto above the west door. In the sanctuary, the main apse has a fine altar by Sanmicheli which incorporates the *Martyrdom of St George*, a very crowded work by Veronese, probably painted around 1555, the year he left his native city to take up his brilliant career in Venice. The two huge paintings here are by Paolo Farinati (right) and Felice Brusasorci (left), both skilled local painters who certainly influenced the young Veronese. Also by Brusasorci is the *Madonna between Archangels* on the fourth south altar.

On the north side, the painted doors high up on either side of the organ are by an artist from Brescia, Girolamo Romanino, and beneath the organ is a painting of *St Cecilia* (patron saint of music) by his compatriot Il Moretto. The fourth chapel has a beautiful *Madonna with Saints and Angel Musicians* by Girolamo dai Libri. In the third chapel, the polyptych in a fine gilded frame includes *Sts Roch and Sebastian*, the *Transfiguration*, and a predella all by Giovan Francesco Caroto, who also painted the altarpiece of *St Ursula and the Virgins* in the first chapel.

Opposite the church façade is Sanmicheli's **Porta San Giorgio** (1525).

PALACES AND FORTIFICATIONS BY SANMICHELI

The architect and sculptor Michele Sanmicheli, born just outside Verona in 1486, carried out numerous buildings in the city and also designed the gates in her defensive walls. He became very well known and was called to Rome to work for the Papacy, and in Venice he was put in charge of the defences, not only in the city itself but also throughout her empire. Among the best palaces he built for the citizens of Verona are **Palazzo Pompei** (*see p. 113*) and **Palazzo Canossa** on Corso Cavour (*map Verona 6*), dating from around the same time. **Palazzo Bevilacqua**, on the other side of the Corso (*map Verona 7*), is an unusually ornate work. Sanmicheli also worked on chapels and altar screens in the churches of San Bernardino, Sant'Anastasia, San Giorgio in Braida and the Duomo.

In the early 16th century he built the town walls on the lines of the older Della Scala ramparts. They are the earliest example of a new type of military engineering that was later developed by Vauban. The **Porta del Palio** (*map Verona 9*) shows Sanmicheli's skill in combining structural beauty with military strength, and his **Porta Nuova** (*map Verona 14*) also survives intact.

ART AND ARCHITECTURE IN VERONA

The architect Michele Sanmicheli (1486–1559; *see above*) designed some important buildings for this, his native town. But it is in the field of painting that Verona is especially interesting, for the numerous works in its churches and museums by local artists, most of them little-known elsewhere. Interestingly the greatest painter born in the town, Paolo Caliari, always known as Veronese, left no works of great importance here since he was active almost entirely in Venice. But nevertheless it is clear to see how much he was influenced as a young man by Verona's local school of painting.

Altichiero was the most important north Italian painter in the second half of the 14th century, a creative interpreter of the style of Giotto: although he was born in Verona, most of his best surviving works are now in Padua. However,

there are frescoes by him here in the churches of Sant'Anastasia and San Fermo (as well as in Santa Maria della Scala). The most famous painter active in Verona in the early 15th century was **Pisanello**. His remarkable fresco of *St George* in Sant'Anastasia is one of the very few of his works to have survived (another, in very poor condition, is in San Fermo). Fewer than ten paintings can today be attributed to him, but one of the loveliest is in the Castelvecchio museum (*see overleaf*). He was clearly fascinated by natural details and by the Gothic world of chivalry, and painted with the care of a miniaturist.

Pisanello's near contemporaries **Giovanni Badile** and **Stefano da Zevio** both also painted charming Madonnas (now also preserved in the Castelvecchio), as well as carrying out frescoes in Sant'Anastasia and San Fermo (Badile died young, but also produced frescoes for Santa Maria della Scala).

Perhaps the most influential native artist of the later 15th century was **Domenico Morone**, whose frescoes in the library of the convent of San Bernardino (now called the Sala Morone) are considered his best works. His son Francesco carried out frescoes in Sant'Anastasia. **Francesco Bonsignori** was at work at the same time as Domenico in San Bernardino (and his works can also be seen in the Castelvecchio). Successors of Domenico include **Francesco Torbido** (altarpiece in San Zeno and frescoes in the Duomo), **Antonio Badile** (San Nazaro e Celso) and **Giovan Francesco Caroto**, all of them born in the 1480s. Caroto was perhaps the ablest and is also the best represented (in Castelvecchio, San Fermo, San Giorgio in Braida, Santa Maria in Organo, San Francesco, San Paolo and Sant'Eufemia). Badile has been recognised as Veronese's earliest master. **Girolamo dai Libri**, also born in the late 15th century and another talented follower of Domenico Morone, earned his second name (*Libri*, books) from his skill as an illuminator. His paintings, which often incorporate beautiful landscapes, can be seen in Sant'Anastasia, San Giorgio in Braida, Santi Nazaro e Celso, San Paolo and San Tomaso Cantuariense.

In the early 16th century artists of the '*maniera*' included Caroto's pupil **Domenico Brusasorci**, who worked on frescoes in Santo Stefano, Santa Maria in Organo and Sant'Eufemia. His son **Felice Brusasorci**, who was particularly skilled in portraiture, also left altarpieces here, and the one in San Giorgio in Braida must have influenced Veronese. Domenico's near contemporary **Paolo Farinati** is well represented with altarpieces and frescoes (San Giovanni in Fonte, San Giorgio in Braida and the Museo degli Affreschi).

The Olivetan monk **Fra' Giovanni da Verona**, born in the city in 1457, left his masterpiece here: the magnificent intarsia choir stalls in Santa Maria in Organo. Such was their fame that he was then called to work in the Vatican.

Left: *Madonna della Quaglia* (*Madonna of the Quail*), an early 15th-century masterpiece by Pisanello, in Verona's Museo del Castelvecchio.

MUSEO DI CASTELVECCHIO

Map Verona 6. Entrance from the drawbridge on the Corso Castelvecchio. Closed Mon. museodicastelvecchio.comune.verona.it.

This magnificent castle, built by Cangrande II della Scala in 1354, was used throughout the following centuries as a citadel, and after the fall of Venice as barracks. It was opened as a museum in 1925 and after War damage was imaginatively recreated by Carlo Scarpa. The details of his work throughout the museum bear close study and this is perhaps the place where you can best appreciate his style and skill in inventing (simple) ways of displaying works of art in order that they can be viewed to best advantage. The collection is superb—and fortunately, intact. In 2015, three masked thieves stole eighteen million dollars' worth of artworks, including Pisanello's famous *Madonna della Quaglia*, and works by Rubens and Tintoretto. They were recovered in 2021, *en route* to Moldova, and returned to Verona.

A drawbridge leads into the lovely courtyard, with a water garden designed by Scarpa and eleven medieval inscriptions relating to the Della Scala family.

The collection
Among the sculptures displayed in the long enfilade of downstairs rooms is a memorable 14th-century statue of *St Cecilia* (with long pigtails and holding her attribute, a portable organ) and another of *Santa Libera*, a polychrome statuette with the same hairstyle: both are thought to be by the same sculptor.

A trove of treasure found in Via Trezza in Verona in 1938 includes precious 14th-century jewels. Also on show are the sword and belt found in the tomb of Cangrande I. Among the famous masterpieces of the collection are three Madonnas: *Madonna del Roseto* by Stefano da Zevio (the Madonna literally immersed in a bed of roses), *Madonna della Quaglia* by Pisanello (the Madonna shown in a garden, inhabited by a quail and goldfinches) and a third by Michele Giambono (although damaged, the Madonna has particularly striking eyes).

There are works by the Venetian artists Jacopo and Giovanni Bellini, Alvise Vivarini and Carpaccio; and by Francesco Morone, son of Domenico the influential Veronese painter and his fellow Veronese Liberale da Verona (also known as a very fine miniaturist) and his pupil Giolfino. The 16th-century artists Giovan Francesco Caroto and Girolamo dai Libri (also represented in the collection) were both influenced by Liberale da Verona. There are plenty of examples of the work of Caroto's pupil Domenico Brusasorci. Major masterpieces are Mantegna's *Holy Family* and Carlo Crivelli's *Madonna della Passione*. There are also works by Tintoretto and Veronese (Verona's greatest painter but who left very few of his works in his native city).

Approached through the south wing of the castle (or from outside it) is the very fine **Ponte Scaligero** (only open to pedestrians), built at the same time as the Castelvecchio by Cangrande II. After its destruction in WWII, it was very well reconstructed, using the original materials.

SAN ZENO

Map Verona 5. Entrance usually on the left of the façade. For opening times and visitor information, see chieseverona.it.

The great church of San Zeno is one of the outstanding achievements of Romanesque architecture in Italy. It was begun in 1120 and completed some 100 years later. The apse was rebuilt in 1398. It has wonderful 12th-century sculpture on the facade and the bronze doors, and a superb painting by Mantegna adorns the high altar.

Exterior of San Zeno

The façade has a magnificent **rose window** which depicts the Wheel of Fortune. It is the work of Brioloto (c. 1200), an artist who worked on a number of buildings in Verona. The lovely band of twin arches is continued round the south side. Flanking the doorway are **five tiers of reliefs** in very good condition with scenes from the Old and New Testaments by two sculptors known simply as Maestro Nicolò and Maestro Guglielmo (1138): on the right, the lowest one shows Theodoric hunting a stag which leads him headlong into Hell; above are the *Creation of Adam; Creation of the Animals; Creation of Eve* and the *Temptation;* and at the top the *Expulsion from Paradise* and *Cain and Abel*. On the left, the lowest panel shows a group of mounted knights and foot soldiers in a battle; the panel above is divided into a series of scenes: the *Visitation, Annunciation,* the *Virgin before the Nativity, Annunciation to the Shepherds,* and the Magi preparing for their journey to Bethlehem; above is the *Adoration of the Magi, Presentation in the Temple,* and the Angel with Joseph; above again, the *Flight into Egypt* and *Baptism of Christ;* and at the top the *Garden of Gethsemane, Betrayal of Judas* and the *Crucifixion*. The doorway itself, dating from the same date and by the same sculptors, has a porch supported on marble lions with a polychrome lunette of St Zeno. St Zeno, Verona's patron saint, is apparently buried in the crypt of the church, and prayers are left for him here.

Interior of San Zeno

The church has a raised presbytery and a trifoliate wooden ceiling which survives from 1386. Some of the piers have capitals from Roman buildings. Also from ancient Rome are the large **porphyry bowl (1)** and stoups at the west end (the font in pink marble dates from the 12th century).

The remarkable **bronze doors (2)**, made for the entrance in the 12th century, have reliefs of scenes from the Old and New Testaments. The frames are decorated with masques, and two of them, especially large, served as door handles. Some of the reliefs are too high up to see clearly, but on the left door at eye level you can see Christ in Heaven and the Devil throwing sinners into the fire. On the west wall, the painted **Cross (3)** is attributed to Lorenzo Veneziano (mid-14th century).

The **first south altarpiece (4)** is by the local painter Francesco Torbido (1520), and the second is made up of 'knotted' columns of red marble resting on a lion and a bull.

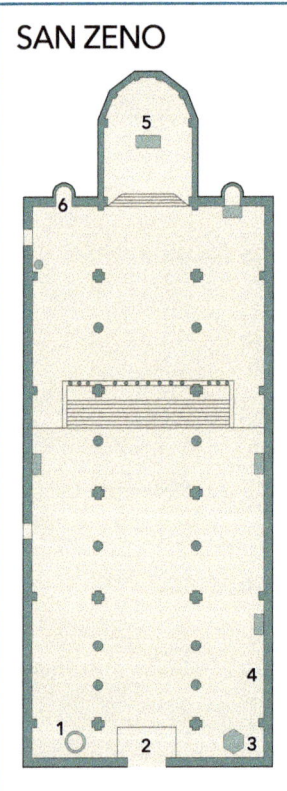

1 Porphyry bowl
2 Bronze doors
3 Painted Cross
4 Altarpiece by Torbido
5 Triptych by Mantegna
6 Smiling St Zeno

In the **sanctuary** is a huge altarpiece in wonderful colours and excellent condition (in its original frame), which is one of the great works by Mantegna **(5)**. This triptych, memorable also for its garlands which unite the three scenes (together with the pilasters with classical tondi in 'relief'), shows the Madonna with angel musicians and eight saints. The figures are depicted as if seen from a low viewpoint. It was painted between 1457 and 1459 in Padua after Mantegna had carried out the frescoes there in the church of the Eremitani, and the year before he moved to Mantua. The altarpiece clearly left a lasting impression on the local school of painting in Verona. The predella is a copy, Mantegna's wonderful original being now in the Louvre.

The frescoes in the apse behind and above the altarpiece are attributed to Martino da Verona (late 14th century). A 12th-century sarcophagus serves as high altar. On the balustrade are statues of Christ and the Apostles thought to be by a German sculptor working c. 1250.

In the north apse is a colossal polychrome **seated figure of St Zeno (6)**, shown smiling, by a 13th-century sculptor.

The crypt has beautiful pink columns in various colours.

San Bernardino

Some way south of San Zeno is the church of San Bernardino (1466; *map Verona 5*), entered through the cloister in front of the west façade, which has pretty carving round the portal. The first chapel on the south side has a barrel vault and was frescoed all over in the early 16th century by the local painter Giolfino. The altarpiece in the second chapel is by Francesco Bonsignori. The damaged frescoes in the fourth chapel are attributed to Domenico Morone and his son Francesco, and Domenico painted the organ doors in the north aisle. The chapel at the end of this aisle is entirely covered with 16th-century paintings in a gilded framework. Outside is a sculpted polychrome *Pietà*. On the right of the sanctuary is a vestibule and circular chapel, a very refined work by Michele Sanmicheli (1557). In the north aisle is a charming organ (1481) on a graceful bracket and a Baroque altar by Francesco Bibiena, better known as a theatre designer. Domenico's best frescoes (1503) are in the Sala Morone (entered from outside the church).

SAN FERMO

Map Verona 7–8. For opening times and visitor information, see chieseverona.it.

A Benedictine church built from 1065 to 1138 survives below a second church rebuilt by the Friars Minor around 1313 in a Gothic style. On the façade is the tomb of Antonio Fracastoro, physician of the Della Scala, who died in 1368. The 15th-century porch on the north side protects a fine portal of 1363.

Interior of San Fermo

The broad interior, without aisles, has a very fine wooden ceiling of 1314 which has a frieze of portrait heads of 416 saints (explained in a panel in the nave), and the various frescoes on the walls mostly date from the same time. Over the west doorway is a **fresco (1)** attributed to Altichiero or Turone. On the south side, beyond the first altar, unfortunately very high up, is a delightful angel **fresco by Stefano da Zevio (2)**. The marble **pulpit (3)** and (in the adjoining chapel) the wall-mounted **tomb of Barnaba Morano (4)**, were made by the same little-known sculptor, called Antonio da Mestre in 1306–1412. Outside is a lovely plain sarcophagus supported by two red marble oxen. The third altar has a **painting by Francesco Torbido (5)**.

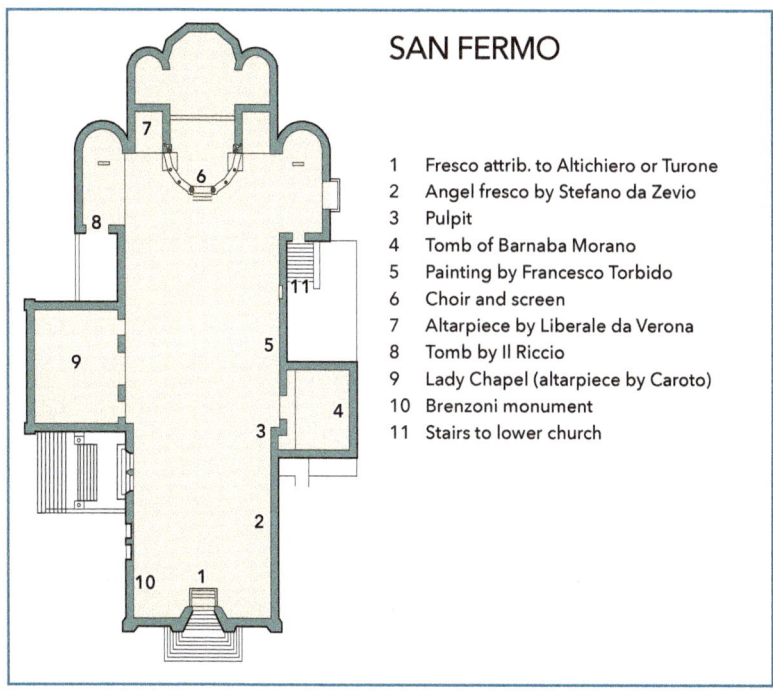

SAN FERMO

1 Fresco attrib. to Altichiero or Turone
2 Angel fresco by Stefano da Zevio
3 Pulpit
4 Tomb of Barnaba Morano
5 Painting by Francesco Torbido
6 Choir and screen
7 Altarpiece by Liberale da Verona
8 Tomb by Il Riccio
9 Lady Chapel (altarpiece by Caroto)
10 Brenzoni monument
11 Stairs to lower church

The **choir (6)** has a curved screen of 1573 and wonderful frescoes on the ceiling of the sanctuary with symbols of the Evangelists and above the triumphal arch (including Guglielmo di Castelbarco offering the church to Prior Gusmerio), all dating from the early 14th century. The chapel to the left of the sanctuary has an **altarpiece by Liberale da Verona (7)** and 14th-century frescoes found a few years ago behind the altar.

In a chapel off the north side is a remarkable **classical tomb (8)** on a very idiosyncratic design, in marble and bronze, made by Il Riccio around 1516 and perfectly preserved. It is the burial place of Girolamo and Marcantonio della Torre. The elaborate **Lady Chapel (9)** has a good *Madonna and Saints* by Giovan Francesco Caroto.

High up on the west wall is the **Brenzoni monument (10)** by Nanni di Bartolo (1439), with a very unusual sculpture of the *Resurrection of Christ* with the soldiers asleep at the tomb. It incorporates an exquisite *Annunciation* frescoed by Pisanello behind, with the Virgin shown in a Gothic chamber, and the angel with huge wings and long robes, but it is unfortunately in very bad condition.

From the south transept, stairs **(11)** lead down to the Romanesque lower church, with simple red decoration on the vaults.

OTHER SIGHTS IN VERONA

Verona has so many important monuments, churches and museums, and they are all widely spread out over a large area of the city. Many visitors will not have the time to visit all of them: a selection is given here, in alphabetical order.

Giardini Giusti

As soon as you have passed through the open portico, with its wooden ceiling and huge lantern, and entered the garden gate, you are immersed in a lovely peaceful green garden (*map Verona 4; open daily until dusk*). Behind the Giusti palace, it was laid out in the 16th century and has survived through the centuries, beautifully maintained. The ancient cypresses and formal box hedges surround fountains and statues. The maze, dating from 1786, is one of the oldest in Europe. At the end of the central cypress avenue, steps lead up to a grotto beneath the rockface, at the top of which a colossal grotesque masque dominates the view. Paths lead up left through a small wood to a tower (with a spiral staircase), which gives access to the upper terrace. There is a panoramic balcony above the mask and the little informal garden here has paths between the lawns and pines and cypresses. On the left, beyond a locked gate, can be seen an attractive old building with a loggia, and there is a view of the old town defences above the upper perimeter wall of the gardens.

During a visit in 1608, Thomas Coryate claimed that he found it 'a second paradise', and John Evelyn and Goethe were particularly struck by the venerable cypresses (Goethe even confessed that in September 1786, he actually picked some cypress branches here, as well as some caper blossom).

'Juliet's Tomb' and the Museo degli Affreschi

This museum (*map Verona 11–15; museodegliaffreschi.comune.verona.it*), in a not particularly attractive part of town, is visited because of its associations with Shakespeare's Juliet: unfortunately spurious, though the tradition goes back some centuries. In the 1930s an empty sarcophagus was placed in the atmospheric crypt below the cloister of the former monastery here and declared to be that of Juliet. But even in Byron's day the tomb was shown to visitors. 'I have been over Verone,' he wrote to Augusta Leigh, 'Of the truth of Juliet's story they seem tenacious to a degree, insisting on the fact—giving a date (1303), and showing a tomb. It is a plain, open, and partly decayed sarcophagus, with withered leaves in it, in a wild and desolate conventual garden, once a cemetery, now ruined to the very graves. The situation struck me as being very appropriate to the legend, being blighted as their love. I have brought away a few pieces of the granite, to give to my daughter and my nieces.'

Today the place is well worth visiting for its museum of frescoes and works of art, which has an impressive display of Roman amphorae found during excavations in the courtyard outside. There are also frescoes by Brusasorci and Paolo Farinati; *sinopie* by Altichiero; and early 16th-century works by Giovan Francesco Caroto and Francesco Morone (*Washing of the Feet*).

Museo Miniscalchi-Erizzo

Palazzo Miniscalchi (*map Verona 3; museominiscalchi.it*) was given a monumental Neoclassical façade on Via Garibaldi in 1880, but the 15th-century building retains its façade on Via San Mamaso, with handsome marble windows and doorway, and its mural paintings dating from c. 1580: it is one of the few palaces left in Verona which retains its exterior painted decoration, although once many palaces in the city had similarly decorated façades.

The house and its contents were left to a foundation in the 20th century by Mario Miniscalchi-Erizzo, and the eclectic collection formed by his family from the 17th–20th centuries is spaciously arranged in this their residence since the 15th century. Here you will find ivories, porcelain, furniture, paintings, arms and armour, and archaeological material, including Roman glass and bronzes.

Museo di Storia Naturale (Museum of Natural History)

Occupying the classically inspired Palazzo Pompei, built by Michele Sanmicheli c. 1530, this museum (*map Verona 12; museodistorianaturale.comune.verona.it*) has displays of flora and fauna, both Italian and international, as well as interesting examples of fossils from Bolca, a village which is famous for them (*see p. 118*).

Sant'Eufemia

Founded in 1262, and rebuilt in 1375 (*map Verona 7*), there are fine tombs on the exterior. Inside are works by Domenico Brusasorci. Also here are works by Giovan Francesco Caroto, Martino da Verona and Moretto.

Santa Maria in Organo

This church (*map Verona 4; usually closed in the middle of the day*), well worth a visit, was built by Olivetan friars in the late 15th century, although it is thought to have been founded in the 7th century. The very unusual façade is part early Gothic and part Renaissance, and the graceful campanile, dating from 1533, is ascribed to Fra' Giovanni da Verona, who also made the beautiful choir stalls inside.

In the interior, the nave, with its wonderful old columns all with different capitals, is frescoed with Old Testament scenes by two contemporaries, Nicolò Giolfino and Giovan Francesco Caroto. The transept chapels have two altarpieces by important painters not elsewhere represented in Verona: Guercino (south side), born in 1591 near Ferrara, and Luca Giordano (north side), born in Naples in 1634. Behind the high altar are magnificent stalls by Fra' Giovanni, inlaid with street scenes and musical instruments. They are his masterpiece and were carried out from 1494 to 1500 while he was a friar in this monastery. The backs of the benches have very pretty paintings by Domenico Brusasorci. In the north transept apse is a delightful life-size Palm Sunday figure of Christ on an ass, dating from the mid-13th century, and frescoes by Brusasorci. The sacristy has more exquisite inlaid intarsia work on the cupboards, again by Fra' Giovanni da Verona, made some years after the choir stalls (in 1519–23). The walls are frescoed with portraits of Benedictine monks by Francesco Morone. The crypt preserves ancient columns and capitals.

Santa Maria della Scala

The name of this church (*map Verona 7; usually closed in the middle of the day*) comes from the Della Scala family, since Cangrande ordered its erection in 1324: the apse survives from that time. On the right side the second altar has a votive fresco and in the chapel to the right of the sanctuary are numerous early 15th-century frescoed scenes from the life of St Jerome, by Giovanni Badile. The very fine wall monument of a certain Guantieri of Florence (d. 1430), is carved from pink Verona marble and includes a fresco of the *Crucifixion* and *Pietà* in the tympanum, also by Badile. In the sanctuary are more good fresco fragments by Badile and Altichiero, and in the chapel to the left of the sanctuary a delightful *Madonna and Saints* by Francesco Ubertini, showing the influence of Perugino, with an angel playing a lute.

Santi Nazaro e Celso

Built in 1463–84 (*map Verona 8*) near the site of a 10th-century shrine. The chapel of San Biagio has a pretty vault over the apse, an altarpiece by Girolamo dai Libri, and interesting frescoes by Bartolomeo Montagna. In the sacristy is a triptych by Francesco dai Libri (Girolamo's father), and part of a polyptych by Montagna. On the second north altar is the best known work by Antonio Badile, who was Veronese's first master.

San Paolo

Reconstructed in 1763, this church (*map Verona 12*) had to be rebuilt after 1944. It contains a good altarpiece of the *Madonna and Saints*, painted in 1526 by Girolamo dai Libri. The painting of the *Madonna and Child*, with saints and donors, was commissioned from Veronese by the Marogna family for their chapel here around 1562. Giovan Francesco Caroto painted the high altarpiece.

San Tomaso Cantuariense
Dedicated to St Thomas Becket, this church (*map Verona 8*) has a fine west front and rose window dating from 1493. It contains a monument to Michele Sanmicheli erected in 1884, centuries after his death, and a painting by Girolamo dai Libri.

VERONA PRACTICAL TIPS

VISITOR CARD

lThe Verona Card gives free admission to museums and monuments (and free public transport); it can be purchased at the Tourist Office or at museums.

GETTING AROUND

- **By car:** The historic centre of Verona is small enough to mean that most sights can comfortably be seen on foot. If you do need to use a car, bear in mind that the centre is closed to traffic during the morning rush-hour and for much of the afternoon, unless you have authorised access.
- **By train and bus:** The main railway station is at Porta Nuova (*map Verona 14*). regional and city buses are operated by ATV (*atv.verona.it*). Bus terminus in front of Porta Nuova railway station.
- **By bicycle:** There is an app for rental bikes: *bikeverona.it/en/how-it-works*.

WHERE TO STAY

€€€ **Gabbia d'Oro**. The 'Gilded Cage', a small luxury hotel, beautifully furnished and with a gracious atmosphere, in the very centre of the old town. *Corso Porta Borsari 4/a, hotelgabbiadoro.it. Map Verona 7.*

WHERE TO EAT

€€€€ **Casa Perbellini 12 Apostoli**. Elegant restaurant in a historic building. It began life in 1750 serving historic Veronese dishes. It now has three Michelin stars. *Vicolo Corticella San Marco 3, casaperbellini.com. Map Verona 7.*

€€€ **Il Desco**. If you enjoy fine dining and Michelin-starred cuisine, then this is the place to come. Reservations essential. Be sure to check opening times, which change. *Via Dietro S Sebastiano 7, ristoranteildesco.it. Map Verona 7.*

€€ **Caffè Dante**. In business since 1865 on Piazza dei Signori. It gets mixed reviews but the location cannot be beaten. *Piazza dei Signori 2, caffedante.it. Map Verona 7 (and 2 Inset).*

€€ **Maffei**. Another long-established place in the heart of historic Verona. Tables outside in summer. *Piazza delle Erbe 38, ristorantemaffei.it. Map Verona 7 (and 2 Inset).*

€–€€ **Antica Bottega del Vino**. Historic wine bar (and restaurant) first opened in 1890, with a cosy atmospheric interior and a list of almost 3,000 vintages. In a quiet alley off Via Mazzini. *Vicolo Scudo di Francia 3, bottegavini.it. Map Verona 7.*

€ **San Matteo Church**. Self-service restaurant and pizzeria in a former church. Quick, efficient and good value. *Vicolo del Guasto 4, off Corso Porta Borsari, san-matteo-churchristorante-pizzeria.it. Map Verona 7.*

FESTIVALS AND EVENTS

Opera season at the Arena runs from mid-June–early Sept (*arena.it*). Box office at Via Dietro Anfiteatro 6/b. The cheapest (unreserved) tickets are for the highest stone steps. For summer events in the Roman Theatre, see *estateteatraleveronese.it.*

The Festa di Santa Lucia, with a street market in Piazza Brà and Via Roma, is celebrated from 10–13 Dec. Carnival celebrations, which have been held in the town since the 16th century, culminate on the Fri before Shrove Tues (*Venerdì gnocolar*). Festival of St Zeno, the patron saint, on 12 April.

SOAVE, THE MONTI LESSINI & VALPOLICELLA

The area to the east and north of Verona is home to the two famous wine regions; Soave and Valpolicella. Soave is a white wine produced in the hills to the east of Verona, around the charming walled town of the same name. To the north are the mountains of Lessinia, an alpine plateau of remote villages and pastures, also known for its fossils. Valpolicella is a collection of hilly towns and villages to the north of Verona, known mostly for its red wine.

THE WINE OF SOAVE

At 16,000 acres, Soave is the largest white wine appellation in Italy. It is grown on the fertile hillsides east of Verona, around the village that bears its name. Vast quantities of wine are produced here, with the quality fluctuating greatly, the more mass-produced offerings sometimes affecting the reputation of the wine as a whole. But the volcanic soil here lends itself to winemaking, and the local grape variety, Garganega, produces wines of deep minerality: All Soave must consist of at least 70 percent Garganega, and much of the best wine is closer to 100 percent. One of the long time best producers is Pieropan, which has vineyards on some of the best sites in the Soave Classico zone, including Calvarino and La Rocca, where the vines cluster around the old Della Scala castle. Other top wineries are Prà and Gini, both located in Monteforte d'Alpone, also famous for its cherries. The Anselmi winery here labels its wines in the IGT category, after Roberto Anselmi chose to remove all of his wines from the DOC system in 2000, in protest at the wine's often mediocre quality. They are still considered one of the premier producers in the area.

Garganega is also the predominant grape in the small adjoining region of Gambellara, which has an increasingly good reputation.

SOAVE

Soave (*map Veneto West C3*) is a pleasant little town overlooked by a hilltop castle which gives its name to the famous white wine, celebrated in a festival here in Sept. The impressive **battlemented walls**, extremely well preserved, were built by the Della Scala (Scaligeri) before 1375. There are two original gates to the town: Porta Aquila in the north and Porta Verona in the south. Both lead to the central **Piazza**

Antenna (named after a mast from which the flag of St Mark was flown in 1405 when Verona voted to join the Venetian Republic) where there is Palazzo Cavalli, a Venetian Gothic palace of 1411, and Palazzo di Giustizia (1375). Opposite Palazzo Cavalli is the duomo (San Lorenzo). A cobblestone path leads up from the piazza to the hilltop medieval **castle** (*also reached by road*), enlarged by the Scaligeri in 1369. The keep is defended by three courtyards, all built at different times and each on a different level. The above-mentioned walls of the castle create the courtyards before sloping downwards to envelop the town. Privately owned (*castellodisoave.it/en; closed Mon*), it was restored and partly reconstructed in 1892. The residence has an armoury on the ground floor, and above are rooms with Gothic Revival painted decorations and imitation furniture. There is a fine view from the battlements, with a walk along the interior.

West of Soave is **Caldiero** (*map Veneto West C3*) has been known for its thermal baths since Roman times and has a modern spa complex with hot springs.

THE MONTI LESSINI

To the north of Verona are the volcanic Monti Lessini (*map Veneto West B2*), with the valleys of the **Tredici Comuni**, a group of 13 towns occupied by the descendants of Germanic settlers who migrated here in the 13th century, and who retained a distinct Cimbrian dialect for centuries. A degree of autonomy and the isolation of the area helped to preserve a Germanic alpine culture here until the 20th century. **Bosco Chiesanuova**, the main resort (*map Veneto West B2*), has a museum illustrating the history of Lessinia—as the region as a whole is known. The wider Lessinia area is pleasant and remote, protected as a regional park since 1990, and particularly pastoral for an alpine area. The lower parts are mostly forested, with cherry trees and chestnut and beechwoods. The flint outcrops in the limestone hills were used in the Palaeolithic era for making tools, and a shelter used by Palaeolithic hunters has been found. Slabs of the local stone were traditionally used as a roofing material and to make drystone walls. **Ponte di Veja**, c. 8km southeast of Sant'Anna d'Alfaedo, is a natural bridge made of limestone, purportedly the inspiration for part of Mantegna's famous Camera degli Sposi fresco in Mantua and the description of the Malebolge in Dante's *Inferno*.

Lessinia is renowned for its fossils. The town of **Bolca** (*map Veneto West C2*) is home to one of the largest and best preserved collections of fossils from the Eocene epoch (approximately 50 million years ago) Bolca is famous above all for its fossilised fish, though various other forms of marine life have been discovered here, reflecting a lagoon type habitat at the time. Highlights include fossils of sharks and jellyfish, and can be viewed at the impressive museum in the town. The fossils at the museum mostly come from the site commonly known as the Pesciara (the 'Fishbowl'), a network of tunnels 2km to the east of Bolca, from which thousands of fish fossils have been extracted. The Pesciara is a museum site of its own, with an excavation cave, and can be reached via a 1km walk from the car park. **Roncà**, closer to Soave, also has a museum dedicated to fossils, including the head of a crocodile and the Eocene precursor to the dugong.

The Val d'Illasi is known for its wrought-iron craftsmen: the most famous workshop is that of the Da Ronco family at **Cogollo** (*map Veneto West C2*), now into its fourth generation (*bertodacogolo.com/en/home-en*). At the head of the valley is **Giazza** (*map Veneto West B2–C2*), the last of the Tredici Comuni to retain some usage of the Cimbrian dialect, with a museum detailing the traditions of the Cimbri.

THE VALPOLICELLA REGION

Valpolicella, near a bend in the Adige in the westernmost part of Lessinia (*map Veneto West B2*), is famous above all for its red wine (*see below*).

THE WINE OF VALPOLICELLA

The DOC of Valpolicella (*map Veneto West B2*) embraces 19 villages stretching from Lake Garda to just north of Verona, with the best wine typically found on the hillsides closest to Fumane, Marano and Negrar. The most valuable grape grown here is Corvina, yielding wines of impressive power and density. DOC regulations require 45–95 percent Corvina, and 5–30 percent of Rondinella in the wine. This, along with the large expansion of the DOC, has led to some renowned producers, notably the Allegrini family in 1997, opting out of the DOC system—a story now familiar in Italy—and producing 100 percent Corvina wines, some of them true classics, though not labelled Valpolicella.

There are various styles in Valpolicella. Straight Valpolicella is a youthful, easy-drinking wine, lighter than some assume, and can be drunk chilled. 'Valpolicella Superiore' on the label means that the alcohol content is slightly higher, and that the wine has been at least a year in the bottle. Recioto and Amarone are made from selected bunches, picked late in the harvest and dried on wooden slats under a straw roof. For Amarone, the sweetness is fermented out, yielding a heavy and often very alcoholic dry wine, quite unique for the climate. To make Recioto, the fermentation is halted before the sugar has converted to alcohol, creating a rich dessert wine. It is probable that *retico*, to which—according to Suetonius—Augustus Caesar was particularly partial, was precisely the same wine, with all its smoky, fruity, marzipan flavours. The newest type of Valpolicella is Ripasso, made by a second fermentation of ordinary Valpolicella on used Recioto or Amarone skins. The result is a full bodied, powerful, alcoholic wine.

Top producers include the Quintarelli estate in Negrar, long considered the gold standard for Amarone; the Tedeschi family near Pedemonte; the large Masi winery, headquartered near Sant'Ambrogio and the Allegrini family in Fumane, long known for its Amarone and the 100 percent Corvina IGT wines of La Poja and La Grola, though the latter returned to the DOC in 2022 as a new blend.

TOWNS IN THE VALPOLICELLA REGION

Sant'Ambrogio has quarries of rosso di Verona marble, used for the pavements of Verona, in some of the floors of Venetian churches and often for well-heads. Just under 4km to the northeast is the church of **San Giorgio di Valpolicella**, an ancient church rebuilt in the Romanesque style in the 12th century, situated in the hilltop hamlet of the same name. It has frescoes dating from the 11th century onwards, and a 12th-century cloister and bell-tower, which dominates the surrounding landscape. In a valley of cherry trees at **Volargne**, the 15th-century Villa del Bene (*open Sun*) has frescoes by Brusasorci, Giovan Francesco Caroto and Bernardino India. Across the Adige from here is **Rivoli Veronese**, scene of one of Napoleon's military victories over Austria (in 1797). The rue de Rivoli in Paris is named after it.

SOAVE AND VALPOLICELLA PRACTICAL TIPS

GETTING AROUND

Regional train stations include Sant'Ambrogio, on the line from Verona to Bolzano. Roncà and Bolca are on regional bus routes only, from San Bonifacio.

WHERE TO STAY

€€ **Villa Quaranta**. An 18th-century villa in a lovely old park, with an open-air pool. *Via Brennero 65, Località Ospedaletto, Pescantina (map Veneto West B2), villaquaranta.com.*

WHERE TO EAT

SOAVE
€€ **Ristorante Al Gambero** and **Osteria del Mare La Scala**, one serving meat and the other serving fish, occupy the former Bolla winery, adjacent to the castle walls (*Corso Vittorio Emanuele 5, ristorantealgambero. it, osteriadelmaresoave.it*). The € **Bigoleria alla Rocca** is a small taverna known for its fresh pasta, especially *bigoli* (*Corso Vittorio Emanuele 155, bigoleriaallarocca.it*).

VALPOLICELLA
€€ **Dalla Rosa Alda**. Simple family-run *trattoria* with a good wine list. It also runs a simple *locanda* (closed Jan and Feb). *Strada Garibaldi 4, Sant'Ambrogio di Valpolicella, dallarosalda.it.*
€€ **Enoteca della Valpolicella**. Not merely a wine bar, but a renowned country restaurant in a 15th-century farm complex. *Via Osan 45, Fumane, enotecadellavalpolicella.it.*

TREVISO & CASTELFRANCO VENETO

Treviso, with its network of canals, is the most Venetian in atmosphere of the towns and cities of the Veneto. It is surrounded by water, with the Venetian lagoon to the south, the river Piave to the north, and the poplar-fringed Sile, with its natural park, to the east. On the flat, alluvial plain nearby is Castelfranco Veneto, birthplace of the great painter Giorgione.

TREVISO

Treviso (*map Veneto East C1*) is a pleasant and prosperous walled city located just 30km to the north of Venice; It was the first territory on the mainland to be ruled by the Venetians. Sitting on the river Sile, the city features many charming canals, giving the town a vaguely Venetian atmosphere. Unlike many other cities in the Veneto, Treviso has preserved much of its medieval street pattern with narrow, winding alleyways intersecting the historic centre. Many of the streets here are arcaded and often feature external frescoes. Some of the finest works of Tommaso da Modena can be found in its churches, whilst the Civic Museum features most of the great Venetian painters of the renaissance. Treviso is also famous for its red radicchio and as the birthplace of tiramisù.

HISTORY OF TREVISO
Finds have proved that there was a Bronze Age settlement on the site of Treviso, before it be-came a Roman municipality in the 1st century BC, known as *Tarvisium*. In the Middle Ages, Treviso was capital of a defensive outpost of the Carolingian empire, and later became a relatively powerful free commune known for its hospitality to poets and artists, especially under the Da Camino family (1283–1312). The city then became the first mainland territory of the Republic of Venice in 1339, a result of the Scaliger War. It later fell under Austrian and then Carraresi control before Venetian rule was consolidated in 1389, the city remaining faithful to Venice until the fall of the Republic. Under Austrian rule from 1815, many of the city's churches were converted to military use. The Austrians were driven out of Treviso by its inhabitants in a revolt in 1848, but man-aged to stay in power after bombarding the city, lasting until 1866 when the region was annexed to Italy. During both world wars it suffered

severely from air raids, notably on Good Friday 1944, when half the city was destroyed in a few minutes. One thousand six hundred civilians were killed in bombings which destroyed 3,783 houses, and 10,261 citizens were either imprisoned for political reasons or deported. In recent years, partly because of the development of its airport (used also as an alternative to Venice airport), Treviso has justly begun to receive an increasing number of visitors.

ARTISTS CONNECTED WITH TREVISO

Works by Tommaso da Modena, a brilliant follower of Giotto at work in Treviso in the early 14th century, can be seen in all four of the town's most important churches as well as in its museums. During his lifetime Tommaso was one of the best-known artists in northern Italy and his fame was such that even the emperor Charles IV commissioned works from him. As his name suggests, he was from Modena, but his best work was done here, especially the fresco cycle in San Nicolò and the St Ursula cycle in Santa Caterina.

Paris Bordone was born in Treviso but spent most of his life in Venice, briefly training in Titian's workshop, unhappily so according to Vasari. Still, the influence of Titian is apparent in his work, which can be seen in the Duomo and the Museo Santa Caterina. Lodewijk Toeput, always known as Pozzoserrato, was born around 1550 in Antwerp, where he worked in the studio of Marten de Vos. Both men visited Rome and Venice, but Vos returned to become one of the most famous Flemish artists of his day, whereas Pozzoserrato settled in Treviso, where he died around 1605. He combines a Flemish style with the influence of Tintoretto, with whom it is thought he worked for a period. He is known particularly for his landscapes and scenes of country fairs and markets.

Luigi Serena is a little-known artist whose works can be seen almost exclusively in Treviso, where he died in 1911. After having studied at the Accademia in Venice together with the better-known Giacomo Favretto, he came to live for the rest of his life here and his works are particularly charming documents of life in the countryside around the town at that time. The light effects in some of his paintings can even be compared to those of the Tuscan Macchiaioli school. He also painted some good portraits. There is a strong collection of his work at the Museo Luigi Bailo, which also has a space dedicated to the local 20th-century sculptor Arturo Martini.

ON AND AROUND PIAZZA DEI SIGNORI

Piazza dei Signori (*map Treviso 1–2*) is the main square and geographical centre of the old town, though part of it is now a major road intersection. The square is lined with palaces and has long been the administrative and commercial centre of the city.

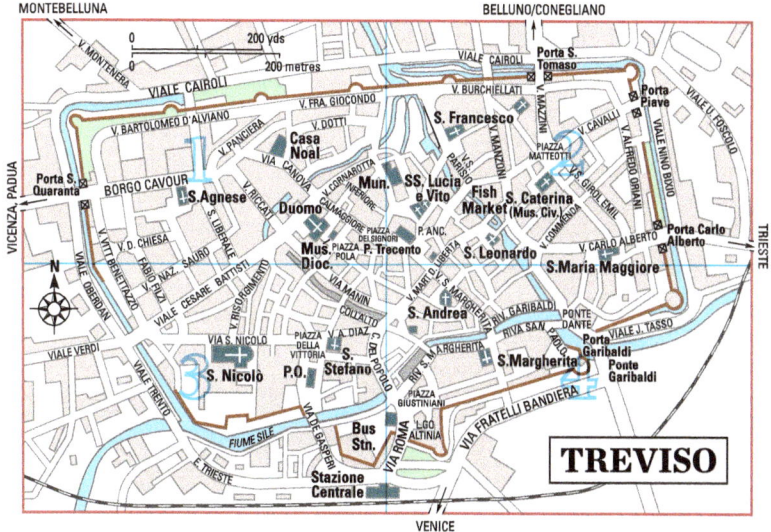

The **Palazzo del Podestà** was rebuilt in antique style in 1877, and is surmounted by the **Torre Civica** (1218), a symbol of the city. The adjoining **Palazzo del Trecento**, first built in the 14th century (though much restored, including after WWII, when it suffered serious bomb damage) is still the seat of the city council. An external staircase leads to the richly decorated first floor, with frescoes from the 14th–16th centuries reflecting the civic use of the building. Behind them in a little cobbled piazza is the former **Monte di Pietà** pawnshop (now owned by a bank), created by Franciscan friars in 1462 to offer low-interest loans to the poor, the building was extended greatly in successive centuries. On the façade is a relief of *Christ as the Man of Sorrows*; the quaint brick campanile of San Vito (*see below*) rises above the roof. The oldest part of the building incorporates the charming 16th-century Chapel of the Rectors (*entrance at no. 3, but not normally open*), with a striking interior featuring frescoes by Ludovico Fiumicelli and six canvases by Pozzoserrato.

To the right, an arched passageway leads to steps down to the two intercommunicating medieval churches of **Santa Lucia and San Vito** (*map Treviso 2; usually open 9-12 every day, 3.30-6 on weekends*), preceded by a portico. A hospice for pilgrims is documented as attached to San Vito as early as 981; the earliest part of the current church is the 12th-century Romanesque apse. The small pretty interior contains Veneto-Byzantine frescoes of the 12th–13th century, a carved tabernacle dated 1363, and an oval ceiling painting of the *Coronation of the Virgin* by Antonio Zanchi (17th century). The church was renovated in 1561, when the halls of the Monte di Pietà were built over it. A small door in the apse leads to Santa Lucia, consecrated in 1389, which has an impressive cycle of frescoes, including, in the Cappella del Crocifisso (with a fine *Crucifixion* scene) the *Madonna del Paveio* (*Madonna of the Butterfly*) by Tommaso da Modena, and a charming balustrade around the altar with half-figures of saints, probably dating from the late 14th century.

On Via Martiri della Libertà, just to the south of the Piazza de Signori, is the **Loggia dei Cavalieri**, a frescoed Romanesque building with Byzantine influences, now used as a covered square for markets and exhibitions.

The attractive **Calmaggiore**, leading northwest out of Piazza degli Signori, is the main shopping street of the town, with arcades on both sides. To the right (south side of the street) a modern shopping arcade has an inscription in the pavement recording that in 1973 part of the main street of the Roman town dating from the 1st century AD was discovered here some 3m below ground level. The Calmaggiore passes the extraordinary exterior of the duomo.

THE DUOMO AND MUSEO DIOCESANO

With its seven green domes and massive squat campanile, the duomo (*map Treviso 1; entrance usually by the side door*), founded in the 12th century, has one of the most eccentric exteriors in Italy, with one flank on Calmaggiore and an oversized **Neoclassical façade and portico** added in 1836. This disjointed appearance is the result of centuries of additions to the originally Romanesque structure, before the decision was taken to rebuild the church in a Neoclassical manner in the 18th century. Construction was interrupted, carried out in multiple stages before the façade was eventually added on. The duomo's campanile is in fact contiguous with the neat Romanesque church of **San Giovanni** to the left, dating from the 12th century, which used to serve as the baptistery (*now only open for exhibitions*). There are two segments of 3rd-century AD Roman frieze embedded into the wall on either side of its entrance. Inside are two small apses with fragments of 13th-century frescoes of the *Madonna and Child*.

Interior of the duomo

On two pilasters in front of the second south chapel are *St John the Baptist* by Alessandro Vittoria and a bas-relief of the *Visitation* attributed to Lorenzo Bregno, with the Virgin embracing St Elizabeth. Steps at the end of this aisle lead up to the marble **Cappella Malchiostro**, named after Canon Broccardo Malchiostro, who commissioned the frescoes and altarpiece from two of the best artists at work in the Veneto at the time, Pordenone and Titian. This was the first artistic encounter of the two, who later came to be great rivals. Highlights of Pordenone's frescoes include the *Adoration of the Magi* on the left wall, a crowded scene dominated by large expressive figures, and the depiction of Emperor Augustus in the semi-dome of the apse. Titian's altarpiece of the *Annunciation* underwent conservation treatment in 2022, revealing a signature and date of 1520. The painting includes the kneeling figure of Malchiostro in the background: the portrayal of the unpopular donor was controversial at the time, and the figure was vandalised in 1526 and subsequently repainted by another artist. On either side are shadowy niches frescoed by Pordenone with the figures of two saints. In the vestibule of the chapel are the jambs of the 12th-century west portal, a lovely *Adoration of the Shepherds* painted by Paris Bordone around 1557, and the *Madonna del Fiore* by Girolamo da Treviso il Vecchio dating from the previous century. Also here is the tomb of Bishop Castellano, who died in the 14th century. A small door near the chapel leads to the sacristy, which can be visited on request, with another canvas by Paris Bordone.

In the **retro-choir** (*unfortunately usually cordoned off*) are frescoes by Ludovico Seitz (1880) and two very fine monuments: a baroque memorial to Pope Alexander VIII, who died in 1691 (and had been a canon in Treviso) with a remarkable portrait-statue by Giovanni Bonazza, and the superb tomb of Bishop Zanetto, who died in 1485, by Antonio and Tullio Lombardo with the help of their father Pietro. (Tullio Lombardo also probably sculpted the supposed portraits of the three martyrs Teonisto, Tabra and Tabrasta on their urn on the high altar.)

The entirely marble coated **Chapel of the Sacrament** is also usually cordoned off so it is difficult to see its good early 16th-century sculptures by Giovanni Battista and Lorenzo Bregno, and the very fine tomb of Bishop Franco in the vestibule.

In the **north transept** is a lovely altarpiece of *St Justina*, with saints and the kneeling donor, painted by Francesco Bissolo around 1530, and a sculpted *St Sebastian* in the outer niche of the first nave pillar.

On the right of the sanctuary, steps lead down to the lovely 11th-century **crypt** with its 68 columns and several tombs of the city's bishops. It has fragments of early frescoes and part of its original mosaic pavement (as well as 16th-century majolica tiles in the apse). A door here (*not always open*) leads into the Museo Diocesano, but this is usually entered from outside (*see below*).

On the right of the huge portico of the duomo is the **Bishop's Palace**, and here, beneath an arch, is a passageway (Via Canoniche) where (behind railings, below street level) you can usually see (if not protected with sand) a circular **Palaeochristian polychrome mosaic pavement** dating from the early 4th century AD, which probably once belonged to a baptistery. Via Canoniche leads round the corner into Vicolo del Duomo and the entrance to the Museo Diocesano.

MUSEO DIOCESANO D'ARTE SACRA

The 12th-century Gothic Canoniche Vecchie, behind the duomo, are home to the Diocesan Museum (*map Treviso 1; opening times unreliable, booking by phone or email may be needed; see diocesitv.it/museodiocesano/orari*). Originally housed in the Episcopal Palace, the collection was moved here in 1988. It is interesting, varied and well displayed. On the ground floor is the **Sacello di San Prosdocimo**, probably dating from the 4th century, with a barrel vault. There is also a room dedicated to archaeology, including two cylindrical altars and some Roman busts. Upstairs the loggia, from which two rooms with paintings and fabrics can be accessed, is a portrait of the Venetian ambassador Francesco Benaglio by Pompeo Batoni.

The best works in the **art gallery** include a *Christ Crowned with Thorns* by Pietro de Saliba (nephew and pupil of the more famous Antonello da Messina); frescoes detached from the Episcopal Palace, including very early (probably mid-13th-century) scenes of *Christ in Limbo* and the *Martyrdom of St Thomas Becket* (which includes a representation of Canterbury cathedral complete with domes, looking like St Mark's in Venice; Henry II is shown enthroned on the right). It is thought that this (unknown) artist also worked on some of the mosaics in St Mark's. There is also a detached fresco of *Christ in Pietà* by Tommaso da Modena and *St Sebastian* by the school of Gentile da Fabriano. Highlights of the **fabrics section** are the very interesting early 13th-century silk funerary winding cloth of Persian origin, for the local monk St Parisio, featuring pairs of parrots drinking from a chalice; and a 16th-century Flemish tapestry.

There are many **sculptures**, mostly taken from the duomo, including a 17th-century German silver statue of St Liberale, patron saint of Treviso.

Liturgical treasures include a 13th-century bronze ewer in the shape of an animal; an altar frontal in gilded wood with a relief of the *Last Judgment*; a very beautiful 15th-century processional Cross and two exquisite croziers; and a 14th-century sarcophagus which belonged to a bishop of Treviso. There are also some English alabaster reliefs and a display of 16th-century antiphonals, English alabaster reliefs and a 16th-century Flemish tapestry.

THE MUSEI CIVICI ON VIA CANOVA AND BORGO CAVOUR

Via Canova (*map Treviso 1*) leads downhill from Piazza Duomo, crossing the Siletto canal. A short way further on are three adjoining late medieval buildings, which together comprise one of the three sites of the Musei Civici. They are the Ca' da Noal, the Casa Robegan and the Casa Karwath. The first two both have colonnades with five Gothic arches, and the former has remnants of frescoes by Domenico Capriolo (dating from the year of his death in Treviso, 1528). Owned by the city since 1935, they are used to host exhibitions on contemporary art, including summer events in the large garden. The road curves round into Borgo Cavour, with groups of ilexes and the church of Sant'Agnese, opposite which is the Luigi Bailo museum.

Museo Luigi Bailo (Museo del Novecento)

Luigi Bailo was an abbot and patron of the arts who played a vital role in the preservation of art in Treviso in the late 19th century, founding the first city museum. This original site of the museum (superseded by the Santa Caterina complex in 2003; *see below*) is part of a Renaissance monastery complex, redesigned and reopened in 2015 in a modern style, though the two cloisters and the adjacent city library retain the monastery's original character. The museum houses the Galleria del Novecento, the city's collection of modern art (*museicivicitreviso.it*).

There is a large space dedicated to the work of Arturo Martini. Born in Treviso in 1889, Martini was one of the leading Italian sculptors of the 20th century and this is the largest collection of his work anywhere. Examples range from his early Modernist sculptures, such as *Motherhood* (1910), to later, more classical pieces and there is also a collection of his ceramics and drawings. The museum also has a section focused on the Trevisan-based contingent of the Ca' Pesaro movement, named after the modern art gallery in Venice, and there is an extensive collection of 19th-century paintings, with Luigi Serena particularly well represented. Other highlights are a curious self-portrait of Francesco Hayez as a young child with his family and an excellent portrait of Canova by Thomas Lawrence.

TWO CITY GATES

At the end of Borgo Cavour is **Porta dei Santi Quaranta**, one of the city gates, with a Lion of St Mark guarding its outer face, by the bridge over a canal. You can see a stretch of the low walls erected in 1509–18 by Fra' Giocondo here and walk clockwise along the pleasant path on top of them, as far as **Porta San Tomaso**, the grandest and most ornate of the city gates (*map Treviso 2*), near where the river Botteniga reaches the town from the north.

THE MUSEI CIVICI AT SANTA CATERINA

The third and largest of the Civic Museum sites is at the end of Via Santa Caterina, in the former 14th-century convent of the Servi di Maria (*map Treviso 2; museicivicitreviso.it*). The entrance is in Piazzetta Mario Botter, named after the Trevisan art restorer, an instrumental figure in the creation of this museum and the preservation of art in the city. The courtyard in front, with a little portico, was restored in 2007 and the wall has a very original silhouette in steel netting of a house painter up a ladder. The museum is divided into three sections: the archaeological collection, the Pinacoteca and the deconsecrated church of Santa Caterina. The layout revolves around two Renaissance cloisters.

Ex-church of Santa Caterina

From the larger cloister, with pleasant places to sit, is the entrance to the deconsecrated church of Santa Caterina, which was begun in 1346 before a serious outbreak of plague interrupted work, which was resumed and completed at the beginning of the 15th century. Under Austrian occupation, the church was converted to a military warehouse, with the church stripped of its furnishings and the interior divided into three floors. After bomb damage during the Second World War, the entire church underwent restoration, the process of which led to the discovery of long hidden frescoes, unearthed through the work of Mario Botter, and prompted the restoration and conversion of the entire complex. Alongside its own frescoes, the church is now also used to display detached frescoes from other churches in Treviso.

The **Cappella degli Innocenti** is the only surviving interior chapel, built onto the south wall of the church in 1430, and the very interesting frescoes survive in a damaged state. The *Crucifixion* and *Massacre of the Innocents* (a fragment with the onlookers at windows) are attributed to an unknown master named the 'Maestro degli Innocenti' from these frescoes, though some scholars identify him with Nicolò di Pietro. The frescoes in the vaults, with the Evangelists and their symbols, are much better preserved.

On the south wall is a remarkable damaged fresco, attributed to Pisanello, of the **Miracle of St Eligius**, an interior scene showing the saint as a farrier in his smithy (Eligius is the patron saint of goldsmiths and metalworkers) with his horse and instruments of his trade. Very unusually, the Devil is represented by the figure of a woman (with her tail issuing from her skirts). A fresco on the same wall of the *Madonna* in lovely flowing red robes with saints and angels is attributed to Gentile da Fabriano. There is also an interesting *St Catherine Interceding for Treviso*, holding up a scale model of the city. The last (earlier) scene here of the *Annunciation* shows the angel in billowing white robes with daisies in his hair.

In the chapel to the right of the sanctuary are two very damaged detached frescoes on easels from the sanctuary itself, both by Tommaso da Modena (dating from 1358 or earlier): of Christ (from a *Noli me Tangere*) and *Christ at Emmaus*. In the centre of the nave and in the sanctuary is one of the artist's greatest works: a superb fresco cycle (also on easels), arranged in groups of four, of the **Story of St Ursula**, dating from 1355–8, from the ex-church of Santa Margherita degli Eremitani. The frescoes were detached by Luigi Bailo in 1883 (his annotations can be seen on the backs) and have survived remarkably well, even though the colours have faded. A touch screen explains the scenes in detail: they include the Ambassadors being despatched by the King of England, as well as St Ursula on her way to Rome with all her companions tucked into a boat, and (in the sanctuary) the largest scene of all showing the saint's martyrdom.

The archaeological collection

The material is arranged in strictly chronological order. Palaeolithic and Mesolithic artefacts include a unique collection of bronze sword-blades dredged from the Sile and its tributaries (Hallstatt period: 7th–6th centuries BC), and five remarkable bronze ritual discs (5th century BC) from Montebelluna, 20km from Treviso, suggesting local contact with the Celts. Bronze and Iron Age finds from Treviso itself include the surface of a ceramic oven and braziers from the 10th–9th centuries BC, the result of archaeological digs in the city centre from the 1950s onwards (including a reconstruction of the various levels identified during excavations). There are also Roman-era artefacts from local burial grounds, notably mosaic pavements, glass, inscriptions (all of them transcribed for the visitor), a small head of Venus, a fine group of busts (1st–2nd centuries AD), a relief of the Dioscuri (Castor and Pollux), large sarcophagi and small Roman bronzes. The last section is devoted to the collection of Luigi Bailo, including small Roman bronzes and a collection of Greek and Roman stone items.

The Pinacoteca

The collection comprises paintings from the 14th–18th centuries, with most of the great Venetian artists of the period represented. The paintings are ordered chronologically: the first room contains early frescoes retrieved from the city in the 19th century, preserved under the initiative of Luigi Bailo, as well as a *Madonna and Child* by Gentile da Fabriano. The next section has two of the masterpieces of the collection: two *Madonnas*, one by Giovanni Bellini and the other by Cima da Conegliano. They are both wonderful paintings, even though scholars agree that both were painted with the assistance of collaborators in the artists' workshops.

The two most famous portraits in the collection are by Lorenzo Lotto (a Dominican friar, the guardian of Santi Giovanni e Paolo in Venice, dating from 1526) and Titian (the Humanist Sperone Speroni, with his hands resting on a golden casket, dating from 1544). Other fine works include a *Madonna and Saints* by Pier Maria Pennacchi (at work in Treviso in the late 15th century), and two versions of the *Adoration of the Magi*, one by Girolamo da Santacroce and the other by Girolamo da Treviso the Younger.

The room dedicated to Mannerism has a very fine large *Crucifixion* by Jacopo Bassano, as well as several works by Paris Bordone, includng a *Holy Family*, a *Resurrection* and a scene of *Paradise*, giving a good idea of the production of this Treviso-born painter. Other works include a damaged frieze of putti by the workshop of Donatello and a miniature Crucifix in boxwood by the great woodcarver Andrea Brustolon. There are also bronze plaquettes attributed to Il Moderno and small bronzes by Girolamo Campagna.

The end section of the gallery is focused on the 17th and 18th centuries, including a small *Preaching of St John the Baptist* by Gian Domenico Tiepolo, a lovely spontaneous work, lightly 'sketched' in oil. There is also a fresco from his father Giambattista, and portraits by Pietro Longhi (a Venetian gentleman in a splendid waistcoat) and his son Alessandro.

The ex-church of Santa Margherita, from which the St Ursula fresco cycle was taken, was restored in 2020 and is now one of two sites in the city hosting the **Museo Nazionale Collezione Salce**, the largest museum in Italy dedicated to poster art. The other site is the church of San Gaetano, located very close to the Museo Santa Caterina.

SAN NICOLÒ

From Piazza della Vittoria (*map Treviso 3*), with its huge war memorial by Arturo Stagliano, inaugurated in 1931, it is a short walk west along the arcaded Via San Nicolò to reach the church of the same name (*closed 12–3.30*), which occupies the far southwest portion of the walled city. This remarkably high Dominican foundation is the largest church in the city, built in brick in the 13th/14th century before construction was interrupted by the collapse of the bell-tower and an outbreak of plague, and was not to be completed until the 19th century.

Interior of San Nicolò

The interior of the church is richly decorated. The splendid triple polygonal apse has tall and narrow lancet windows which continue all around the church. The great ship's keel roof in the nave is almost too high up to see. The massive columns have very well preserved **frescoes**: the one by the stoup at the entrance has a continuous series of scenes by Tommaso da Modena, right round it, including the delightful *St Jerome in his Study*, surrounded by piles of books, *St Romuald*, *St Agnes* and *St John the Baptist*.

In the **south aisle** there is a lovely carved altar with statues of the *Risen Christ* and two saints and the *Madonna and Child*, all by Lorenzo Bregno. The aisle is dominated by the monumental fresco of *St Christopher* (1410), reaching almost up to the vault, with fish in the river at his feet. It is attributed to the local artist Antonio da Treviso. By the door into the sacristy here is the 18th-century organ by Gaetano Callido, beautifully decorated with paintings by Antonio Palma.

In the **chapel to the right of the sanctuary** is an altarpiece of the *Risen Christ*, and beneath it eight portraits (six gentlemen and two ladies), which include Bernardo de' Rossi, Bishop of Treviso who became Lorenzo Lotto's patron when the artist was living in Treviso from 1503–6, and whom he painted in a famous portrait now in the Capodimonte Museum in Naples. Through a little door in this chapel you can see the **sanctuary**, with the splendid tomb of Agostino d'Onigo (c. 1500), which has sculptures by Antonio Rizzo and, on either side, frescoes of pages, which in the past have been attributed to Lotto, though this is now doubted by scholars. The splendid high altarpiece in the apse, in a very fine carved marble frame, was started by Marco Pensaben and finished by Savoldo. The monument on the right wall was set up in 1693 to record the great Dominican pope St Benedict XI (Nicolò Boccasini, 1240–1304), born in Treviso and the founder of this church.

The former convent

Outside on the right of the church is the Seminario Vescovile, the former Dominican convent, from which you can enter the **cloister**, which has a well in the middle of its little garden, and some lovely rooms, most notably the **Chapter House** (*open 8–6*). This charming room is known for the delightful frieze around the top of the walls, one of the best known works by Tommaso da Modena, signed and dated 1352. The fresco cycle depicts 40 significant Dominicans including bishops, cardinals, saints and two popes (St Benedict XI and Innocent V), all at their desks intent on their studies, in the act of reading or writing. The two 13th-century popes are shown next to each other on the right of the right window and are easily distinguished because of their headgear. The level of detail and realism is particularly striking for the time, with the Cardinal Hugh of Provence shown wearing spectacles (the first dated example known in painting). The only wall the cycle does not span across has remains of a *Crucifixion* dating from around 1250.

THE SILE RIVER AND SANTA MARIA MAGGIORE

The waterfront of the Sile river, especially along **Riviera Garibaldi** (*map Treviso 4*), is particularly attractive, with arcaded buildings lining both banks. **Ponte Dante** crosses the Cagnan canal at the point where it runs into the Sile. The bridge is named after Dante as the meeting of the rivers is referenced in the Ninth Canto of 'Paradiso' in the *Divine Comedy*. There is a monument on the bridge from 1865, with the verse inscribed. Dante almost certainly visited the town at the time of Gherardo da Camino, who invited poets and men of learning to his court. Gherardo and his daughter Gaia are also mentioned in the *Divine Comedy*, in the Eleventh Canto of 'Purgatorio'.

Via Tolpada runs north from the Sile to the church of Santa Maria Maggiore.

SANTA MARIA MAGGIORE

This church (*map Treviso 2–4*) was built in 1474 and has a simple brick façade in classic late Gothic style, dwarfed by the tall plain brick campanile with a clock, still working. The interior has a lovely little Renaissance chapel decorated with polychrome marble inlay attributed to Pietro Lombardo, which frames a charming fresco of the *Madonna and Child Enthroned*, shown in a typically Byzantine pose. Known as the '*Madonna Grande*' (the Trevisan name '*Madona Granda*' is sometimes used to refer to the church as a whole), it is much venerated, as the numerous ex-votos here attest. There are two warriors kneeling in adoration on either side and the Child, dressed in red and yellow and tucked into the Madonna's lap, has a golden halo and his arms open wide in the act of blessing, while the Madonna in a white robe wears a jewelled gold crown. The painting predates the existing church structure, with Tommaso da Modena called in to remake an earlier version of the fresco in 1349, and it has since been retouched. There are also two curious little reliquary caskets here, with a pair of spurs and chains.

At the end of this aisle is a recomposed tomb with three very intricate beautiful high reliefs and five statues, all made in the 16th century by Bambaia, and in the opposite aisle is a wood Crucifix dating from the same century.

SAN FRANCESCO

From Piazza San Vito, by the church of San Vito (*map Treviso* 2), Via Campana leads across two canals towards the church of San Francesco. By the especially pretty Buranelli canal is an ancient house with a brick exterior and a projecting upper storey on wooden brackets and a portico along the canal. It was carefully restored by Mario Botter in 1974 and is still in excellent condition with some faded frescoes. At the second bridge, the Ponte San Francesco (very well rebuilt in 2002), there is an old mill and two wooden water wheels still working. The bridge leads to the Piazza San Francesco, with the church of the same name.

This large brick church (*map Treviso* 2) dates from the 13th century, exhibiting both Romanesque and Gothic elements. It is most notable for containing the tombs of children of both Petrarch and Dante: In the floor near the south door is the modest pavement tomb of Petrarch's daughter Francesca, who died in Treviso in childbirth in 1384; In the north transept is the hanging sarcophagus of Pietro Alighieri, the eldest of Dante's six sons, with his effigy. It is a strange coincidence that the children of the two greatest Italian poets, both from Tuscany, should be buried in the same church here in Treviso. But both poets had connections to the Veneto. Petrarch, the son of a Florentine friend of Dante's, lived in the Veneto for many years, firstly in Venice, then Padua, before seeing out the last years of his life in the Euganean Hills (*see Arquà Petrarca, p. 45*), almost all of which were spent living with Francesca. Dante himself lived in Verona after being exiled from Florence. Pietro lived with his father in exile, eventually becoming a delegate and then judge in Verona before retiring to Treviso shortly before his death. He was originally buried in the cloister of the old church of Santa Margherita, the tomb lost for years before being discovered and transferred here in 1935.

In the chapel to the left of the high altar is a fresco by Tommaso da Modena (1360) of the *Madonna and Child with seven Saints*.

CASTELFRANCO VENETO

According to a medieval chronicle, anyone who settled in this *castello* (*map Veneto East B1*) was freed (*affrancato*) of all fiscal obligations, hence the town's name. Founded by Treviso in 1199 to defend its western frontier, it faced its first siege against Padua as early as 1215, later falling under control of the Ezzelini and the Scaligeri before becoming part of the Republic of Venice. The rectangular fortification with its five towers and red brick walls, encircled by a moat (the *castello* proper), still encloses the small, dense centre. The village was divided into four quadrants, divided by the two main orthogonal streets. The main street, Via Francesco Maria Preti, runs east–west and is named after the architect of the brick Teatro Accademico and of the duomo. The eastern entrance is underneath the Torre Civica (1339), with a blue clock face and relief of the Lion of St Mark. The castle can also be entered from the old market square, Piazza Giorgione, to the north. Throughout the town are small porticoed palaces, some of them frescoed. The sky, the clouds, and green fields of the environs of Castelfranco are those of Giorgione, who was born and began to paint here.

GIORGIONE

The great Venetian painter Giorgione (1473/4–1510) was born in Castelfranco in the Venetian hinterland. His nickname Giorgione ('great George') is a testimony to his fame, despite the brevity of his life (he died the plague at the age of just 36). Very little is known about his career and very few paintings can be attributed with certainty to his hand, but he has always been one of the best known Venetian artists. A pupil of Giovanni Bellini and influenced by Flemish and Dutch masters, he had an innovative technique of painting on canvas, applying a rich *impasto* and a broad range of colours. He was particularly interested in landscape, as can be seen in his late masterpiece, *La Tempesta*, in the Accademia gallery in Venice. Other paintings produced for private patrons are similarly suffused with an air of mystery, in an atmosphere derived from Venetian Humanism. Scholars have recognised the influence of Dürer, as well as of Carpaccio and Leonardo da Vinci, and have often found it difficult to distinguish between his hand and that of Titian. As well as in his native Castelfranco, works by his hand can be seen in Padua and in the duomo of Montagnana, where two frescoes attributed to him were recently uncovered.

THE DUOMO

The Palladian-style duomo of San Liberale, on Via Preti (*closed 12–3.30*), whose campanile is one of the towers of the defensive walls, contains **Giorgione**'s famous altarpiece of the *Madonna and Child with St Francis and St George in Armour* (c. 1505) in the south apsidal chapel. It is one of very few paintings definitively attributed to Giorgione; it is also the largest and his only altarpiece. It was commissioned by the

Madonna and Child with St Francis and St George by Giorgione (c. 1505), in the duomo of Castelfranco.

Costanzo family, whose coat of arms is prominent on the lowest step of the Virgin's podium. The superb bright colours of her dress and the fabrics protecting her throne are in contrast to the dark tunic of St Francis and the magnificently painted shining suit of armour of his fellow saint. The chequered pavement is painted in perfect perspective and shows the shadows of the figures and in the background there is a wonderful landscape.

Also in the duomo, in the sacristy, are works by Palma Giovane and Jacopo Bassano and seven fragments of frescoes by Paolo Veronese (*Allegorical Figures*, 1551), brought from the destroyed Villa Soranza.

MUSEO CASA DI GIORGIONE

Opening off the piazza to the left of the duomo is the 15th-century Museo Casa di Giorgione (*museocasagiorgione.it*), where Giorgione lived and worked. The main room has a fascinating chiaroscuro frieze, with symbols of the liberal and mechanical arts, historically attributed to Giorgione, though it is now believed it is probably a collaborative work, begun by him but finished by others. Also in the museum is a reconstruction of Giorgione's studio and living quarters, as well as artworks and objects relating to the artist and the Venetian renaissance in general.

OTHER SIGHTS OF CASTELFRANCO

Outside the walls, the old market square, **Piazza Giorgione**, is lined with 16th–18th-century townhouses, some with frescoed façades. To the east along Borgo Treviso, **Villa Revedin**, on the site of a villa by Vincenzo Scamozzi dating from 1607, is the work of Giambattista Meduna (1852–65) and is now used by the University of Padua, who restored the entire complex in 2015. It is surrounded by the large **Parco Bolasco** (*villaparcobolasco.it*), also laid out in the 19th century with a rustic amphitheatre for equestrian events decorated with over 50 statues, many by Orazio Marinali, which were recuperated from the original 17th-century garden. Also in the garden is a lake with two small islands. The interior of the villa, which contains the elaborately frescoed Sala delle Feste, is only open for events.

VILLAS AROUND CASTELFRANCO

There are some interesting villas in the environs of Castelfranco (*map Veneto East B1*), two of them by Palladio. Not all are open to the public, and others only irregularly so; but if you are passing this way, here are some to look out for:

ISTRANA
Villa Lattes. Built in 1715 for Venetian merchant Paolo Tamagnino, this is one of the first works by Giorgio Massari. It is now a house-museum with a vast collection of musical boxes and dolls collected by the Lattes family in the 19th and early 20th centuries. *museovillalattes.it*.

SANT'ANDREA
Villa Chiminelli. Classic Veneto villa built in 1578 for the nobleman and priest Francesco Soranzo, and extensively frescoed by Veronese's brother Benedetto Caliari. There are three small museums in the grounds dedicated to local culture and industry (*visits by appointment, as for the villa itself, by guided tour once a month*; *villachiminelli.it*).

FANZOLO (DI VEDELAGO)
Villa Emo. One of Palladio's most accomplished works, commissioned by Leonardo Emo around 1558 as the family wished to expand their presence in Fanzolo, having bought the large

Palladio's Villa Emo.

farming estate from the Barbarigo family (it remained in the Emo family until 2004). It survives intact in what must have been a wonderful site: the main approach is now flanked by a small railway station (on the branch line between Castelfranco Veneto and Montebelluna). The central building has a monumental porch. Rather than stairs, the entrance is ramped to facilitate the transport of agricultural goods. At the sides are two long, symmetrical *barchesse*, terminating in little dovecotes. The interior is frescoed with delightful mythological and allegorical rustic scenes, painted by Giovanni Battista Zelotti in 1561–5. villaemo.eu.

PIOMBINO DESE
Villa Cornaro. Begun by Palladio for Giorgio Cornaro in 1551–2. The main body was habitable by 1554; the side wings and loggias were built in later stages and completed in 1596 by Vincenzo Scamozzi. Although its position in the centre of the town, not closely related to the surrounding countryside, is less attractive than other villas, it has an impressive façade with a projecting double loggia and open arcades. Inside is a cycle of 104 fresco panels by Mattia Bortoloni, and six large 16th-century stucco statues of members of the Cornaro family. The villa is privately owned.

LEVADA
Ca' Marcello. Built in 1550, but altered in the 18th century by Francesco Maria Preti, when it was frescoed by Giambattista Crosato and the extensive park (*see camarcello.it*), with many statues, was laid out. It is still occupied by the Marcello family, for whom it was built (*house open only for visits of 20 or more, by reservation*).

CITTADELLA

Cittadella (*map Veneto East A1–B1*), in the northern part of the province of Padua, was built by the Paduans in 1220 as a reply to Castelfranco (*see above*), which had been completed a decade earlier. It was designed to be a strategic outpost and fortification against both Treviso and Vicenza. The old centre is enclosed by medieval walls (and a moat), elliptical in shape and extremely well preserved (though the design can only truly be appreciated from the air). Within the walls the town is symmetrically planned, with the main north–south and east–west streets meeting in the centre. The streets probably follow the lines of the old Roman thoroughfares. The gates, Porta Padova (south), Porta Bassano (north), Porta Vicenza (west) and Porta Treviso (east) are named after the towns to which they lead.

Remarkably, since restoration was completed in 2013, the entire perimeter of the walls is walkable, known as the '**Camminamento di Ronda**' (*muradicittadella.it*). The almost 2km walk begins from the Casa del Capitano by the Bassano gate, and allows views both of the historic centre inside the walls and the landscape outside, including the Euganean hills and Mount Grappa.

All four of the **city gates** are frescoed. The Padua and Bassano gates have the stylised cartwheels of the Carraresi, who were lords of Padua in the 14th century. Porta Treviso has remains of an *Annunciation* and *Coronation of the Virgin*, while the *Crucifixion* adorns Porta Vicenza. The Torre di Malta by the Padua gate was built in 1251 by the notorious tyrant Ezzelino III da Romano and used a prison for his enemies. It now houses the **Archaeological Museum**, with local finds from the Bronze Age onwards.

In the central Piazza Pierobon where the four roads meet is the Neoclassical **duomo** (completed 1826; *duomocittadella.it*). The adjacent **Museo del Duomo** has an art gallery with a *Supper at Emmaus* by Jacopo Bassano (*open Sat and Sun 10–1*), along with wooden statues, textiles and frescoes from the original medieval church. There is also a museum of religious art in the bell-tower.

The annual Fiera Franca fair takes place around the third weekend in October and lasts for three days.

TREVISO PRACTICAL TIPS

GETTING AROUND

- **By air**: Treviso Airport (Antonio Canova) is only about 3km outside the town, to the west. It is linked by bus (no. 6) to Treviso railway station (in c. 15–20mins). There are also taxis available. The airport website has up-to-date information: *trevisoairport.it/en*.
- **By rail**: Treviso is well linked by train to other places in the Veneto. There is a line running west to Castelfranco Veneto (c. 30mins) and Cittadella (c. 45mins), though more frequent trains require a change in Mestre. Trains also run north to Conegliano (c. 20mins) and to Feltre and Belluno (c. 65mins and 1hr 40mins respectively).
- **By bicycle**: The countryside around Treviso is ideal for cycling; in fact, Treviso is the home town of bike maker Pinarello. The GiraSile bicycle route begins at Ponte della Gobba and follows bicycle lanes and secondary roads for some 40km as far as the park of the river Sile. Information on *parcosile.it*.
- **By boat**: For boat hire and boat trips on the river Sile, ask at the Tourist Office in Treviso (IAT, Piazza Borsa 4).

WHERE TO STAY

CASTELFRANCO VENETO
€€ **Al Moretto**. Proud to be the oldest hotel in Castelfranco, warm and welcoming and in an excellent location. *Via San Pio X 10, albergoalmoretto.it.*
TREVISO
There are few hotels in the historic centre of Treviso, but plenty of B&Bs and simpler accommodation. A few kilometres to the east is the lovely **Villa Tiepolo**, at Carbonera, which has rooms and self-catering apartments in the old service wings (*villatiepolopassi.it/en/rooms*).

WHERE TO EAT

CASTELFRANCO VENETO
€€–€€€ **Alle Mura**. Old-established, well regarded place set against the medieval town walls. Specialises in seafood. *Via Preti 69, T: 0423 498098.*
TREVISO
Treviso is home to the famous red *radicchio* and also to tiramisù, both of which not surprisingly feature large on local menus.
€€ **Alfredo Ristorante**. An elegant restaurant in a historic building. *Via Collalto 26, alfredoristorante.it. Map Treviso 3.*
€€ **Le Beccherie**. In a historic building, locally known for its good food, and particularly tiramisù (the word first appeared on a menu here, in 1972). *Piazza Ancilotto 10, lebeccherie.it. Map Treviso 2.*
€€ **Toni del Spin**. Typical *trattoria*, now with an *osteria* and *enoteca* attached Well-established and popular, with locals as well as visitors. *Via Inferiore 7, ristorantetonidelspin. Map Treviso 1.*

LOCAL SPECIALITIES

Treviso is famous for its *radicchio rosso* (red chicory). It is particularly good when grilled but is also served raw as a salad. There are two types, the *precoce* (round or oval shaped) and the *tardivo*, the winter variety, which is highly prized. It has very long, narrow leaves and is grown using a special technique. You will see it in markets, in greengrocer's shops and on restaurant menus all over the Veneto, but Treviso is its heartland.

Treviso is also the home town of **tiramisù**. The story goes that in the 1950s, when Alba Campeol, owner of the Le Becchiere restaurant in Treviso was pregnant with her son, she fortified herself for the rigours of the day with a hearty breakfast of coffee and zabaglione. Later, she invented a dessert that would recreate that delicious combination of tastes: the result was *tiramesù* (as it is spelled in the Treviso dialect), which first appeared on Le Becchiere's menu in 1972. Since 2010, the recipe has been legally registered with the Accademia Italiana della Cucina, Italy's culinary academy. It is not zabaglione that is used to give tiramisù its creamy texture, but mascarpone.

Being linked as it is to water, Treviso is understandably a good place for fish. The picturesque **fish market** has been on the Isola Della Pescheria, an island in the Cagnan canal connected to the mainland by two bridges, since 1856 (before that it was held in Piazza Monte di Pietà, with fishermen travelling from the Venetian lagoon to sell their goods, after Treviso became part of the Republic of Venice). The market takes place every morning from Tues–Sat.

ASOLO, CONEGLIANO & VITTORIO VENETO

Asolo seems sleepy and quiet today, for a place that was once so famed and sought-after. In its hinterland is Possagno, with its associations with Canova; and Maser with its famous frescoes by Veronese. Conegliano was the birthplace of the Renaissance painter Cima. The vineyards of Valdobbiadene yield the world-famous Prosecco.

ASOLO

Asolo (*map Veneto North A3–4*) is a quaint little town, somewhat forgotten by the modern world; in fact, if you come here today, you might be baffled to know how popular it once was and how many famous names it attracted. Known as the 'City of a Hundred Horizons', its sobriquet was coined by the poet Giosuè Carducci for

Asolo, Piazza Garibaldi.

its matchless views onto glistening snow-capped peaks. 'I assure you,' wrote Robert Browning, 'that, even though I have knowledge of and have seen with my own eyes the most beautiful panoramas in Italy and elsewhere, I have found nothing quite like the view one can enjoy from the tower of the Queen's palace.' In fact, though Asolo has attracted people of the arts within Italy since the 15th century, it was largely thanks to Browning that Asolo became so famous to the English-speaking world. Motorised traffic is strictly regulated in the old centre and the old arcaded central streets are peaceful and picturesque, with many of the buildings still retaining traces of fresco on the façades. The town and its surroundings are home to many grand villas, and the hills offer good walking.

HISTORY OF ASOLO

Roman Asolo (*Acetum*) is mentioned by Pliny the Elder in his Natural History. It seems to have been a place of considerable prosperity, with a theatre and baths, evidence of which can be seen at various sites in the town. In the late Middle Ages, the town was presented by Venice to Queen Caterina Cornaro (*see box below*) in exchange for her dominions of Cyprus, and she lived in the castle here from 1489 to 1509. It was during this time that Asolo first became a literary and artistic centre. Cardinal Pietro Bembo, champion of the Tuscan dialect and a key figure in the standardisation of the Italian language, coined the term '*asolare*' (to spend time in amiable aimlessness) from the name of the town. From this was derived *Asolando*, the name chosen by Robert Browning for his last volume of poems (1899). Browning's first visit to Asolo was in 1836, and it is the scene of *Pippa Passes*, published five years later. Eleonora Duse (1850–1924), one of the greatest actresses of her time, also had a house in Asolo, and the traveller and writer Dame Freya Stark (1893–1993) lived here for most of her life. Both are buried in the cemetery of Sant'Anna, just outside the town to the west. Other past visitors to Asolo include Henry James, Ernest Hemingway, Arnold Schoenberg and the architect Carlo Scarpa.

How many a year, my Asolo,
Since—one step just from sea to land—
I found you, loved yet feared you so—
For natural objects seemed to stand
Palpably fire-clothed!
Robert Browning. From the Prologue to *Asolando*, 1889

PIAZZA GARIBALDI AND THE DUOMO

The centre of the town is the sloping Piazza Garibaldi, with a fountain and cafés and, overlooking its higher end (officially Piazza Brugnoli, now a car park), the **Villa Pasini Scotti**, with an impressive terraced garden (remains of the Roman baths lie under it). This is one of a number of local villas bought and restored by Pen Browning (1849–1912), son of Robert. On the bottom corner of the piazza, where

Asumption of the Virgin with St Anthony and St Louis of Toulouse. by Lorenzo Lotto (1506), in the duomo of Asolo. The face of the Virgin is said to be a likeness of Queen Caterina Cornaro.

Via Regina Caterina leads off to the west, is the 15th-century **Loggia del Capitano**, with a fine portico and frescoed façade of 1560. Once the seat of municipal government, it and the adjoining palace now host the **Museo Civico** (*usually open at weekends; museoasolo.it*), with archaeological collections dating from prehistoric to Roman times, and a picture gallery on the first floor. Another part of the collection is focused on those who have made Asolo their home, with rooms dedicated to Caterina Cornaro, Eleonora Duse and Freya Stark, along with Browning memorabilia.

Down steps from here is the **duomo**, of very early foundation (Christianity is said to have been brought to these hills by Prosdocimus, Bishop of Padua), though most of the building that stands today dates from 1747, with the façade added in 1889. It is dedicated to the *Assumption of the Virgin* and contains some fine paintings including, over the high altar, a copy of Titian's *Assumption* (in the Frari in Venice). On either side of the altar are two angels by Giuseppe Bernardi, to whom Canova was first apprenticed. On the south side is the baptistery, with a font by Francesco Graziolo, the favourite architect of Caterina Cornaro. The font was donated to the church by her and it features her coat of arms. In a side chapel (*coin-operated light*) are two paintings of the *Assumption*, one by Jacopo Bassano (1549) and the other, very lovely indeed and worth the trip to Asolo to see, by Lorenzo Lotto (1506; with an interesting predella). Some scholars believe the face of the Virgin in Lotto's altarpiece is actually that of Caterina Cornaro. There is also a *St Jerome* by Sebastiano Bastiani (1488) with very Asolo-like hills on the skyline.

CATERINA CORNARO

Caterina Cornaro was born to a Venetian noble family and betrothed, at the age of 14, to James II Lusignan, King of Cyprus. The Cornaro family had always been influential in Cyprus, and this match was brokered by Caterina's father and uncle. The wedding was celebrated in 1472, but James died only a year later, in 1473, leaving the kingdom to Caterina and her unborn child. When the infant James III died the following year Caterina found herself ruler of Cyprus—but not for long. A number of conspiracies weakened her hold on the kingdom until, in 1489, she ceded her dominions to the Republic of Venice. In return she was granted a large estate at Asolo, which she turned into a famous resort for late Renaissance artists and poets. The cardinal and scholar Pietro Bembo wrote extensively of his life at her court, with his treatise *Gli Asolani* set here and published in 1505. Artists believed to have visited the court include Lorenzo Lotto, Giorgione and Gentile Bellini, who painted her three times. The 19th-century composer Gaetano Donizetti wrote an opera based on her life.

Via Browning, with an arcade down one side and remains of frescoes on the housefronts, leads from the piazza down past the house where Browning stayed (near the bottom of the street; plaque), in the last year of his life while writing *Asolando*, to the yellow **Villa Freya**, where Freya Stark lived, just inside the little Portello di

View of the Villa degli Armeni, with its tall cypress trees standing like sentries.

Castelfranco archway, the southern entrance to Asolo. The villa is privately owned, but the extensive gardens are owned by the province and include the remains of a Roman theatre. They can occasionally be visited by guided tour (*villafreya.it*).

THE CASTLES OF ASOLO

Via Regina Cornaro leads to the remains of the **castle where Caterina Cornaro lived** until she fled for Venice in 1509 after Asolo was conquered by the League of Cambrai. In the late 18th century, during French occupation, the castle's audience chamber was turned into a theatre, with stalls and boxes modelled on La Fenice in Venice. Eleonora Duse often performed here but the fittings were sold to the State of Florida and reassembled in Sarasota there after the Second World War, becoming the Asolo Repertory Theatre. A new simpler theatre, named after Duse, was built in 1932, and still exists today. There is not a great deal else to see at Asolo castle, the western side having been demolished in 1816, though the battlements may be visited and a pleasant café operates here in fine weather. Part of the large garden that surrounded the castle was purchased by Browning (despite local opposition) shortly before his death, his son Pen constructing the Villa La Torricella (in Via Sottocastello), and restoring the adjacent tower, one of three remaining towers of the castle.

From the top end of Piazza Garibaldi, to the left of the Al Sole hotel, a winding path leads uphill past the site of a Roman aqueduct (which still feeds the fountain on Piazza Garibaldi) to the empty **Rocca**, which looms above the town (*open 10–1*

& 4–8 in summer but liable to change, see museoasolo.it). Located on the summit of Mt Ricco, all that exists of this medieval castle are its tall polygonal ramparts, from which there are fine views, with the whole perimeter walkable. It can be reached by car from Via Rocca. Beyond this, a very pretty walk can be taken through woodland where there are picnic tables, marked trails and a spring-fed pool (**Sorgente del Tritone**) inhabited by spotted salamanders.

CONTRADA CANOVA

Off the top end of Piazza Garibaldi, to the left, Via Dante leads into Contrada Canova, passing the Palazzo Beltramini, now the Town Hall. On the left, just before Porta Santa Caterina, is the former **house of Eleonora Duse**, marked with a plaque, its wording composed by the great actress's sometime lover Gabriele d'Annunzio.

Beyond this the road leads past the **Hotel Villa Cipriani**, the former home of Robert Browning, and the church of Santa Caterina, with remains of 14th-century frescoes. The road becomes Via Santa Caterina, passing more grand villas, to the **Casa Longobarda**, built by Francesco Graziolo, Caterina Cornaro's personal architect, as his residence. The façade is very fancifully carved. Above it on a hill to the left is the harmonious 16th-century Villa Contarini, known as **Villa degli Armeni** since it was bought by the Armenian fathers of San Lazzaro in the Venetian lagoon. The complex actually consists of two villas, connected by a tunnel, with the smaller Il Fresco visible from via Santa Caterina. Beyond, the road leads to the lovely **cemetery of Sant'Anna**, with the graves of Eleonora Duse and Freya Stark, and, on clear days, wonderful views of the mountains beyond.

AROUND ASOLO: ALTIVOLE, MASER & POSSAGNO

The countryside around Asolo, once a harmonious ensemble of handsome farms and vineyards, has been much altered by the development of light industry and modern housing. However, the area is still dotted with fine old villas.

VILLA FALIER AND ALTIVOLE

The 18th-century **Villa Falier**, below Asolo on the valley floor in the village of Ca' Falier (*map Veneto North A4*), is where, according to popular legend, the young Canova came to the attention of Giovanni Falier, the Venetian noble who became his first patron. It is said that preparations for a banquet were in the final stages when news reached the kitchens that the pastry chef had spoiled the centrepiece. There was consternation all round until the twelve-year-old grandson of a stone-carver, who was employed as a kitchen-boy, shyly offered to carve something from butter. The result—a figure of a lion—so impressed Falier and his guests that Falier took the boy under his wing and arranged for him to be apprenticed to a master sculptor.

In the cemetery of **San Vito di Altivole**, 5km southeast of Asolo, is Carlo Scarpa's Brion tomb, a private burial ground for the Brion family. A cult piece among modern architects, mostly concrete structures are set in extensive gardens with many water features, inspired by the architect's Venetian upbringing. Scarpa himself is buried in the adjacent cemetery of San Vito. Near Altivole is **Caterina Cornaro's 'Barco'**, designed by her favourite architect Graziolo as a countryside retreat, to accompany her main residence at Asolo. During the heyday of her court, many dinners, banquets, jousts and masques were held here, with performances by the famed Padua-born actor and playwright Ruzante. Today the Barco is mostly ruins, with one dilapidated *barchessa* still standing.

MASER: VILLA BARBARO AND TEMPIETTO

At Maser (*map Veneto North A3*), in a lovely setting at the foot of the vine-clad hills to the east of Asolo, is one of Palladio's most famous works, the **Villa Barbaro**, built in the late 1550s for Daniele Barbaro, diplomat, patriarch of Aquileia and writer on architecture, and his brother Marcantonio (*villadimaser.it*). It is one of Palladio's finest achievements: following the traditional plan of the Venetian Renaissance farm, it has a central manor house with engaged Ionic columns and carved tympanum, and symmetrical porticoed *barchesse*. The interior contains famous and beautiful frescoes (1560–61) by Veronese, cleverly incorporating real architectural elements of the building into witty *trompe l'oeil* scenes (Palladio is rumoured not to have approved of what Veronese did to the purity of his building). The cross-shaped Hall of Olympus is decorated with idealised landscapes with Classical ruins. A manservant and a young girl famously appear from behind *trompe l'oeil* doors. In the central room, Giustina Barbaro, wife of Marcantonio, is depicted on a *trompe l'oeil* balcony with her three children, their nurse and pet dog.

The nearby **Tempietto**, on the main approach road in the village, is Palladio's last religious building (1580). The private chapel's centralised plan with a cylindrical body, fronted by a classical facade with six ionic columns, is inspired by the Roman Pantheon. There are two small bell towers set in proportion with the dome.

POSSAGNO

Possagno (*map Veneto North A3*), in the foothills of Monte Grappa, is best known as the birthplace of the famous sculptor Antonio Canova, born here in 1757 to a family of stonemasons. His house in Possagno can be visited, as part of the wider **Museo Canova** complex (*museocanova.it*), adjoining the larger museum, a *gipsoteca*. Canova renovated his house himself in the late 18th century, and it is still home to original furniture and even clothes, around which are hung many of his paintings (oil paintings on canvas and temperas), as well as some drawings and sculptures, notably in the Turret Room, with a large number of Canovan busts. The *gipsoteca* next door, the largest space of its kind in Europe, was founded by his brother in 1833. Housed in the former basilica of the town, it has an extension by Carlo Scarpa, added in 1957, when the architect was called in to redesign the collection. The space preserves all the plaster casts which were in Canova's studio in Rome at the time of his death, including most of his major works, and which his brother had transported here (although some of them were irreparably damaged in WWI). The museum also displays some of the sculptor's models in clay, terracotta and wax, which illustrate his working method.

From the museum, a broad uphill avenue leads to the **Tempio**, the only building Canova designed, and to the construction of which he dedicated much of his last years. Built as the new parish church and Canova's final resting place, he funded most of the project himself. Indeed, he died before construction was completed, instructing his brother to use his entire estate on completing the project, and his remains were transferred here in 1830 (his heart is in Venice, in his famous mausoleum in the Frari). With its Neoclassical facade and elevated position, surrounded by mountains, the church is the most prominent building in the town. Inside is an altarpiece by Canova of the *Descent from the Cross*, and a bronze *Pietà* designed by him, but completed after his death.

ANTONIO CANOVA

From humble origins in the Veneto, Antonio Canova became a skilled sculptor and one of the pre-eminent figures in the Neoclassical movement, with patrons all over Europe, including the Habsburg court in Vienna and Napoleon Bonaparte in France. In 1802, at Napoleon's express request, he went to Paris to model a nude statue of the emperor as Mars, holding a Victory in his hand. That statue is now in Apsley House, London (former home of Napoleon's nemesis the Duke of Wellington). Even more famous is Canova's sculpture of Napoleon's sister Pauline, who married Camillo Borghese: he portrayed her, half nude, as Venus Victrix (the statue is in the Galleria Borghese in Rome). But it is perhaps his supremely elegant marble groups of mythological figures such as the *Three Graces* and *Eros and Psyche* for which he is justly best remembered. The style he invented for sepulchral monuments, with the effigies often accompanied by mourning figures (and his use of the pyramid form derived from ancient Classical tombs), greatly influenced later funerary sculpture. In 1815 Canova went back to Paris on a papal mission: to retrieve the treasures which Napoleon had seized from Italy. He succeeded in large measure and his fundamental role in this operation, and also as a protector of Italian art in general, has always been recognised. However, soon after his death in Venice in 1822, his fame as a sculptor waned. With a revival of interest in the Neoclassical period in the 20th century, Canova was once again acclaimed as one of Italy's greatest sculptors. His works are to be found in many of the most important museums of the world, but few places give as good an overview of his life and work as here in Possagno. He was also an extraordinarily skilled draughtsman and some very fine painted portraits by him also survive.

VALDOBBIADENE & PROSECCO

Valdobbiadene (*map Veneto North A3*) is a pleasant town set among steep foothills that stretch eastwards to Conegliano, dominated by vineyards producing Prosecco. Though Prosecco is produced across nine provinces in the Veneto and Friuli-Venezia Giulia, it is this area here, with shelter from surrounding mountains creating a beneficial microclimate that has become known as the premier zone for the well-known sparkling wine. As such, it is home to the only two Prosecco DOCGs: Conegliano Valdobbiadene Prosecco and Asolo Prosecco. The hills of Conegliano and Valdobbiadene were designated a UNESCO world heritage site in 2019. The grape used in the wine is called Glera, its name having been changed from Prosecco in 2009, to demarcate more clearly the Prosecco region's geographically protected status. Prosecco, from these DOCGs, is one of the best-selling sparkling wines in the world (over 600 million bottles annually). It is made using the Charmat or Martinotti method, fermented in stainless steel tanks rather than in the bottle (as is done in the traditional method used to make Champagne, Crémant and Cava). Exceptional producers include Bortolomiol in Valdobbiadene, the Adami family in Soprapiana, and Silvano Follador in nearby Santo Stefano.

CONEGLIANO & VITTORIO VENETO

CONEGLIANO

Conegliano Veneto (*map Veneto North B3*) is a wine-growing town with a charming historic centre. The main thoroughfare, the Contrada Granda, encompasses the pretty Via XX Settembre, with many attractive 16th–18th-century houses, and the Piazza Giovanni Battista Cima, named after the Renaissance painter, always known as Cima da Conegliano (c. 1459–1518), who was born here. The **cathedral** has a fine altarpiece by him dated from 1492, whilst the adjacent **Scuola dei Battuti** (*open Sat and Sun 10–12 & 4–6*) was built over the cathedral, with nine ogival arches allowing the continuity of the porticoed street. On the first floor is the Sala dei Battuti, a large room with biblical frescoes by Francesco da Milano and Pozzoserrato, also the original painter of the external frescoes. Next door is the chapter room with five Flemish tapestries from the 16th century. In via Cima, behind the cathedral, is the **Casa di Cima**, where the painter lived, converted in to a small museum with reproductions of his work and some archaeological finds.

From the Piazza Cima, with the Neoclassical Teatro Accademia, the Via Accademia leads to the **castle**, accessible either by walking path or by road. All that is left of this ruined medieval fortress are the ramparts, from which there are excellent views of the surrounding vineyards, and the bell-tower, which hosts the **Museo Civico**. The museum includes an archaeological section, a section dedicated to frescoes and a picture gallery, including paintings from the workshop of Cima da Conegliano.

VITTORIO VENETO

Vittorio Veneto (*map Veneto North B3*) was created in 1866 by merging the lower district of Ceneda with the old walled town of Serravalle. Originally named Vittorio, after Vittorio Emanuele II, first king of a unified Italy, the town began to be referred to as Vittorio Veneto after the final victory here of the Italians over the Austrians in October 1918. This name was officially adopted in 1923 (*for more on WWI in the Veneto, see below*).

THE VENETO IN THE FIRST WORLD WAR

At the outbreak of the First World War, Italy at first remained neutral, only entering the War in May 1915 as an ally of France, Britain and Russia against Austria, having been given the guarantee that the Trentino, South Tyrol, Trieste and part of Dalmatia would all become part of Italy at the end of the hostilities. However, Italy was totally unprepared for war and despite the general conviction that the fighting would be rapidly concluded, it continued bitterly for years. Up until 1917 the front line remained substantially the same, with the Austrians holding the Adige valley and the plateau of Asiago and the Italians defending the Isonzo (although Italy had managed to cross the river and win Gorizia in 1916).

When the Russian front collapsed in October 1917, the forces of Austria and Germany won an important battle at Caporetto (now Kobarid, Slovenia), whose name has entered the Italian language as a synonym for 'devastating defeat'. The enemy quickly advanced to the Piave river, which the Italians defended bravely, and won a famous victory at (the later renamed) Vittorio Veneto in October 1918. The following month the Austro-Hungarian Empire collapsed. Three bitter battles were fought in these same years, 1917 and 1918, for control of Monte Grappa (*map Veneto West D1*), now commemorated with a monumental shrine to the fallen (*see p. 86*).

Italy's northern boundaries were redrawn along the alpine ridge, to include the Trentino and South Tyrol, and most important of all, the port of Trieste. Fiume (today's Rijeka, Croatia) and much of Dalmatia was not included: Pope Benedict XV's famous phrase that it had been an '*inutile strage*' (a 'useless massacre') was often repeated.

Ernest Hemingway's experiences as a volunteer with the US Red Cross form the basis of his *A Farewell to Arms*. For the last year of the War, British troops were sent south from the trenches in Flanders to reinforce the Italian fronts. There are five Commonwealth cemeteries in the woods on the Asiago plateau (*map Veneto West C1–D1*); two near the Piave river in the province of Treviso, at Tezze (*map Veneto North B3*) and Giavera (*map Veneto North A3–A4*); and one in Padua. All of these are described in detail on the website of the Commonwealth War Graves Commission (*cwgc.org*).

Though two parts of a single town, Serravalle and Ceneda retain distinct identities. Serravalle has a medieval character, centred around the pretty Piazza Flaminio, with the **Museo del Cenedese** in the fine 15th-century former Palazzo della Comunità (*museivittorioveneto.it*). Its displays include archaeological material and a collection of 19th-century art, as well as the interiors of the old *palazzo* itself. Just off the piazza, over a bridge across the Meschio, is the **duomo (Santa Maria Nova)**, with a high altarpiece of the *Madonna and Child with St Andrew and St Peter* by Titian over the high altar. Titian had connections to the area: his daughter Lavinia settled in Serravalle through marriage, and he himself owned a farm nearby. He was commissioned to paint the altarpiece by the town council of Serravalle in 1542, and completed it in 1547. Further south, near the Porta San Lorenzo is the little **Oratorio dei Santi Lorenzo e Marco dei Battuti**, originally belonging to the Confraternity of the Battuti (the 'Beaten', so named because of their habit of self-flagellating). It is frescoed with 15th century stories of St Lawrence and St Mark.

In the district of **Ceneda**, south of Serravalle, is the **Galleria Civica** (*Viale della Vittoria 321; museivittorioveneto.it; combined tickets with other museums available*), in a fine townhouse of 1906, preserving original furnishings and with an eclectic collection of paintings from medieval to contemporary, including works by Filippo de Pisis and Virgilio Guidi. The cathedral of Vittorio Veneto, **Santa Maria Assunta**, preserves the remains of the 7th-century bishop St Tiziano of Oderzo in a neo-Gothic crypt. Albino Luciani, later Pope John Paul I, was a much later bishop here, from 1958–69, and the Museo Diocesano is dedicated to him, on the first floor of the Episcopal Seminary to the right of the cathedral. The museum (*entrance on Largo Seminario, closed at the time of writing*) also has a Titian altarpiece, of the *Madonna and Child with St Peter and St Paul*, as well as works by Pordenone and Cima da Conegliano. In the arcaded building to the left of the cathedral is the **Museo della Battaglia** (*closed Mon; combined ticket available with Museo del Cenedese and Oratorio dei Battuti*), with material relating to this decisive conflict of October 1918.

South of the main centre of town, at Via della Seta 23, is the interesting **Museo del Baco da Seta** (*museivittorioveneto.it*), tracing the history of the silk industry in Vittorio Veneto.

ASOLO AND ENVIRONS PRACTICAL TIPS

GETTING AROUND

- **By car**: In Asolo, unless you are a resident (or staying in the town), access to cars is restricted in the evenings and on Sun and holidays. Otherwise there is a car park in Piazza Brugnoli (top of Piazza Garibaldi).
- **By train**: Frequent services from Treviso (in 30mins) to Conegliano and (10mins more) Vittorio Veneto. The nearest train station to Possagno (with a bus connection) is at Bassano del Grappa, and there are also buses from the rail stations of Castelfranco Veneto and Montebelluna. The nearest station to Asolo/Maser is Montebelluna.
- **By bus**: Local buses are run by Mobilità di Marca (*mobilitadimarca.it*). Bus no. 112 links Asolo (1hr) and Maser to Treviso and Bassano, via Montebelluna. Bus no. 130 from Possagno to Valdobbiadene (40mins), Bassano (40mins) and Montebelluna (40mins). Buses between Conegliano and Valdobbiadene (1hr), Vittorio Veneto (20mins). NB: The bus stops for Asolo are on the main road on the valley floor. Shuttle buses from the car park serve the old town every 30mins.

WHERE TO STAY

ASOLO
€€€ **Villa Cipriani**. A 16th-century villa, beautifully appointed and well run. Elegant yet homely. Bar and restaurant and a pretty flower garden. Many of the rooms have stunning views, some have sun terraces. Browning's former home. *Via Canova 298, villaciprianiasolo.com.*
€€ **Al Sole**. Overlooking the central Piazza Garibaldi, a historic old hotel (Eleonora Duse stayed here, in room 202). With high-end La Terrazzo restaurant). *albergoalsoleasolo.com.*

CONEGLIANO
€€ **Villa Soligo**. This 18th century Neoclassical ex-hunting lodge in the heart of the DOCG has spa facilities and an outdoor swimming pool. *Via Marconi, Farra di Soligo, hotelvillasoligo.it.*

WHERE TO EAT

ASOLO
€€€ **Locanda Baggio**. A short drive out of town to the north (Via Foresto Casonetto). Two generations of the Baggio family have dedicated themselves to fine cuisine, carefully sourcing ingredients and combining traditional recipes with experimentation. *Via Bassane 1, locandabaggio.it.*

There are also plenty of places in central Asolo itself: on Piazza Garibaldi there is the storied **Caffè Centrale**, founded in 1796 with good cocktails and an illustrious list of visitors, and on Via Browning the very local and atmospheric **Osteria Al Bàcaro** (*albacaroanticaosteria.it*).
For fish there is €€€ **Bistrot** on Via Pietro Bembo (*evenings only except Sun, ristorantebistrotasolo.com*).

CONEGLIANO
€€€ **Al Salisà**. A good restaurant with a pleasant (enclosed) terrace overlooking the garden. *Via XX Settembre 2, ristorantealsalisa.com.*

LOCAL SPECIALITIES

The Prosecco wines of the two DOCGs of Conegliano Valdobbiadene and Asolo (*see pp. 145–6*).

FELTRE, BELLUNO & THE DOLOMITES

The province of Belluno is the largest and northernmost in the Veneto, though also the least populated, its territory almost entirely mountainous and dominated by the Dolomites. Much of its population clusters along the Piave river, which flows south from the Alps through the provincial capital of Belluno and the charming town of Feltre in the Valbelluna valley. These towns are the cultural centres of the province, while the Dolomites attract visitors for skiing and hiking, with their dramatic peaks and scattered alpine villages. Historically an agricultural region, it today relies heavily on tourism.

FELTRE

Feltre (*map Veneto North A3*), possibly founded by the Rhaetians, became a Roman *municipium* in AD 49, situated on the Via Opitergium-Tridentum (the road from Oderzo to Trento). In the Middle Ages Feltre was a free *comune* and a seigniory of various families before coming under Venice in 1404. The Venetian heads of state dated their dispatches *ex cineribus Feltri*, 'from the ashes of Feltre', after forces of the Holy Roman Empire sacked the city twice (in 1509 and 1510) during the War of the League of Cambrai. The architectural uniformity of the city centre, Feltre's most distinctive asset, is a direct consequence of this double debacle and of the ambitious programme of reconstruction that followed it. The old walled city has numerous 16th-century buildings with projecting roofs, and façades bearing frescoes or graffiti. The centre can be accessed through one of three Renaissance city gates.

PIAZZA MAGGIORE AND VIA LUZZO

From Porta Imperiale, or Castaldi, begins the porticoed Via Mezzaterra, running uphill through the old city to the Renaissance Piazza Maggiore, a cluster of noble buildings around a cobbled space, adorned with a Lion of St Mark and statues of prominent *Feltrini*: the humanist Vittorino da Feltre, tutor to the princes of Mantua; and Panfilo Castaldi, locally famed as the inventor (preceding Gutenberg) of moveable type.

The piazza is laid out on several levels. On the elevated north side stands the church of **San Rocco** (1599), fronted by a fine marble fountain spanning the width of the square. It is attributed to Tullio Lombardo (1520). On the west is the 19th-century Gothic-revival **Palazzo Guarnieri**, on the corner of which you will see the faded name 'Karlsplatz'. In 1917–18, Feltre was occupied by the Austrians and this *palazzo* became the headquarters of their armed command.

On the south side of the square is the unusual **Palazzo della Ragione** or Palazzo del Municipio, actually two buildings meeting at the corner—the one with the rusticated arcade (1558), in the Palladian style, is the former Palazzo dei Rettori Veneti, home of the Venetian governors. Inside, on the first floor, is the small wooden **La Sena theatre** of 1802, designed by the same architect as La Fenice in Venice.

Above the square rises the **Castello di Alboino**, named after the Lombard king who first built a castle here on the site of a Roman watchtower. Since destroyed many times over, the current medieval structure was once equipped with four corner towers, of which one, the clock tower still stands, with exterior decoration by Lorenzo Luzzo in 1518.

Luzzo, sometimes (but not unanimously) identified with the lugubrious name of Morto da Feltre, was born here c. 1485 and his works can best be appreciated in the town. Indeed, the continuation of Via Mezzaterra is named Via Luzzo after him. This section is lined with interesting houses, including the Venetian-Gothic-revival Palazzo Villabruna at no. 23, home to the **Museo Civico** (*closed at the time of writing; visitfeltre.info*). The ground floor houses the archaeological section, with artefacts from the Iron Age onwards, including a statue of Aesculapius dating to the 2nd century AD, and an altar of Anna Perenna, a Roman deity. The upper floors contain furniture, sculptures and paintings. There are works by the Feltre artists Lorenzo Luzzo and Pietro Mariscalchi, as well as a small portrait by Gentile Bellini, a triptych by Cima da Conegliano, a *Resurrection of Lazarus* by Palma Giovane and four views by Marco Ricci. (Perhaps the best work by Luzzo, difficult to see today, is a *Transfiguration* in the sacristy of the ex-church of the Ognissanti on Via Borgo Ruga, outside the walls to the northwest. The old conventual buildings today are part of a psychiatric unit and university campus.)

GALLERIA D'ARTE MODERNA

The 16th-century Palazzo Cumano (*Via del Paradiso 8; open Wen–Sun 10–1 & 3–7 visitfeltre.info*) was acquired by the local sculptor Carlo Rizzarda in 1926 to showcase both his own wrought-iron works and his large personal collection, and donated to the municipality after his death five years later. There are over 400 pieces by Rizzarda himself, including furniture, decorative arts and ironwork, whilst his permanent collection includes 19th- and 20th-century Italian paintings and sculpture by Giovanni Fattori, Francesco Paolo Michetti, Carlo Carrà and Arturo Tosi. The museum has since been bolstered by two large donations. On the top floor is the collection of 20th-century art and sculpture from Feltre-born arts writer Liana Bortolon, including an etching by Chagall and ceramics by Picasso. The local Nasci-Franzoia family donated their vast collection of Murano glass to the museum in 2018, with over 800 modern works (including pieces by Vittorio Zecchin and Carlo Scarpa) showcased across three rooms. This is the largest collection of Venetian glass on display anywhere.

MUSEO DIOCESANO

Also on Via Paradiso is the Museo Diocesano (*open Fri–Sun; museodiocesanobellunofeltre. it*), located in the Palazzo dei Vescovi, the former bishop's palace, first built in the

13th century, though much expanded and altered since. Inaugurated in 2018, the museum hosts a varied collection from the dioceses of both Feltre and Belluno, displayed over 27 rooms. Highlights include a large space dedicated to the wooden sculptures of Belluno-born Andrea Brustolon—described by Balzac as the 'Michelangelo of wood'—and two canvases by Tintoretto; an early *Madonna and Child with Sts Victor and Nicholas* and a reduced copy of his *Last Supper* from San Polo in Venice. There are also a number of works by Sebastiano Ricci (*see below*) and a fresco from 1504, attributed to the school of Andrea Mantegna. The 6th-century Eucharistic Chalice of Deacon Orso is of particular note, as is a remarkably detailed Byzantine cross from 1542. There are also spaces dedicated to goldsmithing, ancient icons and liturgical paraments.

GALLERIA ROMITA AND THE DUOMO

The long tunnel known as **Galleria Romita** (officially Galleria Angelini) runs from Viale Marconi in the north to Via Campo Giorgio in the south. It was built by the Germans during WWII and used as an air-raid shelter. In 2024 it caused a minor sensation when it became infested with millipedes. Today it contains a public baths but part of its length, hung with information panels, is open to visit.

Close to the Via Campo Giorgio end of it is the **Duomo-Concattedrale di San Pietro**, rebuilt in the 16th century after the devastations of the League of Cambrai, it preserves a 14th-century Gothic apse and campanile from the earlier structure. Inside, the sanctuary hosts the most interesting works: the tomb of Andrea Bellati, the last dated work of Tullio Lombardo; the 13th-century throne of Bishop Villalta; and a large wooden Crucifix by Vittore Scienza, painted by Lorenzo Luzzo. The polygonal apse is flanked by two side chapels. The chapel of the Blessed Sacrament, on the left, has a cycle on the life of Christ by Giovanni Battista Volpato. The chapel to the right is dedicated to San Fedele, with an altarpiece by Pietro Mariscalchi. Other works by Mariscalchi can be found among the ten side altars, including a *St John the Baptist* and an *Our Lady of Mercy* (*Pala della Misericordia*). The 11th-century crypt is decorated with frescoes and has a coffered ceiling, painted with scenes from the Passion of the Christ.

Steps behind the cathedral ascend to the **Baptistery of San Lorenzo**, with a 15th-century apse, a 17th-century doorway on the façade and a Renaissance doorway on the side. Inside are a baptismal font of 1399 with a Baroque wooden cove, topped with a sculpture of *St John the Baptist*. Fragments of 14th–15th-century frescoes are preserved on the walls.

Beneath the courtyard of the cathedral is a large **Area Archeologica** (*open March–Oct weekends 10–1 & 4-9 fondacofeltre.it*) with excavations of the Roman city, including sections of private homes and possible civic buildings. There are also ruins of a grand post-Roman building, and an early medieval circular baptistery.

AROUND FELTRE

The sanctuary of **Santi Vittore e Corona** (*map Veneto North A3*), sits on a hillside overlooking the village of Anzù. This Byzantine-Romanesque church of 1096–1101 was built by a feudal lord and later incorporated in to a fortified structure. The narrow façade is adorned with chiaroscuro frescoes, whilst the three-aisled interior is covered in 12th–15th-century frescoes. The three 14th-century cycles are of particular note, attributed to the schools of Giotto and Tommaso da Modena. The earliest frescoes are the depictions of St Peter and St Paul. The church also has fragments of 11th-century sculptures and a marble statue of St Victor (1400). The adjoining convent of 1494, built by monks from Fiesole, has more frescoes in the cloister, depicting the miracles of St Victor.

The 15th-century church of Santa Maria Assunta at **Lentiai** (*map Veneto North A3*) has a coffered ceiling with twenty panels painted by Cesare Vecellio, and a polyptych by the workshop of Titian in the main altar.

BELLUNO

The old town of Belluno (*map Veneto North A2–B2*), a Roman *municipium*, stands on a rocky eminence at the point where the River Ardo flows into the Piave—a position which protected it over the centuries both from foreign incursions and from seasonal floodwaters. Here you immediately feel the nearness of the Alps (the Dolomiti Bellunesi, the most southerly of the Dolomite ranges, rise just to the west) and of the forests that have long been the city's principal asset. From Belluno, in fact, came the piles on which Venice is built; and something of the deep greens and browns of the Alpine woodlands can be seen in the paintings of Sebastiano Ricci (*see below*) and his nephew Marco, who were born here in 1659 and 1679, respectively. The Baroque wood-sculptor Andrea Brustolon (1660–1732) was also a native. The town was badly damaged in the Alpago earthquake of 1873.

ON AND AROUND PIAZZA DUOMO

The **duomo of Santa Maria delle Grazie** is a 16th-century edifice designed by Tullio Lombardo, built on a medieval foundation, with an unfinished façade and a detached campanile (1743) by Filippo Juvarra. It was badly damaged in the earthquake of 1873. The luminous interior has paintings by Jacopo Bassano (third south altar) and Palma Giovane (fourth south altar) and Cesare Vecellio, and the two small marble statuettes in the first north chapel are attributed to Tullio Lombardo. The small baptistery opposite dates from the 16th century.

On the north side of Piazza del Duomo is the red 19th-century **Town Hall** and its historic predecessor, the Palazzo dei Rettori (now the prefecture), a Venetian Renaissance building of 1491 with porticoed façade, mullioned windows, central loggias and an imposing clock-tower (1549) over the eastern corner. The facade is adorned with coats of arms and busts of Venetian rectors. Opposite, the former palace of the bishop-counts (1190), now an auditorium, has been completely rebuilt, the Torre Civica being the only vestige of the original structure. The atrium of the building has a Roman lapidary, while the internal courtyard showcases other ancient artefacts discovered during restoration work (*open weekends 9.30–12.30 & 2.30–6*).

Via Duomo leads past the 17th-century Palazzo dei Giuristi, home to the **archaeological section of the Museo Civico** (*mubel.comune.belluno.it*), with Iron Age finds from nearby excavation sites, and Roman and medieval artefacts, including two Lombard tombstones.

The street continues to Piazza Erbe or **Piazza del Mercato**, on the site of the Roman forum, and surrounded by porticoed Renaissance buildings, the finest of which is the former pawnbroker, the Monte di Pietà (1531), adorned with coats of arms and inscriptions. The fountain in the centre dates from 1410.

SEBASTIANO RICCI

Ricci (1659–1734) is famous as much for the scandals in his private life as for his painting. He was a serial womaniser, and often found himself having to leave town in a hurry when his liaisons were discovered. Nor was he above resorting to desperate measures to cover his traces; in 1678 he was imprisoned for attempting to poison a woman he had made pregnant. Released through the intervention of a local nobleman, Ricci fled to Bologna, and then Parma, where he found patrons and began to produce the works he came to be known for. After running off with the daughter of a fellow painter to Turin, he was again imprisoned and nearly executed, this time saved by the Duke of Parma. All this tends to obscure his value as an artist. Often finishing his paintings in a hurry, his style is sometimes too dashing, and he has been accused of superficiality, but Ricci was a virtuoso talent, and the helter-skelter energy which compelled him to rush his works to completion translates into nervous brushwork which give them an amazing lightness of touch. Ricci has been compared to Veronese. He certainly studied Veronese, and reinterpreted him in a dazzling, colourful style which was to lift early 18th-century Venetian painting out of its doldrums and steer it on a new course, towards the later brilliance of Tiepolo. Ricci was highly sought-after in his own lifetime both in and outside Italy, granted commissions by the Medici and Louis XIV, and travelling to Vienna (Karlskirche, Schönbrunn) and London. He spent four years in England, painting several works including the apse of the chapel of the Royal Hospital Chelsea, before returning to Venice after narrowly losing out in a competition to fresco the dome of St Paul's. Ricci's intemperate eating, drinking and womanising took its toll on his health: he suffered acutely from gallstones, and died on the operating table. His nephew Marco was similarly plagued by scandal, also fleeing Venice after murdering a gondolier in a tavern brawl. He also went on to spend time in London, primarily painting the sets for Italian operas staged in the city.

SAN PIETRO

South of Piazza Erbe is Via Mezzaterra, lined with Venetian-style townhouses, many of which are frescoed. Turn left into Vicolo San Pietro for the Gregorian church of

San Pietro, a 14th-century edifice rebuilt in 1750, with a bare façade and, inside, paintings by Sebastiano Ricci (over the high altar) and Andrea Schiavone, as well as two remarkable wooden altar panels carved by Andrea Brustolon.

THE MUSEO CIVICO AND SANTO STEFANO

From Piazza del Mercato, continue north along Via Rialto, beyond the ancient Porta Dojona, to the spacious **Piazza dei Martiri**, the main promenade and commercial centre of the town, and Piazza Vittorio Emanuele II, where the large Palazzo Fulcis (restored in 2017) hosts the **art collection of the Museo Civico** (*mubel.comune.belluno.it*). There are two *Madonnas* by Bartolomeo Montagna, as well as several works by Marco and Sebastiano Ricci, who worked in this building, painting three canvases for the room known as the Camerino d'Ercole (*at the time of writing on display in the former upper-floor grain loft, awaiting repositioning*). Many other local painters are also represented here, along with sculptures by Andrea Brustolon and a large porcelain collection.

Via Roma leads from the museum to the late Gothic church of **Santo Stefano** (1468), with a large 15th-century doorway on the side. Inside, the Cappella Cesa, with a large wooden altarpiece by Matteo Cesa, has frescoes attributed to Jacopo da Montagnana (c. 1487). Next to the sanctuary are two large angels holding lamps by Andrea Brustolon, who also made the Crucifix in the left aisle (both transferred here from other churches in the city closed during Napoleonic rule). A 3rd-century Roman sarcophagus was excavated from underneath the church during construction; once displayed in the piazza outside, it is now in the Palazzo Crepadona, the civic library (Via Ripa).

THE DOLOMITES

The northern Veneto, where the Dolomites merge with the white limestone peaks of the eastern Alps is renowned above all for its ski resorts, the most famous of which is **Cortina d'Ampezzo** (*map Veneto North A1*). Yet the region has a year-round appeal, with the jagged outlines of the mountains provide some of the most distinctive landscapes in all of Italy. In late spring, the valleys and alpine meadows become a lush green, and the historically pastoral villages have a charming character. The protected area of the **Parco Nazionale delle Dolomiti Bellunesi** (*map Veneto North A2; for information, see dolomitipark.it*) covers the southernmost ramifications of the Dolomites, including the great limestone massifs of the Talvena (2542m), the Schiara (2565m), the Monti del Sole (2240m) and the Alpi Feltrine (Sass de Mura, 2550m). These mountains join typically alpine landscapes, characterised by bold peaks and powerful vertical walls, with the grassy meadows and shady forests and valleys of the Prealpi. The park's flora is one of its prime assets, especially in the warmer southern sections, and includes numerous native species and rarities. Magnificent beechwoods yield at higher altitudes to fir and larch. The park is home to herds of chamois and roe deer.

THE CADORE

The Cadore is the mountainous district surrounding the upper valley of the Piave and its western tributaries, stretching all the way to the Austrian border. The region only became wholly a part of Italy in 1918, ceded after the First World War. There was heavy fighting here along the old frontier line, with many fortifications and trench lines still visible. There is a strong regional identity; the *Cadorini* traditionally speak Ladin, a Romance language, especially around Cortina and the former Tyrolean villages, though in much of the province the dialect is something of a Ladino-Venetian hybrid. The area is framed by some of the most dramatic peaks of the Dolomites, including the famous Tre Cime di Lavaredo and Monte Antelao.

Pieve di Cadore (878m; *map Veneto North B1*), the chief town of the region, is a summer and winter resort beneath the southern foothills of the Marmarole, best known as the birthplace of Titian c. 1488. It was also the site of the Battle of Cadore in 1508, when Venetian forces defeated the advancing troops of the Holy Roman Emperor, triggering the creation of the League of Cambrai and subsequent war.

On Piazza Tiziano, with a statue of the artist, is the Palazzo della Magnifica Comunità Cadorina (*magnificacomunitadicadore.it*), rebuilt twice in the 16th century, containing a small archaeological museum. The museum hosts pre-Roman and Roman finds, many from nearby Lagole, an ancient thermal bathing site (next to the larger man-made Lago di Cadore), excavated from 1949 onwards. Among the materials found are ex-votos with inscriptions in the ancient Venetian language. The parish church next door has an altarpiece of the *Madonna and Child with Saints* by Titian, as well as several paintings by members of his family, including a large *Last Supper* by his cousin and pupil Cesare Vecellio above the high altar, and several works by his nephew Marco Vecellio. To the south of the piazza, along Via Arsenale is Titian's birthplace (*closed for restoration at the time of writing; see magnificacomunitadicadore.it*), a typical Cadore stone house which has been converted in to a small museum, with reproductions of his drawings and faithfully furnished rooms. Further along Via Arsenale is the modern Museo dell'Occhiale (*museodellocchiale.it*), an eyewear museum with optical memorabilia from the Middle Ages onward, the local area being the historic epicentre of the industry in Italy.

On the hillside overlooking Pieve is the fortress of **Monte Ricco**, built in the later 19th century on the site of an ancient castle, and used as a logistics centre and warehouse during the First World War, along with the nearby Batteria Castello.

CORTINA D'AMPEZZO

Cortina d'Ampezzo (1210m at the church; *map Veneto North A1*) is a summer and winter resort, one of the most popular and famous in Italy, long frequented by high society. It lies in a sunny upland basin, and the view of the mountains on all sides is magnificent; the town is at the centre of the Ampezzo Dolomites Natural Park, home to some of the most well known mountain groups of the Dolomites, such as the Tofane, Monte Cristallo and Sorapiss. Cortina was chosen, along with Milan, as the host of the 2026 Winter Olympics. The resort has been especially popular with writers; Aldous Huxley wrote much of *Point Counter Point* here in 1926–7, while

Hemingway set the short story 'Out of Season' here, written when visiting in 1923.

Corso Italia, lined with hotels, is the main street of the town. The **basilica** here has a wooden tabernacle by Andrea Brustolon and an altarpiece by Antonio Zanchi, and the campanile is built from the same dolomite rock as of the mountains. The **Mario Rimoldi Museum**, also on Corso Italia, is dedicated to modern art, with works by Filippo de Pisis (who often stayed in Cortina) and other 20th-century Italian painters.

In the northwest of the town are two more small museums: the Rinaldo Zardini **Palaeontological Museum**, named after a local photographer and collector, with a large collection of Triassic fossils, mostly of marine life and all found locally, dating from an age when the region was a tropical sea, and the mountains atolls; and an **Ethnographic Museum** detailing the history of the Ampezzo community.

A spectacular road across the Dolomites, built by the Austrians in 1901–9, leads west from here to Canazei and Bolzano, while to the northeast is the **Lago di Misurina** (1737m), one of the most beautifully situated lakes in the Dolomites.

FELTRE AND BELLUNO PRACTICAL TIPS

GETTING AROUND

- **By train**: For Feltre, there are direct trains from Treviso (70mins) or Padua (80mins). From Belluno there are also direct trains to Venice (1hr 45mins), and a slower regional train to Conegliano (1hr). The main station serving the Venetian Dolomites is Calalzo di Cadore, with trains running from Belluno. (1hr).
- **By bus**: There are buses run by DolomitiBus (*dolomitibus.it*) between Feltre and Belluno (they cover most of the province; no. 20 goes to Lentiai). For Santi Vittore e Corona at Anzù (4km away), buses from Feltre are operated by La Marca (*mobilitadimarca.it*; the 126 line to Valdobbiadene). Bus 914 on the urban line by DolomitiBus goes to Anzu as well, though only twice a day. Buses to Cortina (bus station in Via Marconi) are run by Cortina Express from Treviso and Venezia (*cortinaexpress.it*). Other services all over the Dolomites are run by DolomitiBus (*website as above*). Local buses and ski buses are run by SE.AM Servizi Ampezzo (*serviziampezzo.it*). The integrated suedtirolmobil.info covers Cortina as well.
- **By bicycle**: The villages of Cadore are connected by the 'Lunga Via delle Dolomiti' cycle-pedestrian path.

WHERE TO STAY

CORTINA D'AMPEZZO
€€€ **De la Poste**. This is the classic place to stay in Cortina, in the very heart of the town. It is the oldest hotel in the resort (opened in 1804), and has a celebrated restaurant. It is especially famous for its wood-panelled bar, once frequented by Hemingway and still one of the main meeting spots in the town.

Closed out of season. *Piazza Roma 14, .delaposte.it*.
FELTRE
€€ **Doriguzzi**. A pleasant central hotel which claims to be the oldest in town. Modern bedrooms. Favoured by cyclists. *Viale del Piave 2, hoteldoriguzzi. it*.

WHERE TO EAT

BELLUNO
€–€€ **Taverna**. A simple *trattoria* with good local dishes, right in the heart of town behind the Teatro Comunale. *Via Cipro 7, ristorantetaverna.it*.
CORTINA D'AMPEZZO
€€ **Baita Piè Tofana** (with rooms). A lodge, popular with hikers and climbers, with good traditional food and fabulous views. Ten mins from the centre of Cortina. Evenings only. *Località Rumerlo, baitapietofana.it*.

FESTIVALS AND EVENTS

The **Palio di Feltre** is a pageant, held on the 1st Sun in August, to celebrate the 'donation' of Feltre to Venice in 1404. Its origins, however, go back to the reign of the previous ruler, the Duke of Milan: after the Duke's death in 1388, it was agreed that a horse race and Mass should be held each year on the anniversary. Under Venetian rule, this tradition evolved into a celebration of the handover to Venice, with the winner receiving a prize of 15 ducats. The current event, founded in 1979, is stretched over the whole weekend, centred around a competition between the town's four districts. Celebrations begin on Fri with each district hosting a dinner in their neighbourhood, while on Sat there is an archery competition and relay race. On Sun, there is a morning procession along Largo Castaldi to attend Mass, with participants dressed in medieval garb. In the afternoon there is another procession along Via Mezzaterra and Piazza Maggiore before the four districts compete in the Prà del Moro arena in a tug-of-war and horse race to determine the overall winner, and the new holder of the 15th-century ducat banner.

LAKE GARDA

Lake Garda (Lago di Garda; *map Veneto West B1–A2*) is the largest of the northern Italian lakes, partly in the Veneto (the eastern shore) partly in Trentino (the north) and partly in Lombardy (the west). Its mild climate permits the cultivation of olives and lemon trees, and the vegetation is characterised by thick cypress woods. Most of its resorts were developed in the 1920s and 1930s, although some grand hotels had already been built at the end of the 19th century for Austrian and German visitors—and summering on the lake is much older than that: the ancient Romans greatly appreciated the climate of Lacus Benacus (their name for it being derived from a Celtic word meaning 'horned').

The inspiring beauty of the lake has made it traditionally popular with writers. Goethe saw his first olive trees here in 1786. Byron—somewhat inevitably—was here too, at Desenzano in 1816, and Tennyson came in 1880. D.H. Lawrence lived on by the lake in 1912 and 1913; he describes the lemon gardens in *Twilight in Italy*.

Citrus cultivation here dates from at least the 16th century and reached its height in the early 19th century. This was the northernmost locality in the world where citrus fruits could be grown commercially. A few of the characteristic hothouses (*limonaie*), built of tall stone struts roofed over with wooden slats in winter, and protected by glass panes in front, still survive at Gargnano, San Vigilio and Torri del Benaco. These shelters are unique to Garda.

Fishing is still practised in a few localities. The *carpione* (*Salmo carpio*), a kind of large trout found only in Garda, is endangered now. Instead, menus often feature *lavarello* (*Coregonus lavaretus*), freshwater whitefish (also known as *coregone*).

The breezier upper part of the lake, where the water is deepest, is popular for sailing and windsurfing, and there are regattas in summer. The predominant winds (which can swell into violent storms) are the *sover* (or *soar* or *sora*), from the north, in the morning, and the *ora*, from the south, in the afternoon. Good places to swim include the peninsula of Sirmione, the Isola dei Conigli off Moniga, the Baia del Vento between Salò and Desenzano, and the Isola San Biagio.

THE LOMBARD SIDE OF THE LAKE

SIRMIONE

Sirmione (*map Veneto West A2*) stands at the tip of a narrow promontory 3.5km long and in places only 119m wide, in the centre of the southern shore of the lake. It was a Roman station on the Via Gallica, halfway between Brescia and Verona. Now it is a popular resort, very crowded with tour groups in season (though deserted in winter). There are many enjoyable walks on the peninsula, and you can swim in the

Sirmione: the 'Grotte di Catullo' viewed from the water.

lake on the east side. The peninsula tip is covered with the remains of a vast Roman villa, thought to have belonged to the poet Catullus.

Sirmione: castle and churches

The picturesque 13th-century **Rocca Scaligera** (*open Tues–Sun 8.30–7.30*), where Dante is said to have stayed, marks the entrance to the town. Completely surrounded by water (copper-headed Pochard ducks inhabit its moat), it was a stronghold of the Della Scala family, lords of Verona. The massive central tower, 29m high, has a good view.

Via Vittorio Emanuele (closed to cars) leads north from the castle through the scenic little town towards the ruins of Catullus' vast villa at the end of the peninsula. A road on the right leads to the 15th-century church of **Santa Maria Maggiore** (or Santa Maria della Neve), which preserves some antique columns in its porch, one of the outermost ones being a Roman milestone. There are traces of frescoes in the interior, including a lion of St Mark with drawn sword. At the end of Via Vittorio Emanuele is a spa with a hotel that uses warm sulphur springs rising in the lake.

Via Catullo continues, passing close to **San Pietro in Mavino**, a Romanesque church of 8th-century foundation with early frescoes. At the end of the road is the entrance to the so-called Grotte di Catullo.

Sirmione: 'grottoes of Catullus'

The Grotte di Catullo (*closed Mon; opening times vary; see museilombardia.cultura. gov.it*) are the sprawling ruins of a large Roman villa, called '*grotte*' because before excavation, the vaulted substructures seemed like natural caverns. This is the most important example of Roman imperial domestic architecture in northern Italy. It is set amid olive groves on the end of the headland, with splendid views out over the lake and of the rocks beneath the clear shallow water. The extensive ruins belong to a succession of country houses dating from of the 1st century BC to the late 3rd century AD, when the building was abandoned. It is conceivable that the villa may have belonged to the family of the Valerii Catulli. Many wealthy Romans came to Sirmione for the summer, and Catullus—who is known to have had a villa here—speaks of '*Paene peninsularum, Sirmio, insularumque ocelle*' ('Sirmione, gem of all peninsulas and islands'). The site was only properly investigated in the 19th and beginning of the 20th centuries. Near the entrance is a small antiquarium, with pottery and exquisite fragments of frescoes dating from the 1st century BC. Of the villa itself, little that is readily comprehensible remains, as it was plundered for building material over the centuries and its site is now covered by an olive grove. The most conspicuous survivals are the vast substructures and vaults (the eponymous *grotte*), built to support the main upper floor, which occupied an area over 160m long and 100m wide. There are also a number of huge cisterns, as well as a baths complex and the ruins of what would once have been long, graceful seaview terraces with a covered walkway (cryptoporticus) below the western colonnade.

DESENZANO

Desenzano del Garda (*map Veneto West A2*) is a pleasant resort. From the quay, a bridge crosses the entrance to a picturesque harbour for small boats, with cafés, restaurants and the Galleria Civica (temporary exhibitions) around it. Behind this, the **Piazza Giuseppe Malvezzi** opens out, with pretty arcades and a monument to St Angela Merici (1474–1540), foundress of the Ursuline order, who was born here. Just out of the piazza is the **duomo**, with a *Last Supper* by Giambattista Tiepolo (or possibly his son Gian Domenico) in the Cappella del Santissimo Sacramento. The duomo also has a number of works by Andrea Celesti, a Venetian painter who worked widely around Lake Garda. His wife was from Toscolano, which is where he died in 1712.

A short way further north, on Via Crocefisso, is the entrance to the excavations of a **Roman villa** (*closed Mon; for times, see museilombardia.cultura.gov.it*), mostly dating from the 4th century AD but on the site of an earlier edifice of the 1st century AD. It is the most important late Roman villa in northern Italy, of great interest for its colourful 4th-century mosaics. The grandiose design of the reception rooms of the main villa includes an octagonal hall, a peristyle, an atrium with two apses, and a triclinium with three apses, all with mosaics. Other, less grand rooms to the south may have been baths. An antiquarium (beneath which the Roman edifice of the 1st century AD, with an underfloor heating system, was discovered) has finds from the site, including remains of wall paintings. Separate excavations to the north have revealed a residential area, with part of an apsidal hall and baths, to the east. The villa was discovered in 1921, and excavations have continued, even though the site is in the centre of the town.

The Lion of St Mark is normally depicted in peaceful guise, holding a book. In Santa Maria Maggiore in Sirmione, it is shown ready for war.

BATTLEFIELDS NEAR LAKE GARDA

The low moraine hills south of Lake Garda, formed by the ancient glacier of the Adige, have been the theatre of many battles: during Prince Eugene's campaign in the War of the Spanish Succession (1701–6); during Napoleon's enterprises (1796–1814); and during the Wars of Italian Independence (1848–9, 1859 and 1866).

San Martino della Battaglia
From Rivoltella, halfway between Sirmione and Desenzano, a by-road leads away from the lake up to the tower (74m high) of San Martino della Battaglia (*map Veneto West A3*), which commemorates Vittorio Emanuele II's victory over the right flank of the Austrian army on 24th June 1859. The interior (*open March–Sept Mon–Sat 9–12.30 & 2.30–7, Sun and holidays 9–7; Oct–Feb Tues–Sun 9–12.30 & 2–5.30; solferinoesanmartino.it*) contains sculptures and paintings relating to the campaign.

Solferino
At nearby Solferino, Napoleon III, in alliance with Vittorio Emanuele, defeated the rest of the Austrian army on the same day. The Austrians were under the personal command of the 29-year-old emperor Franz Joseph, the last time he ever led his troops into battle. An ossuary chapel in the little town (follow Via Ossario) displays the skulls of the 7,000 dead, collected from the battlefield and placed in grisly formation here, completely covering the sanctuary walls of the chapel. The Swiss businessman Henry Dunant was an eyewitness of the conflict and was so appalled by the suffering he witnessed of wounded soldiers abandoned and left to die uncomforted that he personally organised aid and relief work to tend them, regardless of which side they were on (the altarcloth in the chapel is embroidered with the words '*Omnes Fratres; Tutti Fratelli; Alle Brüder; Tous Frères*'). Dunant's *A Memory of Solferino* was the inspiration for the foundation of the International Red Cross. The museum on the square in front of the ossuary chapel has mementoes of the battle (*open March–Sept Tues–Sun 9–12.30 & 2.30–7; Oct–Feb by appointment, solferinoesanmartino.it*). The little Albergo 'Alla Vittoria' offers coffee. It is also possible to climb the square Rocca, known as the 'Conning Tower of Italy' (*La Spia d'Italia*), from where there are fine views of the lovely countryside that hosted these two most sanguinary encounters.

Villafranca di Verona
Villafranca (*map Veneto West B3*) preserves a castle of the Della Scala, built in 1202 to provide reinforcement against Mantua to the south. It was enclosed by a large wall with seven small towers, which forms the majority of the castle complex as it can be seen today. The town gives its name to the armistice of

Villafranca, the result of a meeting here on 11th July 1859 between Napoleon III and Austrian emperor Franz Joseph. Through the secret deals he negotiated with Cavour, Napoleon III had done much to set the independence ball rolling in Italy. When that ball began to reach full momentum after the bloody battle of Solferino, the French leader began to be wary and concluded an armistice with Austria, in effect halting Italian expansion into Austrian territory. It wasn't until the 1860s, when Prussia defeated Austria at Königgrätz, that Italy's dreams of independence came nearer to fulfilment. The Palazzo Bottagisio, the site of the meeting, is now home to a museum dedicated to the Risorgimento.

THE REPUBLIC OF SALÒ

The Republic of Salò or Italian Socialist Republic (*Repubblica Sociale Italiana* or RSI) was formed in September 1943 as a puppet state of Nazi Germany, set up by Hitler in a last attempt to re-establish the Fascist government of Italy. In 1943, four days after the Armistice, the Germans brought Mussolini here having released him from prison. It was an ideal place to govern from, as the borders of the German Reich had reached Limone, only 20km north, with the annexation of the Trentino-Alto Adige. Germany and Japan were the only countries to recognise the Republic, which carried out brutal policing activities throughout Italy. It ended with the Liberation of Italy by the Allies in 1945 and Mussolini's execution by partisans a few days later as he fled northwards towards the Alps. For the brief months of its existence, the Republic commandeered numerous grand villas on the shores of Lake Garda, for use as ministries, hospitals and residences, including for Mussolini himself (at Gargnano) and for his mistress Clara Petacci (at Gardone Riviera). Many of those buildings are now hotels. Signboards have been placed outside the buildings today, with a map showing the extent of the Republic, the number of properties taken under its control, and detailing who and what they were used for. The huge Villa Alba at Gardone, for example, built in 1910 for a wealthy businessman from Magdeburg, served as a military communications and radio control centre. The Hotel Bellariva at Fasano housed officials from the German Embassy and was linked to the embassy building itself by an underground tunnel. At Maderno, the Hotel Golfo was the seat of the Fascist Party of the Republic and headquarters of the Black Brigades.

SALÒ
Salò (*map Veneto West A2*), the Roman *Salodium*, is an appealing town with a slightly old-fashioned atmosphere. It has two gates, one surmounted by a lion, the other by a clock. It was the birthplace of Gaspare Bertolotti (also known as Gaspare da Salò, 1540–1609), generally considered to be the first maker of violins. But all these

things are eclipsed by Salò's notoriety in recent Italian history as capital of Mussolini's short-lived puppet republic (*see above*).

Near the waterfront is the **cathedral**, a fine building in a late-Gothic style built at the end of the 15th century, with a good Renaissance portal (1509). It contains an altarpiece of *St Anthony* (1529) by the prolific painter from Brescia called Girolamo Romani, known as Romanino, who often produced particularly colourful and original works. Palazzo Fantoni is the seat of the **Biblioteca Ateneo**, which has its origins in the Accademia degli Unanimi, founded by Giuseppe Milio in 1564. The Unanimi were a group of around 20 well-born young men of Salò who got together to discuss ethics and other questions: probably much like the Academy of the Olympians in Vicenza, whom Goethe describes as convening to argue about whether invention or imitation had contributed more to the fine arts. Milio was a poet and a writer on horticultural subjects, and was apparently keen on bee-keeping (the emblem of the Unanimi was a beehive). Today the library has over 25,000 volumes, many of great historical interest.

Boat trips can also be made at certain times from April–Oct to the privately-owned **Isola del Garda** (Garda Island), where guided tours of the grounds and neo-Venetian mansion of the Borghese Cavazza family are given. Booking is required. For information, times, departure ports and prices, see *isoladelgarda.com*.

In the André Heller Foundation botanical garden above Gardone Riviera.

GARDONE RIVIERA

Gardone Riviera (*map Veneto West A2*) lies in a sheltered position and was once famous as a winter resort. Its parks and gardens are planted with rare trees. On the lakefront and in the hills behind rise grand villas, many of them built by German and Austrian industrialists who came here for the mild winters. Today they have become summer hotels (most of them closed between late October and Easter). On the waterfront, by the boat landing, is a short *lungolago* with cafés, bars and pizzerias. Gardone's villas were also commandeered as residences during the Republic of Salò (*see above*): Villa Fiordaliso was the

The neo-Venetian Borghese Cavazza mansion on Isola del Garda.

home of Claretta Petacci, Mussolini's mistress. It is now a hotel and restaurant. The huge, Neoclassical Villa Alba (1904–10), on the landward side of the main road, now a conference centre and wedding venue, was built for a German businessman, Richard Langensiepen, who had large holdings of land on the lake which he used for the commercial cultivation of flowers.

Above the main road, at Via Roma 1, is a **botanical garden** belonging to the André Heller Foundation (*hellergarden.com*). The gardens were originally laid out by the doctor, dentist and botanist Arturo Hruska over a long period between 1910 and 1971. Since their acquisition by Heller they have been planted with works of contemporary sculpture and turned into a 'garden of ecological awareness', filled with Tibetan prayer flags, palm trees with their trunks painted to resemble peace flags, Buddha statues, a Torii gate rising above smoking undergrowth (the smoke being produced by nozzles which emit water vapour), pools overstocked with large koi carp and staff in tie-dye shirts. Hruska's botany is somewhat overwhelmed. The statuary includes works by Heller himself (spitting heads), Miró, Keith Haring, Roy Lichtenstein and Mimmo Paladino. When you buy your ticket you will be given a handlist and map.

Via Roma continues to wind uphill to **Gardone Sopra**, a very pretty little enclave of narrow streets and clustering houses with a few cafés and restaurants. At the Accadueocafé on Via Carera you can sit out under a vine trellis with a glass of good house white wine and a sandwich or bruschetta, looking out at the lake below, which shimmers through the trees. Also in Gardone Sopra is the famous Vittoriale, last home of Gabriele d'Annunzio (*see below*). Pleasant walks along marked trails can be taken in the hills behind Gardone and Salò.

GABRIELE D'ANNUNZIO

Gabriele d'Annunzio (1863–1938) was born Francesco Rapagnetta, the son of a well-to-do and politically prominent landowner. He married the daughter of a duke but was not a model husband—among his mistresses was Eleonora Duse, for whom he wrote a number of plays (no longer performed today). He also wrote a play set to music by Debussy; Marcel Proust was at the opening night and said the best thing about it were the lead actress's legs.

D'Annunzio began his career as a poet: his first verses, *In Early Spring*, were published when the author was just 16; they were closely followed by *New Song* (1882), which established his fame. His best-known poetic work is the anthology *In Praise of Sky, Sea, Earth and Heroes* (1899). His novels raised eyebrows because of their self-seeking, amoral Nietzschean-superman heroes, but stylistically they were dull and academic.

Outside Italy D'Annunzio is much better known for his military exploits. In 1914–16 he called for Italy to enter the First World War on the side of Britain and France, rather than honour the Triple Alliance, the secret agreement between Germany, Austria-Hungary and Italy formed in 1882. He volunteered for dangerous duty in several branches of service, notably the air corps, and lost an eye in action. When Italy lost Istria at the Treaty of Versailles, he and a few hundred supporters occupied the port city of Fiume and held it for 18 months, until forced to withdraw by the Italian navy. He made peace with Mussolini, but never held an important government position (his legions were the first to wear the black shirt that became emblematic of the Fascists). He spent his last years writing here on Lake Garda. When he died in 1938 he was given a state funeral.

VITTORIALE DEGLI ITALIANI

The Vittoriale degli Italiani (*vittoriale.it; museum closed Mon*), the famous last residence of Gabriele d'Annunzio (*see above*), was created for him by a local and otherwise unknown architect called Giancarlo Maroni, who lived here from 1922 until his death in 1952. Evidently the eccentric martial poet worked in close collaboration with his architect and together they created its elaborate and gloomy décor as well as the garden surrounding it (with an amphitheatre).

Near the entrance (you will be given a map of the complex with your ticket) is the **Museo d'Annunzio Segreto**, highly recommended, with film and stills documenting d'Annunzio's life (unfortunately there is nowhere to sit while you watch) and exhibits including his huge collection of shoes. Beyond this stretch the gardens and villa itself, the **Prioria** (shown on a 30-min tour), which has been preserved as a museum. The interior, including an Art Deco dining room, is crammed with a jumble of Art Nouveau *objets d'art*, chinoiserie, mementoes, sacred objects, Indian works of art, and even an organ. Off the dark hallway is a reception room with an inscription that D'Annunzio made Mussolini read on his visit here: 'Remember that you are made of glass and I of steel.' The garden in front of the villa harbours odd statuary and columns surmounted by projectiles. A path descends through the pretty woods of the Acquapazza valley towards the main road. The gardens also include a **dog cemetery** (D'Annunzio was famously fond of dogs).

Opposite the villa an **auditorium** houses the biplane from which D'Annunzio dropped leaflets on Vienna announcing Italian victory in 1918. Viale di Aligi leads past a fountain filled with small dogfish to a building that houses the motorboat in which D'Annunzio took part in the assault on Fiume. The boat is named *MAS 96*, 'MAS' standing for *Memento Audere Semper*: Remember Always to Dare. Beyond lies D'Annunzio's grand **mausoleum** at the top of the hill, where he and his architect are buried. The mausoleum is circular, in imitation of the imperial mausolea of Hadrian and Augustus in Rome or of Theodoric in Ravenna. At the top are ten sarcophagi containing the remains of ten heroes of Fiume, which D'Annunzio claimed for Italy and was unwilling to relinquish when it was declared a free buffer state at the end of the First World War. Concrete sculptures of dogs loll on the mausoleum roof. In the interior is a huge bronze Crucifix by Leonardo Bistolfi (1926). From here, a path leads through woods to the prow of the ship *Puglia*, donated to D'Annunzio by the Italian Navy and reconstructed here as a monument.

TOSCOLANO-MADERNO

Toscolano-Maderno (*map Veneto West A2*) is a lively resort, formed of two small settlements, each with its own port at the two sides of a peninsula formed by deposits brought down by the Gaino stream. Up until recently the peninsula was covered in olive plantations. Today it has holiday villas and bungalows and a large working paper mill.

As you approach from Gardone, you come into **Maderno**, with a bustling main square on the waterfront and very narrow streets behind (driving along them not recommended). On the waterfront square is the 12th-century church of **Sant'Andrea**, which shows remains of Roman and Byzantine architecture, especially in the decoration of the pillar capitals, doors and windows: an older church seems to have been incorporated in the building. The interior has remnants of frescoes and, in the sanctuary (on the left), a painting of the *Virgin and Child* by Veronese. Another painting by Veronese, of the bishop Herculanus (Ercolano), is in the 18th-century parish church which stands across the square from Sant'Andrea.

To reach **Toscolano**, you cross the Gaino. Signed from the old hump-backed bridge is the **Museo della Carta** (*ecomuseovalledellecartiere.it; café and shop*), arranged in a pretty old paper mill, one of many that operated in this valley from the 15th century until the mid-20th. The short, easy walk to the museum, up the narrow, gorge-like valley, is interesting, lined with information boards about the paper mills and hydroelectric station.

On the north side of the promontory, in Toscolano, where Isabella Gonzaga of Mantua came to spend time in the summer, is the church of **Santi Pietro e Paolo**, with paintings by Andrea Celesti, a Venetian artist who was much in favour in the *Serenissima* until, for reasons unclear, he fell foul of Doge Alvise Contarini (legend has it that he painted a likeness of the doge with ass's ears). By 1688 he was at work in Toscolano (the native town of his wife). The **Santuario della Madonna di Benaco**, behind Santi Pietro e Paolo on the lake, has a barrel vault and numerous 15th-century frescoes. Four Roman columns stand in front of the church. Nearby, entered from the car park in front of the modern paper mill, is an enclosure with scant remains of a **Roman villa**, occupied from the 1st–5th centuries AD, with remnants of mosaic, a baths complex and nymphaeum. Only a small part of the villa survives. In its heyday it must have been magnificent indeed, opening out directly onto the water. In ancient Roman times, Toscolano, called Benacum, was the chief settlement on the west shore of the lake. The villa has been identified as belonging to the family of the Nonii Arrii, specifically to a certain Marcus Nonius Macrinus, a 2nd-century consul from a patrician family of Brescia. Opening times are subject to change (*see visittoscolanomaderno.info or ask at the Infopoint in Toscolano-Maderno*).

GARGNANO AND LIMONE

Beyond Toscolano the landscape becomes prettier. **Gargnano** (*map Veneto West A2*) is a very attractive little port. Several large stone pavilions where lemon trees were once cultivated can be seen on the terraced hillside. San Francesco is a 13th-century church with a cloister. Mussolini lived in Gargnano, at Villa Feltrinelli (now a hotel), from 1943 until three days before his death. An inland road from Gargnano to Limone has spectacular views: it passes the hill sanctuary of **Madonna di Monte Castello**, which has the finest view of the whole lake.

Limone sul Garda (*map Veneto West B1*) takes its name from its lemon groves, said to be the first in Europe. Up until the beginning of the 20th century, Limone was surrounded by terraced lemon and citron gardens and was accessible only by boat before the shore road from Gargnano was built in 1931. In previous centuries it was a very romantic spot, possibly the inspiration for one of Goethe's best-known lyrics: *Kennst du das Land, wo die Zitronen blühn* ('Do you know the land where the lemon trees blossom; where golden oranges gleam amidst dark foliage…?'). Goethe had sailed down from Torbole past Limone, where he admired the lemon gardens. Limone's development as a resort in the 1950s and 1960s has bequeathed it a number of unattractive buildings, sadly.

LAGO DI LEDRO

At the mouth of the Valle di Ledro, a valley of great botanical interest, is the Lago di Ledro (*map Veneto West A1–B1*), nearly 3km long, with the little resort of Pieve di Ledro at its northern end. The lake is proud of its clean water and is a good place to come for a swim. When the water is low, on the east side of the lake near **Molina di Ledro**, you can see some of the c. 15,000 larchwood stakes from lake dwellings of the early Bronze Age, discovered in 1929. There is a fascinating museum here (Museo delle Palafitte; *palafitteledro.it*), where a clutch of thatched Bronze Age huts (3rd–2nd millennium BC) has been reconstructed on a wooden platform above the water.

In 2024, when it was announced that a 39m red fir from the Valle di Ledro was to be cut down and sent to the Vatican, as the St Peter's Square Christmas tree, protests from environmentalists ensued. The fir tree was felled nevertheless.

THE NORTH END OF THE LAKE

RIVA DEL GARDA
The northern end of the lake is in the region of Trentino, which until 1918 belonged to Austria-Hungary, and has a distinctly more alpine feel. Riva del Garda (*map Veneto West B1*), the Roman *Ripa*, is a lively, somewhat overgrown little town. Sheltered by Monte Rochetta to the west, it became a fashionable winter resort at the turn of the 20th century—Thomas Mann and Franz Kafka both came to take the waters here. The centre of the old town is **Piazza III Novembre**, overlooking the little port. Here are the 13th-century Torre Apponale, the 14th-century Palazzo Pretorio, the 15th-century Palazzo Comunale and some medieval porticoes. The Rocca, a 14th-century castle encircled by water, heavily restored, now houses the **Museo Alta Garda**, or MAG (*museoaltogarda.it*). It has two main sections: a Pinacoteca with local painting and sculpture from the 14th–19th centuries, including works by the Neoclassical painter Giuseppe Craffonara (born in Riva in 1790) and the *Last Supper* of Pietro Ricchi, a pupil of Guido Reni known for his candlelit night scenes. The *Last Supper* was painted for the refectory of the Inviolata (*see below*) c. 1645. The second section has archaeological finds from the north Garda region, including a display of extraordinary stone stelae from Arco (4th–3rd millennia BC), of suggestively human form and decorated with incised daggers, spears and talismanic objects.

North of the waterfront, on Largo Marconi (between Via Negrelli and Viale dei Tigli) is the **church of the Inviolata**, with a fine Baroque interior and paintings by Pietro Ricchi (*see above*).

Torbole sul Garda (*map Veneto West B1*), a summer resort on the lake's northeastern tip, played a part in the war of 1439 between the Visconti and the Venetians, when fleets of warships were dragged overland by teams of oxen and launched into the lake here. Goethe stayed at Torbole in 1786.

THE EASTERN SHORE OF LAKE GARDA

The east side of Lake Garda is bounded by the cliff of Monte Altissimo di Nago (2078m). This is the northern peak of Monte Baldo, the high ridge which lines the shore as far as Torri del Benaco. Part of it is a protected area once known as *Hortus europae* from its remarkable vegetation, which varies from lemon trees and olives on its lower slopes to beech woods and Alpine flowers on the summit. The highest peaks are Cima Valdritta (2218m) and Monte Maggiore (2200m). There are numerous marked hiking trails.

MALCESINE AND CASSONE
Malcesine (*map Veneto West B1*) is a likeable resort with a little port. It was the seat of the Veronese Captains of the Lake in the 16th–17th centuries, and their old

Torri del Benaco, viewed from its castle ramparts.

palace is now used as the Town Hall. The little garden on the lake is open to the public. Narrow roads lead up to the castle of the Scaligeri, of Lombard origin but in the hands of the Della Scala from 1277. It was restored by Venice in the 17th century and later was used as an Austrian defence post. It is open to the public and contains a museum of Natural History, illustrating the flora and fauna of the lake and of Monte Baldo. There is also a room dedicated to Goethe, who had been forced by unfavourable winds to land for a night at Malcesine, and while sketching the castle was almost arrested as an Austrian spy. The next day he docked at Bardolino, where he mounted a mule to cross into the Adige Valley for Verona. There is a fine view from the top of the tower. Concerts are often held in the castle. A cableway runs to the top of Monte Baldo, and there are pleasant walks in the area.

To the south, the coast becomes less wild. At **Cassone** (a suburb of Malcesine) there is a small Museo del Lago (*closed Mon*) in a building on the waterfront that was once a fish incubating plant. Further on, the road passes a cemetery and the early-12th-century church of San Zeno, and at **Pai** there is a magnificent view of the opposite shore of the lake. The coast here is known as the Riviera degli Olivi, from its many olive trees.

TORRI DEL BENACO

During the years of Venetian rule, Torri del Benaco (*map Veneto West A2*), the Roman *Castrum Turrium*, was the chief town of the Gardesana, a federation comprising ten towns between Malcesine and Lazise and headed by a Capitano del Lago. Today Torri has a pretty horseshoe-shaped port and the town itself is lively and attractive. In places you can still see stretches of its fortifying walls. At one end of the terrace of the waterfront **Gardesana hotel** (once the headquarters of the Gardesana council) is a monument to Domizio Calderini, a Humanist scholar born in Torri in 1444. The Latin epitaph is by his friend, the great Tuscan poet Poliziano. Behind it, the **Oratory of the Holy Trinity**, now a war memorial chapel, has 15th-century frescoes, including a *Last Supper* with fine fish.

Looming above the port are the swallowtail battlements of the impressive **Castello Scaligero**, a castle of the Della Scala dating from 1383 (*usually closed Mon and in the middle of the day*). It contains a small museum illustrating the history of fishing on the lake and the production of olive oil. There is a also a section dedicated to the rock carvings found in the district (*see below*), the oldest supposedly dating from 1500 BC. A splendid **limonaia** of 1760, which protects a plantation of huge old lemon trees—as well as citrons, mandarins and oranges—against its south wall, can also be visited: the scent of the blossom is delicious in spring. This is one of very few such structures to survive on the lake where once lemons were cultivated in abundance. Unfortunately it backs onto a field where boys play football, and at the time of writing, most of the glass panes had fallen victim to their over-enthusiastic kicks.

PUNTA SAN VIGILIO TO GARDA

The headland of **Punta di San Vigilio** (parking on the main road) is a romantic and secluded place, now occupied by a fine restaurant, Locanda San Vigilio, which is also a hotel. The complex includes a walled lemon garden and a café-bar on the waterfront, with tables out on the harbour mole. Their charming motto, "*En somnii explanatio*" (Here is the explanation of the dream), is taken from lines carved on a statue in the next-door chapel.

In the hills behind San Vigilio, a path leads to the **rock carvings of the Roccia de la Griselle**. A short way towards Garda, on the left, you will see the path (marked 'Graffiti') It leads uphill and then forks right into woodland. Follow the 'Graffiti' signs. A narrow path takes you to a flat rock (the second one you come to) covered with incised images of ships and weapons.

Roccia de la Griselle. One of the incised designs of ships.

From Punta di San Vigilio, it is possible to walk (in c. 30mins) all the way along the foreshore to town of **Garda** (*map Veneto West A2*), at the head of a deep bay, which developed as a resort after the Second World War. It was famous in the Roman and Lombard periods, and was later a fortified town; it still retains some fine old houses and a string of agreeable cafés. A very simple market is held on the waterfront.

BARDOLINO

The hills become lower and the landscape duller as the basin at the foot of the lake opens out. Bardolino (*map Veneto West A2*), another ancient place retaining some commercial importance, is well known for its **wine**, made from the Molinara, Corvina and Rondinella grape varieties. The crisp, dry, refreshing rosé known as Chiaretto is made in a style similar to the rosé of Provence. It is thought that the Romans introduced the technique simultaneously to both Cisalpine and Transalpine Gaul.

A tower and two gates remain from an old **Scaligeri castle**. In a little courtyard, is the tiny Carolingian church of **San Zeno**, which retains its 9th-century form with a tower above the crossing and ancient paving stones. It has four old capitals and fragments of frescoes. The 12th-century church of **San Severo** has contemporary frescoes.

LAZISE AND PESCHIERA
Lazise (*map Veneto West A2*), with a very pretty waterfront, retains part of its medieval wall and a castle of the Scaligeri, with Venetian additions. The 16th-century double-arched Venetian customs house on the lakefront attests to its former importance. San Nicolò is a 12th-century church with 16th-century additions and 14th-century frescoes.

Peschiera del Garda (*map Veneto West A2–A3*), an ancient fortress and one of the four corners of the Austrian 'quadrilateral' (the other three are Verona, Mantua and Legnago), stands at the outflow of the Mincio from Lago di Garda. The impressive fortifications, begun by the Venetians in 1553, were strengthened by Napoleon and again by the Austrians. Close by is Italy's most famous children's theme park, **Gardaland**, which opened in 1975, inspired by Disneyland. Today it receives around 3 million visitors a year.

LAKE GARDA PRACTICAL TIPS

GETTING AROUND

- **By train:** The Venice–Milan line serves Peschiera del Garda, Desenzano del Garda–Sirmione and Lonato, from which there are frequent country bus services to outlying points. Regional trains connect the lake stations to Verona or Brescia in less than 30mins; fast trains stop at Desenzano–Sirmione only, making the run in c. 20mins.
- **By bus:** Bus services run several times daily by the roads on the west and east banks from Peschiera and Desenzano to Riva. Frequent service from Verona via Lazise and Garda to Riva, and from Brescia to Desenzano, Sirmione, Peschiera and Verona, and between Salò and Desenzano, and Desenzano, Salò and Riva. Run by ATV, see www.atv.verona.it.
- **By boat:** Boat services (including two modernised paddle-steamers built in 1902 and 1903) are run by Navigazione Laghi (*navigazionelaghi.it*). These operate from around mid-March–early Nov (the timetable changes three times a year). A daily boat service runs between Desenzano and Riva in 4hrs, calling at various ports en route—but not all services follow the same route. Check the

website for details. Hydrofoils run twice daily in 2hrs 40mins (with fewer stops). All year round a car ferry operates between Maderno and Torri di Benaco in 30mins (every 30mins, but less frequently in winter) and there is a summer ferry from Limone to Malcesine in 20mins (hourly). Tickets are available allowing free travel on the lake services for a day. Tours of the lake in the afternoons in summer are also organised.

Motor and sailing boats can be rented from Garda Yachting Charter (*gyc.it*). The north tip of the lake around Riva is reserved for sailing boats.

• **By cablecar**: For details of the cablecar (*funivia*) service from Malcesine to Monte Baldo, see *funiviedelbaldo.it*.

WHERE TO STAY

Lake Garda has been a famous resort for well over a century and there is no shortage of places to stay, for all budgets. Most are seasonal, open from Easter until the end of Oct.

GARDONE RIVIERA
€€–€€€ **Bella Riva**. Family-friendly hotel right on the lake at Fasano, between Gardone and Maderno. In an old villa used for German embassy staff during the Republic of Salò, renovated with modern décor. Pleasant gardens right on the lakefront, with swimming pool. *Via Podini Mario 1/2, bellarivagardone.it*.
€€€ **Grand Hotel Fasano e Villa Principe**. A former hunting lodge of the emperors of Austria set in a lovely park with garden terrace overlooking the lake. *Via Zanardelli 190, Località Fasano del Garda, ghf.it*.

€€€ **Villa del Sogno**. The former villa of a German industrialist, used as a convalescence home by German officers during the Republic of Salò. Set in a beautiful garden with swimming pool and tennis court, the hotel is gracious and old-fashioned, impeccably run, with a vast and ample terrace overlooking the water, divided into a variety of sitting areas, for breakfast, pre-dinner cocktails, or dinner in the candlelit gazebo. *Via Zanardelli 107, villadelsogno.it*.
SAN VIGILIO
€€€ **Locanda San Vigilio**. Well-appointed rooms in the 15th-century house and its outbuildings right on the lake. Rooms vary a great deal; the nicest ones are in the house itself. Excellent restaurant attached. *locanda-sanvigilio.it*.
TORRI DEL BENACO
€–€€ **Albergo Gardesana**. Comfortable, friendly hotel overlooking the harbour and the castle. Very good value. Restaurant. Parking. *Piazza Calderini 5, gardesana.eu*.

WHERE TO EAT

DESENZANO
€€€ **Esplanade**. Fresh seasonal cuisine with a garden overlooking the lake. This has been an acclaimed place to eat for many years. *Via Lario 10, ristorante-esplanade.com*.
€€ **Cavallino**. Well established seafood restaurant with seasonal dishes and good wines. *Via Murachette 29, ristorantecavallino.it*.
GARDONE RIVIERA
€€€ **Lido 84**. Fine dining in a magnificent setting. Michelin-starred. Booking essential. *Corso Zanardelli 196, ristorantelido84.com*.

GARGNANO
€€€ **La Tortuga.** A gourmet's delight, known for fine food and excellent wines. By the harbour. *Via XXIV Maggio 5, ristorantelatortuga.it.*

LAZISE
€€ **Porticciolo.** Traditional cuisine of the lake area, especially fish. On the waterfront. *Lungolago Marconi 22, ilporticcioloristorante.it.*

MALCESINE
€€€ **Vecchia Malcesine.** A high-quality offering just south of the harbour. Michelin-starred. Booking essential. *Via Pisort 6, vecchiamalcesine.com.*

€ **Osteria Santo Cielo.** Very close to the park that surrounds the Town Hall, south of the port, a snug vaulted tavern serving salads, platters of cold meat and cheese and other snacks, to be washed down with a beaker of house wine. Informal, delightful. *Piazza Turazza 11.*

PESCHIERA
€€ **Albergo-Ristorante Papa** (with rooms). Good local food and wine. *Via Bell'Italia 38–40, albergo-papa.com.*

SALÒ
€€ **Gallo Rosso.** Excellent small restaurant in the historic town centre. *Vicolo Tomacelli 4, ristorantegallorosso.it.*

€ **Osteria dell'Orologio.** Wine bar with good selection of snacks and light meals downstairs and full restaurant service upstairs. *Via Butturini 26, osteriadellorologiosalo.eatbu.com.*

SAN VIGILIO
€€€ **Locanda San Vigilio.** Superb restaurant with an excellent wine list. In a lovely secluded spot. Eat either in the narrow loggia overlooking the water or in the old living room (with an open fire in chilly weather). *locandasanvigilio.it.*

SIRMIONE
€€€ **La Rucola 2.0.** Acclaimed restaurant very close to the castle. Michelin starred. Reservation essential. *Vicolo Strentelle 3, ristorantelarucola.it.*

€€€ **Osteria del Vecchio Fossato.** Inventive menu, warm, cosy, old-world atmosphere. A restaurant with a contented following. *Via Antiche Mura 16, osteriadelvecchiofossato.it.*

LOCAL SPECIALITIES

Lake fish (*coregone/lavarello*) and local wines are the things to look for. White wines made from the Lugana grape are invariably good. You rarely go wrong with a delicate Bardolino Chiaretto rosé. And Soave (white) and Valpolicella (red) are well known (*for more on those wines, see pp. 117ff*).

PRACTICAL INFORMATION

GETTING AROUND

BY PUBLIC TRANSPORT
The public transport network, composed of buses and trains (and ferries on Lake Garda) is extensive, though local buses sometimes cater mainly to schoolchildren or those commuting to and from work and are timetabled accordingly. Bus companies vary and timetables change seasonally. Website addresses are given in each individual chapter of this guide.

Trenitalia, the state operator (*trenitalia.com*), runs a mixture of high speed services, called Frecciarossa, and cheaper but slower regional trains, labelled Regionale (R) or Regionale Veloce (RV). Italo is a private high-speed alternative to Frecciarossa (*italotreno.com*).

By taxi: Taxis are hired from ranks or by telephone; there are no cruising cabs. Before engaging a taxi, make sure it has a meter in working order. Fares vary from city to city. No tip is expected but it will be appreciated if you round up the fare. Supplements are charged for late-night journeys and for luggage. If your destination is outside the town limits, it is worth asking roughly how much the fare is likely to be. Uber in Italy will just book you a regular taxi. There are other taxi apps (eg FreeNow and ItTaxi).

DRIVING IN ITALY
Regardless of whether you are driving your own car or a hired vehicle, Italian law requires you to have a red warning triangle (you can hire one from ACI for a minimal charge and return it at the border). In the Dolomites between Nov and April, you must have winter tyres.

Unless otherwise indicated, cars entering a road from the right are given precedence. Trams and trains always have right of way. If an oncoming driver flashes his headlights, it means he is proceeding and not giving you precedence. In towns, Italian drivers frequently change lanes without warning. They also tend to ignore pedestrian crossings.

Roads in Italy
As 80 percent of goods transported travel by road, there are a lot of lorries and trucks. Italy's motorways (*autostrade*) are indicated by green signs or, near the entrance ramps, by large boards of overhead lights. All are toll-roads: at the toll booths, choose the 'Biglietto' line (not Telepass). At the entrance to motorways, the two directions are indicated by the name of the most important town (and not by the nearest town), which can be momentarily confusing. Dual-carriageways are called *superstrade* (also indicated by green signs). Italy has an excellent network of

secondary highways (*strade statali*, *regionali* or *provinciali*) indicated by blue signs marked SS, SR or SP; on maps simply by a number.

Parking

Many cities have closed their centres to traffic (except for residents): the restricted zones are known as ZTLs. Access is allowed to hotels and for the disabled. It is always advisable to leave your car in a guarded car park, though with a bit of effort it is almost always possible to find a place to park free of charge, away from the town centre. However, to do so overnight is not advisable. Always lock your car when parked, and never leave anything of value inside it. A lot of parking spaces operate the '*disco orario*' system (marked by a sign), which allows you to park free for 2hrs. You indicate the time that you parked on the adjustable disc. Hire cars are usually fitted with a disc in their windscreens. They are also available at petrol stations and tobacconists.

GENERAL TIPS

DISABLED TRAVELLERS

All new public buildings are obliged to provide facilities for the disabled. Historic buildings are more difficult to convert, and access difficulties still exist. Hotels that cater for the disabled are indicated in tourist board lists. Airports and railway stations provide assistance, and certain trains are equipped to transport wheelchairs. Access to town centres is allowed for cars with disabled drivers or passengers, and special parking places are reserved for them. For further information, contact the tourist board in the city of interest.

OPENING TIMES

Museum opening times often change without warning. Many small museums are open only at weekends or by appointment. National museums are usually closed on Mondays and many are closed on the main public holidays: 1 Jan, Easter, 1 May, 15 Aug and 25 Dec. Archaeological sites and parks generally open at 9 and close at dusk. Where possible, website addresses have been given in the text of this guide. It is always advisable to check before you visit. Entrance fees vary.

Churches open early in the morning (often for 6 o'clock Mass), and most are closed during the middle of the day (from noon until 3, 4 or 5pm), although cathedrals and larger churches that have become tourist destinations may be open throughout daylight hours. Smaller churches and oratories are often open only in the early morning, but the key can usually be found by inquiring locally. The sacristan will also show closed chapels and crypts, and a small tip should be given. Some churches ask that sightseers do not enter during a service, but normally visitors may do so, provided they are silent and do not approach the altar in use. When entering any place of worship in Italy you should cover your legs and shoulders, and generally dress with decorum. An entrance fee is often charged for admission to treasuries, cloisters and bell-towers. Coin-operated lights are still used in many churches to illuminate frescoes and altarpieces so it is useful to arm yourself with a stock of 50 eurocent and 1 euro coins.

PERSONAL SECURITY

Pickpocketing is a widespread problem in towns all over Italy: it is always advisable not to carry valuables and to be particularly careful on public transport. Crime should be reported at once to the police or the local *carabinieri* office (found in every town and small village). A statement has to be given in order to get a document confirming loss or damage (essential for insurance claims). Interpreters are provided. For all emergencies, T: 112. The switchboard will co-ordinate the help you need. For medical assistance: T: 118.

PHARMACIES

Pharmacies (*farmacie*) are usually open Mon–Fri 9–1 & 4–7.30 or 8. A few are open also on Saturdays, Sundays and holidays (listed on the door of every pharmacy). In all towns there is also at least one pharmacy open at night (also shown on the door of every pharmacy).

PUBLIC HOLIDAYS

Italian national holidays are as follows:
- 1 January, *Capodanno*, New Year's Day
- 6 January Epiphany
- Easter Sunday and Easter Monday
- 25 April (Liberation Day)
- 1 May (Labour Day)
- 2 June (Festa della Repubblica)
- 15 August, *Ferragosto* (Assumption)
- 1 November (All Saints' Day)
- 8 December (Immaculate Conception)
- 25 December (Christmas Day)
- 26 December (St Stephen)

Each town keeps its patron saint's day as a holiday.

TELEPHONING

For all calls in Italy, dial the city code (for instance, 049 for Padua), then the telephone number. For international and intercontinental calls, dial 00 before the telephone number. The country code for Italy is +39.

TIPPING

Service charges are normally included and tipping in Italy is not routinely expected. It is normal to round up the bill and leave a few coins in appreciation.

ACCOMMODATION

A selection of places to stay, chosen on the basis of character or location, is given at the end of each section of this guide. They are classified as follows: €€€€ (€900 or over), €€€ (€350–900), €€ (€150–300) or € (€150 or under), but these classifications are only intended as a general guide and should not be taken as exact rates, since these vary seasonally and on different days of the week. It is advisable to book well in advance, especially between May and October; if you cancel the booking with at least 72 hours' notice you can claim back part or all of your deposit. Service charges are included in the rates. By law breakfast is an optional extra, although a lot of hotels will include it in the room price. When booking, always specify if you want breakfast or not.

EATING IN THE VENETO

RESTAURANTS

A very short selection of places to eat is given at the end of each section of this guide. Prices are categorised as follows: €€€€ (€80 or more per head), €€€ (€60–80), €€ (€40–50) and € (€30 or under), but as with the prices given for hotels, these are intended as a general guide only. Websites of restaurants have been given where possible: most take a day off during the week and some are not open on Sun evening. It is always worth checking and it is always a good idea to reserve.

Prices on the menu do not include a cover charge (shown separately), which is added to the bill. The service charge (*servizio*) is now almost always automatically added. Very simple establishments may not offer a written menu.

BARS AND CAFÉS

Counter-top bars and cafés are open from early morning and people tend to pop in for a coffee and a snack which they have standing up at the bar. The traditional rule is that you order at the bar (don't be intimidated by the throng, just call out your order), then pay the cashier, then present your receipt to the barman in order to get served, though in some places you pay the barman when you have finished your drink or snack. A small tip will be appreciated. If you sit at a table, where you will get waiter service, the charge is usually higher. When going for an evening *aperitivo*, you can order at the bar but there is almost always table service, and nibbles (sometimes quite hearty; sometimes just a few crisps or peanuts) will be served with your drink.

COFFEE

Italy has excellent coffee. *Caffè* (which essentially mans *espresso*) can be ordered *lungo* (diluted), *corretto* (with a liquor) or *macchiato* (with a dash of hot milk). *Cappuccino* is generally considered a breakfast drink. A glass of hot milk with a dash of coffee in it, *latte macchiato* is another early-morning favourite. In summer you will find *caffè freddo* (iced coffee). Most bars now offer lactose free milk, oat milk etc.

SNACKS

Gelato (ice cream) is always best from a *gelateria* where it is made on the spot: the best ones can have long queues outside them in summer. *Panini* (sandwiches) are made with a variety of cold meats, fish, cheeses or vegetables, for example spinach (*spinaci*), *melanzane* (aubergines), *zucchini* (courgettes) fried in vegetable oil. When you ask for one, the barman will usually ask if you want it heated up. Slices of pizza and *arancini* (rice croquettes with cheese or meat inside) are also easy to find. Sweet snacks include breakfast pastries (croissants, either plain or filled with chocolate, confectioner's custard or jam) and different varieties of tart (*crostata*).

PASTA

Pasta is an essential part of most meals throughout Italy. A distinction is drawn between *pasta comune* (e.g. spaghetti) produced industrially and made of a simple flour and water paste, and *pasta all'uovo* (tortellini, ravioli and so on), made with egg.

Pasta comes in countless forms. An ordinary Italian supermarket usually stocks about 50 different varieties, but some experts estimate that there are more than 600 shapes in all. The differences of shape translate into differences of flavour, even when the pasta is made from the same dough, or by the same manufacturer. The reason for this is that the relation between the surface area and the weight of the pasta varies from one shape to another, causing the sauce to adhere in different ways and to different degrees. Even without a sauce, experts claim to perceive considerable differences in flavour, because the different shapes cook in different ways.

Northern Italy is home to *pasta fresca*, usually home-made, from a dough composed of flour, eggs, and just a little water. Typical pasta shapes of the Veneto region include tagliatelle and *bigoli* (a stout form of spaghetti), known in dialect at *bigoi*.

REGIONAL CUISINE

The cuisine of much of the Veneto is basically Venetian with local variations. Fish and seafood form the basis of many main courses. Specialities include *seppioline nere* (cuttlefish cooked in their own ink) and dishes involving *baccalà* (salt cod). Look out also for *folpi* or *moscardini*, baby octopus. In the Po delta, you will find eel and sturgeon. Poultry is also popular: you will see a lot of duck, and the preference for poultry over pork or beef gets stronger the closer you are to the coast. A popular first course is tagliatelle in *brodo d'anatra* (duck broth). Thick soups are also popular. The best of these is *pasta e fasioi* (pasta and beans), which is eaten lukewarm, having been left to 'set up' for an hour or so before being served. *Radicchio trevigiano* (long, narrow radicchio from Treviso) is popular all over the region, eaten in salads, grilled, fried, in risotto or as a sauce for tagliatelle. In Padua, you will also see *rovinassi* as a pasta sauce: these are chicken or duck livers (and other offal), mixed with onions and other vegetables into a tasty ragout.

Cornmeal polenta is often used as a staple, as is rice, which is grown all along the Po valley. First courses are traditionally rice-based, either a risotto or a rice soup (the Veneto is said to have the most varieties of risotto anywhere in Italy; *Vialone nano* is the local risotto rice variety, grown around Verona). *Risotto nero* is made with cuttlefish ink. *Risi e bisi* (rice mixed with peas) typically has a consistency somewhere between a risotto and a soup.

Other popular traditional dishes are *bovoloni*, *bovoletti* or *bogoni* (snails in butter, garlic, and parsley); *piccioni torresani allo spiedo* (pigeon on the spit) and *cappone alla canavera* (capon cooked inside an ox bladder). *Sopa coâda* from Treviso is a pigeon and vegetable broth, called '*zuppa alla scaligera*' in Verona as it was said to have been served at the court of the Della Scala. The great speciality of Verona, however, is gnocchi, served in melted butter or tomato sauce, or with a meat ragout. The most famous of these ragouts (often also served with polenta) is the *pastissada de caval*, a rich stew of horsemeat and aromatic herbs. The story is that it was invented after the Battle of Verona, which was fought between Theodoric and Odoacer in AD 489 (Theodoric won). So many horses fell on the battlefield that a use had to be found for their meat. *Risotto al tastasal* is another popular favourite; the rice is flavoured with chopped salami.

Other Veneto dishes include fish from Lake Garda, notably *lavarello*, and *boliti misti* or *lesso* (boiled meat) with *pearà*, a sauce of breadcrumbs, butter, ox marrow, parmesan cheese, salt and pepper (*pearà* means peppered). In the mountain regions you will generally find a lot more meat and dairy, including delicious cured meats and cheeses.

Among the sweets is the Veronese *pandoro*, a great fluffy cake eaten at Christmas, and the ring-shaped Easter *brasadela*. *Bussolà vicentino* is a ring-shaped cake made very simply from flour, eggs, butter and sugar. The rich dessert *tiramisù* is also a Veneto invention, claimed by Treviso. Very Paduan is the *torta pazientina*, a sponge cake layered with *zabaglione* cream.

WINE

The Veneto is famous for its wines. More detail about some of them (Valpolicella, Soave, Prosecco) is given in the relevant chapters of this guide.

Italy's *appellation controlée* is the DOC (*di origine controllata*), which specifies maximum yields per vine, geographical boundaries within which grapes must be grown, permitted grape varieties and production techniques. Superior even to DOC is the DOCG (*di origine controllata e garantita*). This is not to say that DOCG wines are automatically superior. A plethora of regulation, as well as over-expansion, has led some winemakers to choose to exit the DOC system, wanting to experiment with alternative grape varieties or different vinification techniques. Instead they label their vintages IGT (*indicazione geografica tipica*), classifying them as wines of special regional character. An IGT wine, therefore, is not necessarily of lesser quality than a DOC. Indeed, in some cases it may be particularly interesting. Wines designated *vino da tavola* are simple table wines. It can be excellent, but the quality is not guaranteed.

Red wines are *vini rossi* on the wine list; white wines, *vini bianchi*; rosés, *chiaretti* or *rosati*. Dry wines are *secchi*; sweet wines, *amabili* or *dolci*. *Vino novello* is new wine. *Passito* wines are made from grapes that have been specially dried before pressing, to concentrate the sweetness.

GLOSSARY OF TERMS

Androne, in a Venetian palace, the central ground-floor hall

Amphora, antique vase, usually of large dimensions, for oil and other liquids

Annunciation, the appearance of the Angel Gabriel to Mary to tell her that she will bear the Son of God; an image of the 'Virgin Annunciate' shows her receiving the news

Apostles, those who spread the Christian word, traditionally twelve in number, in other words the disciples (excluding Judas but with his replacement Matthias), and later including St Paul and his followers

Apse, vaulted semicircular end wall of the chancel of a church or of a chapel

Architrave, the lowest part of an entablature (*qv*), the horizontal frame over a door

Assumption, the ascension of the Virgin to Heaven, 'assumed' by the power of God

Attic, the topmost storey of a building, hiding the spring of the roof

Basilica, originally a Roman building used for public administration; in Christian architecture, an aisled church with a clerestory (*qv*) and apse

Bas-relief, sculpture in low relief

Bucranic, featuring a form of Classical decoration featuring carved ox heads (bucrania) and garlands

Campanile, bell-tower (pl. *campanili*)

Cavea, the part of a theatre or amphitheatre occupied by the tiers of seats

Chiaroscuro, distribution of light and shade, apart from colour, in a painting

Comune, in medieval central and northern Italy, a self-governing town

Condottiere, captain-general of a city militia; soldier of fortune at the head of an army

Corinthian, order of Classical architecture easily identified by its column capitals decorated with curling acanthus leaves

Cornice, the uppermost part of an entablature (*qv*); the raking cornice is formed by the angled cornices enclosing the sides of the tympanum (*qv*), e.g. above a portico. A cornice can also refer to any projecting strip of ornamental moulding at the top of a building under the roof or at the top of a wall beneath the ceiling

Decumanus maximus, the main east–west street of a Roman town

Diptych, painting or tablet in two sections

Doctors of the Church, St Ambrose, St Augustine, St Gregory and St Jerome

Doric, order of Classical architecture characterised by stout, fluted columns widening towards the bottom, meeting the pavement directly, with no base, and capped by a simple ring capital

Dormition, the death of the Virgin Mary, often portrayed in art as a 'falling asleep'

Duomo, the principal church of a town

Engaged, of a column, not free-standing; forming a part of the pier or section of wall to which it is attached

Entablature, the continuous horizontal element above the column capitals (consisting of architrave, frieze and cornice) of a Classical building

Evangelists, the authors of the four Gospels, Matthew, Mark, Luke and John, often depicted in art through their symbols, respectively the man/angel, lion, bull and eagle

Exedra, a recessed area, square or curved, projecting from a room or other space

Ex-voto, tablet or small painting expressing gratitude to a saint

Ghibelline, in medieval Italy, during the internecine squabbling for power, the faction that supported the Holy Roman Emperor over the Pope

Gipsoteca, a gallery of sculptures and casts made of plaster

Gold-ground, of early medieval altarpieces, with the saints and holy figures painted against a background of gilding

Grotesque, painted or stucco decoration in the style of the ancient Romans (found during the Renaissance in Nero's Domus Aurea or 'Golden House' in Rome, then underground, hence the name, from 'grotto'). The delicate ornamental decoration usually includes patterns of flowers, sphinxes, birds, human figures etc, against a light ground

Guelph, in medieval Italy, during the internecine squabbling for power, the faction that supported the Pope over the Holy Roman Emperor

Incunabulum, (pl. incunabula), any book printed before 1500, in the same century as the invention of movable type

Intarsia, inlay of wood, marble, or metal

Ionic, order of Classical architecture characterised by slender fluted columns mounted on a base and capped by a capital with twin scrolls

Krater, ancient Classical mixing vessel, conical in shape

Loggia, covered, arcaded or colonnaded gallery or balcony, usually at ground or first-floor level

Lombard, pertaining to a Christian people who arrived in Italy in the 6th century, dominating much of it and establishing duchies. They were conquered and superseded by Charlemagne in the 8th century

Lunette, semicircular space in a vault or ceiling, or over a door or window, often decorated with a painting or relief

Mastio, of a castle, the keep

Metope, a panel inserted between triglyphs (*qv*) in the frieze of a Doric temple

Municipium, town or settlement founded before the Roman conquest and later Romanised and given certain privileges; today, a *municipio* is a Town Hall

Ogival, in architecture, featuring ogees, in other words peaked curves

Orans, praying (Latin). In art, the *Virgin Orans* is usually shown with her hands raised

Palaeochristian, from the earliest Christian times up to the 6th century

Pendentive, concave spandrel beneath a dome, linking it to the rectilinear architecture of the main body of the building

Peristyle, court or garden surrounded by a columned portico

Piano nobile, the 'noble floor', referring to the first floor of a palazzo, where the grandest rooms were to be found

Pietà, group (usually featuring the Virgin) mourning the dead Christ

Pietre dure, hard or semi-precious stones, often used in the form of mosaics to decorate cabinets, table tops etc.

Pilaster, shallow pier or rectangular column projecting only slightly from the wall

Polyptych, painting or tablet in more than three sections

Predella, small painting or narrow rectangular panel, usually in sections, attached below a large altarpiece

Pronaos, vestibule or anteroom in front of the main chamber of a temple

Putto (pl. putti), sculpted or painted figure of a little naked boy

Ragione, lit. 'reason'. A *Palazzo della Ragione* in a medieval town was the *Palais de Justice* or magistrates' court

Rhaetians, an ancient people, an alliance of pre-Roman alpine tribes

Risorgimento, the 'Resurgence', the period of 19th-century Italian history characterised by an upswelling of national feeling, dominated by characters like Garibaldi, who ultimately led the country to unification and to freedom from Austrian, Bourbon and papal rule

Rocca, a castle or fortress, the word deriving from the Persian *rukh* (hence a 'rook' in chess)

Romanesque, style of architecture pre-dating the Gothic, largely from the 12th century, characterised by massive columns and round arches. The equivalent of Norman in Britain

Rusticated, of masonry cladding, having deep grooves or channels cut between the blocks, giving a sturdy appearance

Scaena, in an ancient theatre, the backdrop behind the stage

Sinopia, large sketch for a fresco made on the rough wall in a red earth pigment called *sinopia*, because it originally came from Sinop on the Black Sea. Pl. *sinopie*

Situla, bucket- or beaker-shaped vessel for ritual use

Stele, upright stone bearing a commemorative inscription

Stoup, vessel for Holy Water, usually near the entrance of a church

Tabernacle, wall recess fronted by a decorative framework or a free-standing ornamental casket, meant to house sacred objects; small street shrine with a votive image

Terraferma, 'dry land', used by Venice to describe her holdings on the Italian mainland, as opposed to overseas

Thermal window, semicircular in form, divided into three lights by two vertical elements. The name comes from its use in the architecture of ancient Roman baths (*thermae*). Often used in Palladio's architecture

Tondo (pl. *tondi*), round painting or relief

Trabeated, of a door or window aperture or colonnade: having a horizontal lintel as opposed to an arched one

Transept, one of two lateral 'arms' in a church, opening to left and right from the top of the nave, before the steps into the sanctuary or chancel

Tribune, in architecture, a raised platform; in a church, the raised area at the vaulted or apsidal east end

Triclinium, the 'dining room' of an ancient Roman house, furnished with couches

Triglyph, section of the frieze of a Doric temple decorated with three inscised vertical lines

Triptych, painting or tablet in three sections

Trompe l'oeil, literally a 'deception of the eye'. Used to describe illusionist decoration, painted architectural perspectives, etc

Tuscan, when referring to a column, possessing a simple Doric-style capital, mounted on a base, and unfluted

Tympanum, the triangular or semicircular space enclosed by a pediment and raking cornice, above a portico, doorway or other aperture

INDEX

Numbers in italics are picture references. More detailed references are given in bold.

Abano Terme 43
Abbazia di Praglia 43
Abbazia di Santa Maria delle Carceri 49
Accommodation 178
Adria 57
Agugliaro 78
Alberti, Giuseppe 70
Allegrini, winemakers 119, 120
Alpini regiment 85
Alpini, Prospero 88
Altavilla Vicentina 78
Altichiero **17**, 31, 32, 101, **105**, 111, 113, 114
Altinum 10
Altivole 143
Altopiano dei Sette Comuni 88
Ammannati, Bartolomeo 22
Andreolo de' Santi 97
Annigoni, Pietro 31
Anselmi, Giorgio 85
Anselmi, Roberto 117
Antenor 15; (tomb of) 36
Anthony of Padua, St 27
Antonino Veneziano 71, 73
Antonio da Mestre 111
Antonio da Treviso 129
Anzù 152
Arosio, Filippo 22
Arquà Petrarca 45
Asiago 88, 147
Asolo 138ff, *138*, *140*, *142*
Aspetti, Tiziano 28
Attila the Hun 10
Austria, Austrian rule in the Veneto 9, 15, 45, 53, 86, 120, 121, 127, 146, 147, 150, 162, 163, 172
Badia Polesine 55
Badile, Antonio 107, 114
Badile, Giovanni 103, 107, 114
Bagnolo 78

Balzac, Honoré de 152
Bambaia (Agostino Busti) 131
Barbieri, Giuseppe 94
Bardolino 171
Basaiti, Marco 22
Bassano del Grappa *82*, 83
Bassano family, artists 83
Bassano, Francesco the Elder 84
Bassano, Francesco the Younger 27, 88
Bassano, Jacopo 64, 84, 88, 129, 134, 136, 141, 153
Bassano, Leandro 13, 68, 84
Bastiani, Sebastiano 141
Batoni, Pompeo 125
Battaglia Terme 43
Bellano, Bartolomeo 17, 30
Bellini, Gentile (brother of Giovanni) 151
Bellini, Giovanni 13, 22, 53, 68, 108, 128
Bellini, Jacopo (father of Giovanni) 108
Belluno 153
Belzoni, Giovanni Battista 21, 23
Bembo, Cardinal Pietro 139, 141
Bernardi, Giuseppe 141
Bertesina 78
Bibiena, Francesco 110
Bissolo, Francesco 125
Bistolfi, Leonardo 167
Bolca 118; (fossils from) 113
Bolzano Vicentino 78
Bonazza, Antonio (son of Giovanni) 49
Bonazza, Giovanni 125
Bonin, Paolo 66
Bonino da Campione 97, 98
Boninsegna, Bonaventura 101
Bonsignori, Francesco 107, 110
Bordone, Paris 122, 124, 125, 129
Bortoloni, Mattia 135
Bosco Chiesanuova 118
Breganze 78
Bregno, Giovanni Battista 125

Bregno, Lorenzo (brother of Giovanni Battista) 124, 125, 129
Brenta Canal 39
Brioloto 109
Briosco, Andrea (*see Riccio, Il*)
Browning, Robert 139, 141, 142, 143
Brusasorci, Domenico 64, 104, 107, 108, 113, 114, 120
Brusasorci, Felice (son of Domenico) 104, 107
Brustolon, Andrea 129, 152, 153, 155, 157
Buonconsiglio, Giovanni 51
Burchiello, canal boat 39
Byron, Lord 40, 45, 46, 49, 113, 159
Ca' Falier 143
Cadore region 156
Calderari, Ottone 60
Caldiero 118
Caldogno 78
Caliari, Benedetto (brother of Veronese) 134
Caliari, Gabriele (father of Veronese) 99, *100*
Callido, Gaetano 129
Campagna, Girolamo 28, 95, 129
Campagnola, Domenico (son of Giulio) 36, 44
Campagnola, Giulio 36
Canaletto, Antonio 70
Canera, Anselmo 75, 80
Canova, Antonio 22, 84, 143, **145**; (birthplace and museum) 144
Caorle 11
Capriolo, Domenico 126
Carducci, Giosuè 138
Carlevarijs, Luca 70
Caroto, Giovan Francesco 104, 105, 107, 108, 112, 113, 114, 120
Carpaccio, Vittore 13, 108
Carpioni, Giulio 64, **65**, 72, 73
Carrà, Carlo 151
Carraresi family 15, 34, 35, 48, 50, 121, 136
Carriera, Rosalba 13
Cartigliano 88
Cassone 170
Castelfranco Veneto 132
Castelgomberto 79
Castello del Catajo 44
Castello di San Pelagio 44

Cattaneo, Danese 28, 30
Catullus, villa of 160
Celesti, Andrea 67, 88, 167
Cesa, Matteo 155
Chagall, Marc 151
Chess game (Marostica) 87
Chioggia 11, *12*
Chioggiotto, Il (*see Marinetti*)
Cima da Conegliano 13, 48, 64, 128, 146, 148, 151
Cimbri, ancient people 88, 118, 119
Cini, Count Vittorio 47
Cittadella 135
Cogollo 119
Colli Euganei 43; (wine) 52
Colzè 79
Commonwealth war cemeteries 147
Conegliano Veneto 146
Cornaro Piscopia, Elena 24
Cornaro, Queen Caterina 11, *140*, 141, **141**, 142, 143
Cortina d'Ampezzo 156
Coryate, Thomas 112
Cosini, Silvio 28
Costozza 79
Craffonara, Giuseppe 169
Cricoli 75
Crivelli, Carlo 108
Crosato, Giambattista 135
Curtoni, Domenico 94
D'Annunzio, Gabriele d' 45, 143, **166**; (home of) 166
Dante 7, 17, 96, 98, 130, 160; (tomb of son of) 131
Da Romano family (Ezzelini) 15, 35, 48, 50, 84, 86, 87, 132, 136
Della Scala family (Scaligeri) 59, 87, 88, 91, 97, *97*, **108**, 117, 132, 160, 162, 170, 171; (tombs of) 96
Della Valle, Andrea 44
Desenzano del Garda 161
Dickens, Charles 41
Dolo 40
Dolomites 155
Domenico da Lugo 102
Domenico da Venezia 66
Donatello 17, 29, 30, **31**, *31*, 32, 36

Dorigny, Louis 70, 75, 79
Dos Passos, John 86
Due Carrare 44
Dueville 79
Dunant, Henry 162
Dürer, Albrecht 85
Duse, Eleonora 139, 141, 142, 143, 166; (grave of) 143
Dyck, Sir Antony van 65
Emerson, Ralph Waldo 48
Enego 88
Eraclea 11
Este 48
Euganean Hills 43
Evelyn, John 112
Ezzelini family (*see Da Romano*)
Fabricius, surgeon 24
Falconetto, Giovanni Maria 17, 26, 27, 28, 34, 35, 44, 102
Fallopius, scientist 24
Fanzolo 134
Farinati, Paolo 101, 103, 104, 107, 113
Fascist government (Salò) 163
Fasolo, Giovanni Antonio 79, 80, 81
Fattori, Giovanni 151
Feltre 150
Ferrari, Ettore 54
Fiorentino, Giallo 55
Fogolino, Marcello 68
Fontana, Domenico 62
Food and drink, general 178ff
Foza 88
Francesco da Milano 146
Francesco dai Libri 114
Franco, Battista 41
Fratta Polesine 55
Fumane 119, 120
Fusina 41
Galileo 24
Gallio 88
Garda, Lake 159ff
Garda (town) 171
Gardaland 172
Gardone Riviera 164, *164*
Gargnano 168
Gaspari, Antonio Francesco 49
Gattamelata, *condottiere* 31, *31*

Gentile da Fabriano 127, 128
Giambono, Michele 22, 101, 108
Giavera 147
Giazza 119
Giocondo, Fra' 127
Giolfino, Nicolò 99, 102, 108, 110, 114
Giordano, Luca 71, 114
Giorgione 22, 51, 132, **132**, *133*; (house of) 134
Giotto 17, *20*, 21
Giovanni da Verona, Fra' 103, 107, 114
Giovanni degli Eremitani, Fra' 24
Girolamo dai Libri 101, 105, 107, 108, 114, 115
Girolamo da Santacroce 129
Girolamo dal Santo 36
Girolamo da Treviso the Elder 124
Girolamo da Treviso the Younger 129
Giulio Romano 44, 70, 102
Giusto de' Menabuoi *14*, 17, 21, 22, **26**, 27, 29
Goethe 34, 62, 72, 73, 112, 159, 168, 170
Goldoni, Carlo 13, 39
Grappa (drink) 83, 85; (mountain) 86
Graziolo, Francesco 141, 143, 144
Greppi, Giovanni 86
Grisignano di Zocco 79
Gualtiero 35
Guardi, Francesco 70
Guariento 17, 21, 22, 34, 84
Guercino 114
Guidi, Virgilio 148
Haring, Keith 165
Hayez, Francesco 126
Heller, André 165
Hemingway, Ernest 83, 86, 139, 147, 157
Hitler, Adolf 40
Howard, Thomas, Earl of Arundel 8; (burial place of) 32
Huxley, Aldous 156
India, Bernardino 75, 80, 120
Istrana 134
Jacopo da Montagnana 155
Jacopo da Verona 35
James, Henry 139
Jappelli, Giuseppe 23, 43, 49
Jefferson, Thomas 81

Jesolo 10
Juvarra, Filippo 153
Laghetto della Costa 46; (finds from) 48
Lago di Garda 159ff
Lago di Ledro 168
Lago di Misurina 157
Lawrence, D.H. 159
Lawrence, Thomas 126
Lazise 172
League of Cambrai, War of 150, 156
Le Court, Juste 31
Ledro, lake 168
Lendinara 55
Lentiai 153
Lessinia region 118
Levada 135
Liberale da Verona 101, 102, 108, 112
Liberi, Pietro 54, 67
Lichtenstein, Roy 165
Lido di Jesolo 10
Limone sul Garda 168
Livy 15
Lombardo, Antonio (brother of Tullio) 27, 28, 125
Lombardo, Pietro (father of Tullio) 31, 44, 125
Lombardo, Tullio 27, 28, 44, 125, 150, 152, 153
Lombards 6, 10, 47, 151
Longa 79
Longare 79
Longhena, Baldassare 54, 57, 73
Longhi, Alessandro (son of Pietro) 53, 129
Longhi, Pietro 70, 129
Lonigo 79
Lorenzo da Bologna 70, 74
Lorenzo Veneziano 67, 68, 99, 101, 109
Loreo 57
Lotto, Lorenzo 128, 130, *140*, 141
Lugo di Vicenza 79
Lusiana Conco 88
Luvigliano 44
Luzzo, Lorenzo 151, 152
Maestro Guglielmo 109
Maestro degli Innocenti 127
Maestro Nicolò 102, 109
Maffei, Francesco 54, **54**, 64, 72

Maganza, Alessandro **65**, 67, 69, 73, 74, 75
Maganza, Giovanni Battista (son of Alessandro) 69, 81
Malcesine 169
Malcontenta, Villa 40, *41*
Mantegna, Andrea 17, 22, 32, 85, 108, 110, 118
Margutti, Domenico 86
Marieschi, Michele 70
Marinali, Angelo (brother of Orazio) 70
Marinali, Francesco (brother of Orazio) 78
Marinali, Orazio 77, 79, 80, 84, 134
Marinetti, Antonio ('Il Chioggiotto') 13
Mario, Alberto 55
Mariscalchi, Pietro 151, 152
Maroni, Giancarlo 166
Marostica 87
Martial, Latin poet 10
Martini, Arturo 122, 126
Martino da Verona 110, 113
Maser 144
Massari, Giorgio 77, 80, 134
Massari, Muttonio 80
Matteotti, Giacomo 55
Meduna, Giambattista 54, 134
Memling, Hans 64
Michele da Firenze 101
Michele da Verona 102
Michetti, Francesco Paolo 151
Minello, Antonio 28, 51
Minello, Giovanni (son of Antonio) 27
Minio, Tiziano 35
Mira 40
Miretto, Nicolò 25
Miró, Joan 165
Misurina, lake 157
Moderno, Il 129
Molina di Ledro 168
Monselice 46
Montagna, Bartolomeo 27, 44, 64, 67, 68, 71, 74, 88, 114, 155
Montagna, Benedetto (son of Bartolomeo) 66
Montagnana 50
Monte Baldo 169
Monte Grappa 86
Monte Ricco 156
Montecchio Maggiore 80

Monteforte d'Alpone 117
Montegalda 80
Montegrotto Terme 43
Monteviale 80
Monti Lessini 118
Moretto, Il 105, 113
Morone, Domenico 107, 110
Morone, Francesco (son of Domenico) 99, 101, 107, 108, 110, 113, 114
Moroni, Andrea 33
Morto da Feltre (*see Luzzo*)
Mosca, Giovanni Maria 28
Mussolente 86
Mussolini, Benito 40, 163, 164, 168
Muttoni, Francesco 71, 72, 77, 80, 81
Nanni di Bartolo 101, 112
Napoleon, Napoleonic rule 9, 40, 53, 86, 96, *96*, 120, 145, 172
Napoleon III 162, 163
Negrar 119
Nove 88
Orgiano 80
Padua 25ff
  Baptistery 26
  Basilica of St Anthony (Santo) 27
  City walls 34
  Commonwealth War Cemetery 34
  Duomo 26
  Eremitani 21
  Gattamelata statue 31, *31*
  Loggia e Odeo Cornaro 35
  Market places 24
  Museo Diocesano 26
  Museo La Specola 35
  MuSME 36
  Orto Botanico 34
  Palazzo Liviano 24
  Palazzo della Ragione 24, *25*
  Pedrocchi café 23
  Piazza del Capitaniato 26
  Piazza dei Signori 26
  Prato della Valle 33
  Reggia Carrarese Chapel 34
  S. Francesco 36
  S. Giustina 33
  S. Maria dei Servi 36
  S. Michele 35

Padua contd
  S. Rocco 35
  Scoletta del Carmine 36
  Scrovegni Chapel 17, *20*
  Tomba di Antenore 36
  University 23
Pai 170
Paladino, Mimmo 165
Palladio 30, 59, 60, **60**, 64, *64*, 65, 68, 71, 72, **77**; (Basilica in Vicenza) 66; (bridge at Bassano) *82*, 85; (Teatro Olimpico) 62; (villas by) 40, *41*, 50, 55, 75, , 78, 79, 80, 81 134, 135, *135*, 144; (museum) 70; (first burial place of) 68
Palma, Antonio (father of Palma Giovane) 129
Palma Giovane 47, 51, 134, 151, 153
Palma Vecchio (great-uncle of Palma Giovane) 70
Paolo Veneziano 13, 27, 64
Parco Nazionale delle Dolomiti Bellunesi 155
Pennacchi, Pier Maria 128
Pensaben, Marco 130
Peschiera del Garda 172
Petacci, Claretta 165
Petrarch 22, **45**; (house of) 46; (tomb of daughter of) 131
Piave river 147
Piazzetta, Giovanni Battista 32, 53
Picasso, Pablo 151
Pietro de Saliba 125
Pieve di Cadore 156
Pigafetta, Antonio 72
Piombino Dese 135
Piovene, Antonio 60
Pisanello 101, *106*, **107**, 108, 112, 127
Pisani, Girolamo 81
Pisano, Giovanni 21
Pisis, Filippo de 148, 157
Pittoni, Francesco (uncle of Giovanni Battista) 71
Pittoni, Giovanni Battista 65, 68
Pittoni, Girolamo 67, 68
Pizzocaro, Antonio 77, 79, 81
Po Delta, Polesine 54, 56
Poiana Maggiore 80
Ponte di Veja 118

Ponti, Giò 24
Pordenone 124, 148
Porto Tolle 57
Possagno 144
Pozzoserrato 122, 123, 146
Praglia, Abbey of 43
Preti, Francesco Maria 135
Prosdocimus, St 33, 141
Prosecco 145
Quarto d'Altino 10
Quinto Vicentino 80
Radicchio 137
Recoaro Terme 88
Republic of Salò 163
Rhaetians 150
Ricchi, Pietro 169
Ricci, Marco (nephew of Sebastiano) 65, 151, 155
Ricci, Sebastiano 65, 152, **154**, 155
Riccio, Il 17, 22, 30, **30**, 33, 36, 112
Ridolfi, Bartolomeo 80
Risorgimento, sites associated with 23, 74, 163
Riva del Garda 169
Rivoli Veronese 120
Rizzarda, Carlo 151
Rizzo, Antonio 130
Roana 88
Roccia de la Griselle, rock carvings 171, *171*
Rocco da Vicenza 68
Romanino (Girolamo Romani) 105, 164
Romeo and Juliet 98, 113
Roncà 119
Rosolina 57
Rossetti, Biagio 53
Rotzo 88, 89
Rovigo 53
Rubini, Agostino (nephew of Alessandro Vittoria) 62
Rubini, Lorenzo 65, 72
Rubino, Giovanni 28
Ruzante (Andrea Beloco) 35, 144
Salò 163
San Martino della Battaglia 162
San Pelagio 44
San Vigilio, Punta di 171
San Vito di Altivole 143

Sandrigo 80
Sanmicheli, Michele 30, 50, 53, 78, 91, 96, 101, 102, 104, 105, **105**, 110; (monument to) 115
Sansovino, Jacopo 28, 51, 64, 102
Sant'Ambrogio 120
Sant'andrea 134
Santi Vittore e Corona, sanctuary of 152
Sarego 80
Savoldo, Giovanni Girolamo 130
Scaligeri (*see Della Scala*)
Scamozzi, Vincenzo 40, 44, 47, 49, 60, 62, *63*, 75, 77, 79, 81, 86, 135; (monument to) 71
Scarpa, Carlo 47, 108, 139, 143, 144, 151
Schiavone, Andrea 155
Schoenberg, Arnold 139
Scienza, Vittore 152
Scrovegni, Enrico 17; (tomb of) 21
Seitz, Ludovico 125
Serena, Luigi 122, 126
Shelley, Mary 48, 49
Shelley, Percy Bysshe 43, 49
Sile river 130
Sirmione 159, *160*, *161*
Soave 117
Solferino 162
Squarcione, Francesco 22
Stagliano, Arturo 129
Stark, Dame Freya 139, 141; (grave of) 143
Stefano da Ferrara 25
Stefano da Zevio 101, 107, 108, 111
Stefano dell'Arzere 36
Stella, Paolo 28
Stra 39
Sustris, Lambert 44
Tentorello 68
Tezze 147
Thiene 81
Tiepolo, Giambattista 13, 27, 32, 40, 49, 53, 65, 75, 79, 80, 84, 129, 161
Tiepolo, Gian Domenico (son of Giambattista) 65, 75, 129
Tintoretto, Jacopo 13, 22, 64, 104, 152
Tirali, Andrea 47
Tiramisù 137
Titian 22, 32, 102, 124, 128, 147, 148, 156;

(birthplace of) 156
Tommaso da Modena 122, 123, 126, 128, 129, 130, 131
Torbido, Francesco 102, 107, 109, 111
Torbole sul Garda 169
Torri del Benaco 170, *170*
Toscolano-Maderno 167
Tosi, Arturo 151
Tredici Comuni 118
Treviso 121ff
Turchi, Alessandro 101
Turone 101, 111
Ubertini, Francesco 114
Val d'Illasi 119
Valdobbiadene 145
Valpolicella 119
Valsanzibio 44
Vancimuglio 81
Vecellio, Cesare (cousin of Titian) 153, 156
Veneti, ancient people 5, 15, 58
Venetian lagoon 10
Venice, Venetians 6, 10, 11, 15, 39, 41, 50, 53, 59, 84, 87, 121, 132, 150, 153, 169, 172
Verona 90ff
  Arena 94
  Castel San Pietro 104, *104*
  Castelvecchio *106*, 108
  Della Scala tombs 97
  Duomo 101
  Giardini Giusti 112
  Juliet's house and tomb 98, 113
  Museo degli Affreschi 113
  Museo Archeologico 104
  Museo Lapidario Maffeiano 94
  Museo Miniscalchi-Erizzo 113
  Museo di Storia Naturale 113
  Piazza Brà 91
  Piazza delle Erbe 95, *95*
  Piazza dei Signori 95, *96*
  Roman gates *90*, 94
  Roman theatre 103
  S. Anastasia 98, *100*
  S. Bernardino 110
  S. Eufemia 113
  S. Fermo 111
  S. Giorgio in Braida 104

Verona contd
  S. Maria in Organo 113
  S. Maria della Scala 114
  SS. Nazaro e Celso 114
  S. Paolo 114
  S. Stefano 104
  S. Tomaso Cantuariense 115
  S. Zeno 109
Veronese, Paolo 22, 34, 51, 69, 74, 104, 105, 108, 114, 134, 144, 167
Vicenza 59ff
  Basilica 66
  Corso Palladio 60
  Duomo 67
  Loggia del Capitaniato *64*, 65
  Monte Berico 74
  Museo Civico 64
  Museo Diocesano 67
  Museo Palladio 70
  Piazza delle Erbe 66
  Piazza dei Signori 65
  Roman Theatre 72
  S. Corona 68
  SS. Felice e Fortunato 73
  S. Lorenzo 71
  S. Maria dei Servi 66
  Teatro Olimpico 62, *63*
  Villa La Rotonda 75
  Villa Valmarana 75
Vigardolo di Monticello 81
Villas, general 77
  Angarano 86
  degli Armeni *142*, 143
  Badoer 55
  Badoer Fattoretto 40
  Barbarigo 44
  Barbaro 144
  Benvenuti 49
  Beregan Cunico 81
  Ca' Marcello 135
  Caldogno Nordera 78
  Chiericati Lambert 79
  Chiericati Porto Rigo 81
  Chiminelli 134
  Contarini degli Scrigni 49
  Cordellina Lombardi 80
  Cornaro (Piombino Dese) 135

Villas contd
Cornaro (Romano d'Ezzelino) 86
Diedo Malvezzi Basso 78
Duodo 47
Emo 134, *135*
Falier 143
Feriani 79
Ferramosca-Beggiato 79
Ferretti Angeli 40
Foscari (La Malcontenta) 40, *41*
Foscarini dei Carmini 40
Fracanzan Piovene 80
Gazzotti Grimani Curti 78
Ghellini 81
Ghislanzoni Curti 78
Godi Malinverni 79
Grimani Sorlini 80
Kunkler 49
Lattes 134
Lazara Pisani 40
Loschi Zileri Motterle 80
Molin Grimani Avezzù 55
Nani-Mocenigo 47
Negri Piovene 86
Piovene Porto Godi 79
Pisani 39
Pisani Bonetti 78
Pisani Contarini 40
Pisani Placco 50
Poiana 80
Porto 79
da Porto Casarotto 79
da Porto 'La Favorita' 80
Rezzonico 86
Rocca Pisana 79
Rotonda (Vicenza) 75
Saraceno 78
Saraceno delle Trombe Bettanin 78
da Schio 79
da Schio Piovene 79
Sesso Schiavo Nardone 80
Thiene 80
Trissino Trettenero 75
Valier 40
Valmarana 75
Valmarana Bressan 81
Valmarana Morosini 78

Villas contd
Valmarana Scagnolari Zen 78
Verlato Putin 81
dei Vescovi (Luvigliano) 44
Widmann-Rezzonico-Foscari 40
Zaborra 44
Villafranca di Verona 162
Villaverla 81
Vittoria, Alessandro 30, 50, 67, 70, 124
Vittoriale degli Italiani 166
Vittorio Veneto 146
Vivarini brothers 84, 108
Volargne 120
Volpato, Giovanni Battista 152
War, First World 86, 88, 146, **147**, 156
White, Jessie 55
Wine 180 (*see also Bardolino, Colli Euganei, Prosecco, Soave, Valpolicella*)
Zamberlan, Francesco 54, 88
Zanchi, Antonio 49, 50, 67, 123, 157
Zaniberti, Filippo 56
Zecchin, Vittorio 151
Zelotti, Giovanni Battista 41, 44, 64, 72, 79, 80, 81, 135
Zompini, Gaetano 85
Zuccarelli, Francesco 70

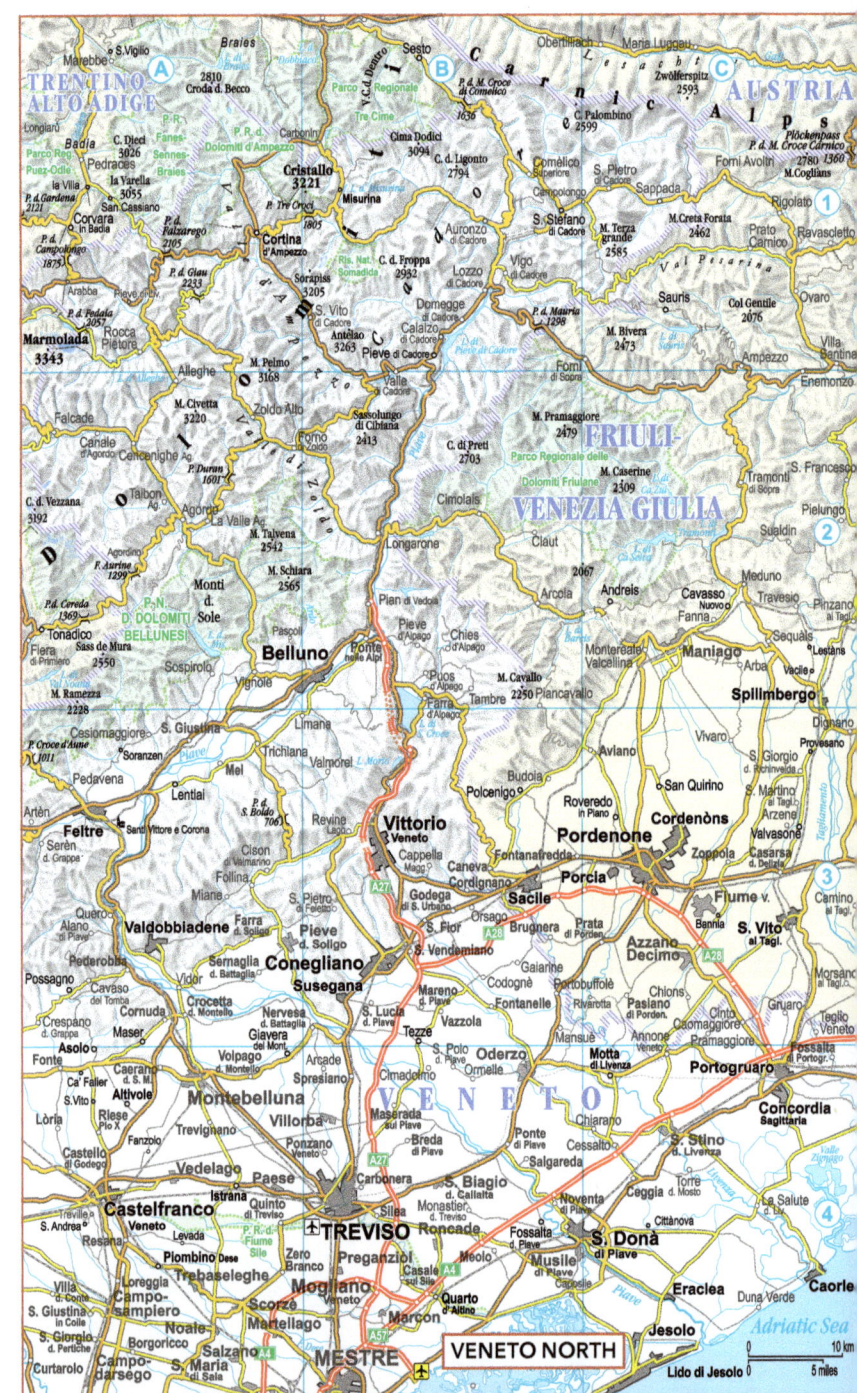

MAPS 193

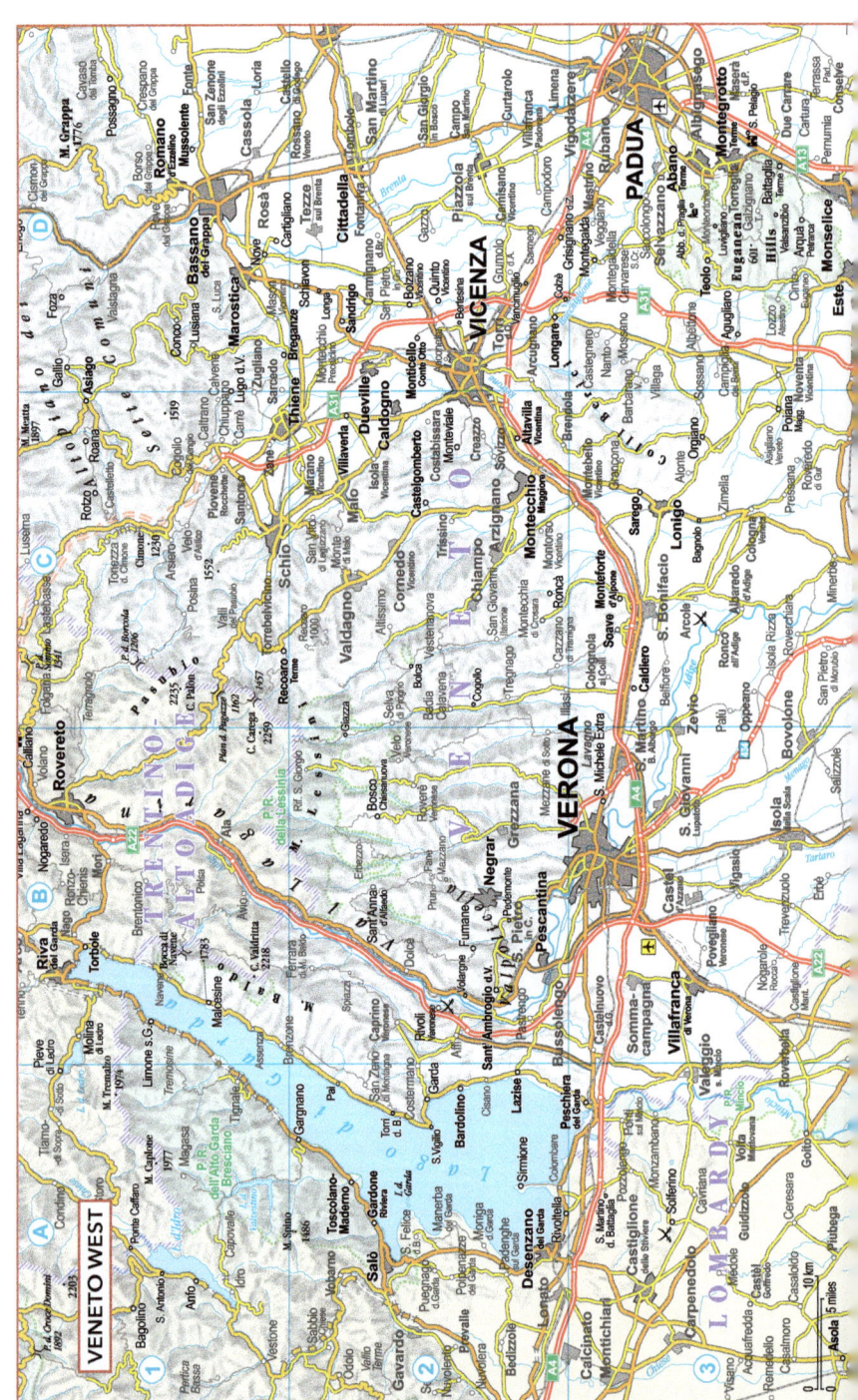

MAPS **195**

VENETO OVERVIEW

About the authors and contributors

ALTA MACADAM is the author of over 40 Blue Guides to Italy. She lives in the hills above Florence with her husband, the painter Francesco Colacicchi. She has worked for the Photo Library of Alinari and for Harvard University's Villa I Tatti. She is at present external consultant for New York University at the photo archive of Villa La Pietra in Florence, and as author of the Blue Guides to Florence, Rome, Tuscany, Venice, Central Italy, Umbria and Lazio, she travels extensively every year to revise new editions of the books.

CHARLES FREEMAN is a freelance academic historian with widespread interests in Italy and the Mediterranean. His *Egypt, Greece and Rome, Civilizations of the Ancient Mediterranean* (Oxford University Press, 3rd ed. 2014) is widely used as an introductory textbook to the ancient world and is supported by his *Sites of Antiquity: 50 Sites that Explain the Classical World* (Blue Guides, 2009). His *The Horses of St Mark's* (Little Brown, 2004) is a study of the famous horses through their history in Constantinople and Venice. He is a Fellow of the Royal Society of Arts.

ANNABEL BARBER is the Editorial Director of the Blue Guides. She is author of *Blue Guide Budapest* and co-author of *Blue Guide Rome* and also works as a translator.

And with special thanks to SIDNEY LEIGH, who conducted additional research for this edition.

www.ingramcontent.com/pod-product-compliance
Lightning Source LLC
Chambersburg PA
CBHW050029090426
42735CB00021B/3425